MOONLIGHTING

Tales and misadventures
of a working life with eels

Michael Brown
with drawings by the author

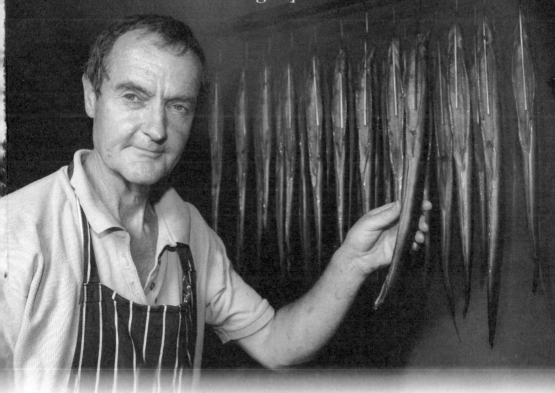

Merlin Unwin Books

Chapter One

It all began with a phone call in the spring of 1973. It was David Forrest, a good friend from university days whom I hadn't seen in a while.

'Why don't you come down to Somerset and see these things called elvers – they migrate up river at night on the high tides and the locals fish for them – it's called elvering. If you've got a bit of time, come and see.'

Time was something I had a great deal of. After university where I'd read languages, I had joined the marketing department of ICI in London. They were a good company to work for, though I never quite understood what marketing was all about, but this was the early Seventies: restless, exciting times, Carnaby Street, the Hippy Trail and mini everything. I was itching to get out. Below, through the windows of the Knights-bridge office, swirled exotic and colourful sights while inside everywhere I looked were men I could see myself becoming if I stayed: grey-suited family men whose daily lives travelling the same train, going home to wives and families, seemed honourable but monochrome; lives of quiet desperation. I wanted more, I wanted to be free and to travel, I wanted to be outside in the open air. Apart from that, I hadn't the faintest clue what I wanted.

I left, pompously telling friends that I wanted to have a go at being a writer. This was as much to justify to my poor parents who had invested considerably in my education the lunacy of leaving a solid career with great prospects, as they saw it, as having anything to do with a talent to write. But I had learnt the importance of a label: it made things plausible, allowable. To say, 'Mum and Dad, I'm off travelling' didn't go down as well as, 'I want to travel and write.' It gave it a greater sense of purpose and acceptability; it was easier for them to sell on to their friends.

I travelled overland roughly in the direction of Australia and very soon discovered that I was not a natural writer, I had very little to say, and I was excruciatingly slow: most of what I wrote I seemed to cross out. Filled with doubts and unsure of myself, thoughts and ideas seemed to dry up and wither on the page. It was not an auspicious start. However more by luck than anything else I managed to land a few articles with the travel section of the Sunday Telegraph whose editor was spending much time building a new life in another country and needed a bank of material from contributors he could feed weekly into his column. I was thus able to murmur impressively,

'Well, I'm a freelance writer actually. I'm working on a travel piece.'

It was an impecunious living with its highs and lows but, unencumbered, it gave me a certain freedom to look for something I really wanted to do.

Following David's phone call, I met him a few days later at Taunton station. He was driving a rattly old grocery van still with the shelves in the back.

'This is what we use to take the elvers up to London airport,' he explained as we ground up a hill on our way to the farm at Curry Rivel, 'and down there is the moor, or the Levels, where we'll be fishing tonight. There's a tide on. I'll drop you on the river, you can fish and I'll pick you up later. We're sending out a shipment tomorrow; I've got to get the boxes ready.'

There was something very invigorating about David's whirlwind pace. It certainly beat staring at a blank piece of paper in my room in London.

David had studied agriculture and marketing at Wye College before coming on to Reading university where we had shared a house in my last year and where he was remembered for his culinary achievements: his tossed pancakes, which we had difficulty removing from the kitchen ceiling. A great networker, before the word was fashionable, with dozens of contacts everywhere in every field; he had enormous energy and was one of those people who fizzed with ideas, trailing in his wake a litter of abandoned plans. Already by this time he'd set up and sold several small businesses, and worked for a charity in one of the poorest areas of northern India. He liked to have several things on the go at once; very often you'd enquire about his latest project, only to find that he was onto a new one.

It was while he was working for a market research company in London that he had been asked by a client to find a source for things called elvers - baby eels, also known as glass eels - for the lucrative Japanese market where they were farmed and grown on to adult eels. David had happened to mention this to a friend who was doing his practical year as an agricultural student on a farm near Curry Rivel in Somerset.

'You're in luck,' said the friend, 'I think I can help; we have elvers down here; they fish for them on the local river, the Parrett, and the farmer I'm working for has special holding tanks for them; he buys them in from the fishermen. They are sold to dealers in Gloucester.'

Never one to waste time, it wasn't long before David had left his market research and was shipping elvers live by air to Japan.

Later that night, I stood on the raised banks of the river Parrett and watched the rising water. Even there, miles inland, the tide was still pushing, the river swelling. The elver net I had been given was a hand-held dip net, deep bellied, about three feet long and half as wide and deep, like a pelican beak, covered in fine mesh. I'd been told to tuck it tight into the bank facing the direction of the sea from whence the elvers were supposed to come. Every now and then, feeling every bit the professional fishermen, I checked it, lifting it up for inspection by its long handle with a sweeping motion to hold the catch in the back of the net, as I'd been shown, but there was nothing. Not a sign of an elver.

Behind me the lights of a small pub, the Black Smock, cast soft light on the little road that wound beside the river. From a village across the moor came the sound of church bells. The river had stopped pushing now, the tide beginning to turn and run back. Gradually its cargo of flotsam, reeds and sticks slid past in reverse. Lifting the net again I peered into the bottom of it and there against the fine sieve mesh I saw my first elvers: a squiggle of tiny translucent creatures, about three inches long and as thin as a bootlace, unmistakeably eel shaped. They made a tiny rustling sound in the bottom of the net. Tipping them into my bucket I laid the net back in the river, tight into the bank, mouth facing downstream and waited a few minutes before lifting it again. This time there were more, a small ball of elvers, perhaps half a kilo and now the sound they made was louder, like fat frying. I looked at them as they swirled and writhed round the bottom of the bucket, forming a small puff of white foam in the centre – the slime secreted by their activity and locally known as vump.

From David, I had learned a little about their life cycle which began with a migration and ended with one, an outward and a return journey

5

forming a circle – like the moon – but one that could take anything up to twenty years or more to complete. Those tiny fish in my net seemed so young and delicate, yet they were already hardened travellers. They had drifted nearly three thousand miles from their spawning grounds in the Sargasso Sea, the other side of the Atlantic, where they had started life as larvae – leptocephalus – shaped like sycamore seeds, little sails that made the most of wind and tide and the Gulf Stream current to carry them across the ocean in countless millions.

After three years they reached the continental shelf where they metamorphosed into the recognisable shape of the elver, or glass eel. Only seven cms long, and weighing no more than a third of a gram, perfectly formed, beautiful as spun glass, they were driven by their migratory instinct to seek freshwater. They entered every European river, stream and freshwater outlet from southern Portugal to northern Europe, straining to reach upstream, inland where they could live and grow to adulthood. Years later when they reached maturity the adult eel would head back down river and back out to sea, re-crossing the Atlantic in months not years, to find again the dark Sargasso weed where they would spawn and die.

And they were now out of water, out of their natural environment, yet still swirling round the bottom of my bucket as if desperate still to continue their migration up-river. They had an urgency, a vigour. They were extraordinary creatures. As I peered at them, intrigued, in wonder, I had not the faintest idea then that they and their species would become so much part of my working life for the next thirty years.

★★★★★

David and I were staying with the local farmer, Anthony Lang, his partner in the Japanese venture. Anthony provided the holding tanks from which to ship the live elvers that came up-river on each set of spring high tides. David would travel down from London for the week of the elver tide and stay at the farm. He had certainly landed on his feet.

Home Farm was a lovely old Somerset farmhouse, long, low, built of the local blue lias stone, with a walled garden and an orchard at the back. Jane Lang, Anthony's wife, was an attractive lady in her early forties, mother of three, and a very good cook. The heart of the house was a large warm kitchen with a big table and an Aga, always full of noise, dogs, children, phones ringing, people calling in, and passers-by; a sort of unofficial meeting place with Jane at the centre of it. Bow windows with seats looked out over her immaculate walled garden and flowering borders. She had a keen eye for colour – the garden, she said, was her peace and sanity. Papers came with breakfast, the FT for Anthony, which David would borrow and read, stretched out like a lord, in the window seat. I was never quite sure how he had managed to reserve this extraordinary accommodation each time he came to fish the tides but I wasn't complaining.

Anthony Lang, the farmer, was in his mid-forties with rugged good looks and breezy confidence, a natural leader, full of enthusiasm and a born salesman. He had grown up in the area and was steeped in the life of the land he farmed. He knew everyone in the vicinity, knew the moors like the back of his hand, had fished for elvers as a boy for fun and for a feed. 'Wonderful with duck egg, the elvers just dipped in a bit of flour'.

Though he had inherited the farm from his uncle, it had come saddled with death duties. He could have sold land to settle them but he wanted to keep the farm intact so was steadily paying them off. With sheep and cattle and arable, he farmed well, had a good eye for stock and had built up a prize breeding flock of Dorset Down sheep. But he also had the entrepreneur's eye for a business opportunity, ready to try any profitable sideline that might boost the farming income. Which was how he had come to elvers.

Some years before, in the late Sixties, he'd happened to read with interest an article in the business pages about a market for elvers and their commercial value. At that time there was no commercial fishing for them in Somerset – locals only caught them for a feed. Coincidentally, at around the same time, on his rounds of the farm, he'd seen a man studying the river and the old mill at the edge of his property and had fallen into conversation with him. The man's name was Mike Hancock. Hancock was eyeing the river for eels – big eels –for which he had a ready market.

'Well,' had said Anthony, 'I don't know much about eels, but I do know about elvers. You'd better come up to the office for a chat.' Hancock was also looking for somewhere to set up a holding site to store the eels he would buy and sell. He was a convincing character, very persuasive, also with an eye for an opportunity. It was agreed they would be partners in an eel venture: Anthony, as landlord and backer, would put in a borehole and tanks to hold live fish, while Hancock would run the operation. And so it was that over the following years, Hancock had established a huge network of elver fishermen around the local river Parrett, buying in elvers each spring by the tonne, selling them to the dealers in Gloucester, while in the summer and autumn he bought and sold adult eels from all over the south of England.

It had worked well for a number of years. Eventually they'd fallen out. Hancock was ambitious, felt he was doing all the work for none of the profit. Wanting to go it alone, he had found and built a perfect site near the town of Chard, some ten miles away, but − as Anthony saw it - in Anthony's time and with Anthony's materials. The split between the two had been sulphurous and left a mark of deep distrust. But the fact was Hancock was still lord of the river, with the allegiance of most of the elver fishermen whom he controlled with an iron fist. It was a virtual monopoly and what newcomers like David managed to buy off the river with a small team of catchers was only ever going to be the crumbs from under his table.

At breakfast each morning at Home Farm, after a night's fishing, the talk was of the night before, of how the fishing had gone, and Anthony would want to know how we had done compared to Hancock and his men. There'd always be much growling. 'He wasn't straight. I could have put the blighter inside if I'd wanted to.'

In a way this was to be our legacy, this rivalry, but as I was to discover, it was not something that was in any way unique in the world of elvers: from Spain and France, to the Severn at Gloucester, rivalries and bad blood thrived in the hothouse elver world. There was skulduggery and there was also eel-duggery. And eel-duggery was just as murky.

Much of the equipment used in Hancock's day had vanished or quietly mouldered away. David was therefore desperately short of kit: nets for catching the elvers, trays for storing them live on the riverbank before they reached the safety of the tanks. To recruit fishermen in those days, like soldiers, you needed to give them the means to catch. Each day, after a gargantuan breakfast, we moved to a beautiful timbered barn beside the house where we'd frantically make and repair nets for the night's tide. In those days fabrication began with an ash pole handle about six feet long onto which was fixed, using willow canes, the actual dip net part, shaped like a cupped hand, deep and bowed. Onto this was glued and tacked the fine sieve mesh that allowed the water through but held the elvers back. In the old days the locals had used net curtain or mesh stocking, even granny's knickers, anything as long as they caught elvers. I loved the net making. It was like being paid to make model boats or planes. After sitting so long at a table in London, wrestling with some travel piece, it felt so satisfying to be doing something practical, to be making something, even if it was only out of ash pole, withy and netting.

I wasn't the only one to enjoy the net making sessions. Once when we were desperately trying to finish the nets in time for the evening tide, Jane Lang came out with sandwiches of fresh brown bread and beef for lunch. Beef off the farm with a sweet marbling of fat and a dab of horse-radish in fresh, brown bread. Just finish the netting, I thought, and then I'd have a break, so I put the plate on a big splitting log behind me. The job finished, I turned in anticipation. The plate was there on the log but it was bare. Puzzled, I looked round, thinking someone else had taken them but the barn was empty. Except for Major. He was the Lang's spaniel, a large, handsome fellow who liked company and would sit amongst the clutter of wood and netting on the floor of the barn. He was sitting to attention, looking away, just a little too nonchalantly I thought. When interrogated, he wagged his tail, denied it instantly but I could tell by the hopeful look in his eye that the beef had been very delicious and he was wondering if there were any more.

At the end of each tide or as soon as there were sufficient elvers for a shipment, the fish were packed in polystyrene boxes, driven to Heathrow and put on a plane to Japan. Each box held one kilo of elvers – some 3,000 baby eels – with a little ice and water and a vented lid for air. David had spent hours improving the design of the original boxes that came from France which were too shallow and prone to tip over. The new box was more robust, deeper and locked into the ones above and below to give greater stability.

I had nothing to do with this part of the operation – I was on net-making duties - but I could feel the tension, saw all the planning and preparation that went into a pack. It was a highly risky business. From the tanks in Somerset to the eel farm in Japan was a journey of 24 hours, sometimes more, and it put the elvers at the very limit of their endurance. Any delay, any hitch, spelled disaster. Kept moist and cool, the elvers could live out of water for limited time, taking oxygen out of the air, respiring through their skin. It was this remarkable ability that made their export to foreign lands possible at all. Even before the First World War, the Germans had collected elvers from Gloucester for restocking their rivers and lakes, transporting them on wooden trays laid with damp moss and stacked inside great wooden chests.

The day after each shipment David would pace up and down, taut as a bowstring, waiting for a phone call to learn whether they'd arrived safely. That anxious wait for news of success or failure was something I was to get to know well in the years to come.

That Spring I helped for three tides and then it was May and the season was over. But something had happened. I had enjoyed hugely the teamwork, the direct involvement, the buzz and excitement of the business. And though utterly different to my native Dartmoor in Devon, I had fallen in love with the Somerset Levels, the quiet intimacy of the moors, the willows, the water and the wide open skies. I told David that, if needed, I'd like to help again the following year.

★★★★★

In the Spring of '74, I arrived in Somerset to find them all reeling from the news that the Japanese market had closed overnight. A virus had been found in European stocks shipped from France and the doors had come down. No further exports. The market was gone. David was bitterly disappointed and embarrassed, the Langs were not happy, the venture was falling apart. Anthony drew on old contacts and managed to sell the fish that had already been purchased to a dealer in Gloucester. With the demise of Japan, David's business associates melted away; they were busy with other things. But I had time: anything to get away from wrestling with that blank piece of paper. We returned to London and got on the phone. Speaking to government agencies, river authorities, any possible leads for a market for elvers, the same name kept coming up, that of Alex Behrendt of Two Lakes, Romsey.

Alex was German, his father had been a Fischmeister and he was born and brought up on fish farms in East Germany. During the war, he'd fought in the German army under Kesselring retreating up through Italy, before being taken prisoner and placed in a POW camp in the south of England. On his release, he'd met and married an English woman and had started a trout fishery, near Romsey in Hampshire, the first of its kind in the country. He'd gone on to develop it into a highly successful business. I got his number and phoned him up.

The voice was crisp, direct, heavily accented,

'Ja, vot you vant?' Alex was always forthright. But as soon as I got into conversation with him, I sensed this was the man, this was our breakthrough. He was so well informed. I described our catching efforts in Somerset and the ban on elvers to Japan.

'Ja, I heard about that. Now look, I read German trade press, all fishing journals. And each week at this time of year, there is adverts for glassaale, that means elvers. Wiz a phone number beside. I give you some and you can ring them up.'

I thanked him profusely.

'And Michael, I can call you Michael, right, you tell me how you get on.'

Over the next days I ran up huge bills phoning the numbers Alex had given me. Most were not interested, had already bought in their seasonal requirement and didn't want more but this was already exciting, it showed me that there was another market beside the Far East and we could contact them in the future. And then I struck lucky. A very strong south German accent with a twang that I could only just understand said yes, he would take elvers, up to 200kgs on the next tide. His name was Alois Haas with a fish farm called Fischzuchtkoenigsee, right up against the Austrian border.

'Ah ja, I know zis man,' said Alex, delighted, when I told him of our progress, 'he was also in the army with me in Italy.'

Returning to Somerset and the farm for the next elver tide, David and I managed, through buying in and from what we caught ourselves, to collect the elvers we needed over the course of the week. We then packed them in the poly boxes and put them on the plane at Heathrow. And waited for a phone call from Haas to inform us of their safe arrival. It was not to be. There had been a disaster. What elvers were left, said Haas, were good, but most of the boxes had been damaged and the fish had escaped. He had managed to salvage some two thirds of the load we'd sent him, for which he would pay us, but the rest must have been scattered somewhere between London and Munich.

David now revealed another side to his character, turning overnight into a kind of forensic loss adjustor and sleuth. Through chatting to staff at the cargo bay where we'd loaded at Heathrow and listening to conversations, he soon pieced together the real story: a fork lift operator had carelessly driven the stacks of boxes at such speed that they'd tipped over. They were all talking about it. The shipment was insured and eventually, after many months, compensation was paid.

This episode marked the end of another season, which had more than dented David's enthusiasm and highlighted for him the unreliability of the business of elvering. Furthermore the timing and commitments of the elver season were beginning to clash with projects he had become involved in. Through international funding he had managed to secure a grant to carry out a study on eel populations worldwide, looking at their distribution, exploitation and cultivation. This was taking up more and more of his time. Moreover he had been commissioned by Fishing News publication to write a book on the subject. It was all happening for him. I could sense his interest in the Somerset venture beginning to wane.

One evening when we'd been fishing to make up the elvers for the Haas order, we talked over the possibility of my taking over from him – if the Langs were agreeable. He would then be free to get on with his new life. Later, alone with my net on the river, I went over our conversation and felt hugely excited as I realised in a rush of clarity that it would be the perfect solution to my quest. Elvering seemed to provide all the ingredients, the things I was looking for: to live and make a living in the country, to run a small business which was seasonal and which would give me time to travel and perhaps to write. Little did I know that the only thing I'd ever write would be cheques.

Meanwhile, as we set off over the summer in separate directions, we decided to remain working together in a loose partnership until plans were clearer. It was agreed that I would look for other elver rivers and attempt to secure a market for the following season.

Two things had recently happened which were indirectly linked but which were to have a big impact on future events. Listening to the radio one day, I had heard a programme about the way writers observed nature. They talked of Gilbert White, and of Graham Williamson's Tarka the Otter, but the piece that really caught my attention was when they turned to Gavin Maxwell and a passage of writing in the Ring of Bright Water where he describes the seasonal arrival of the elvers on the west coast of Scotland. I listened in astonishment. I had no idea elvers were found in any quantities other than in the West Country and Gloucester. Potentially here was another source of supply.

Around this time, too, I had read a book by John Ridgway, *Journey to Ardmore*. Ridgway was still very much a household name, having rowed with Chay Blyth across the Atlantic, an extraordinary feat of endurance. His book fascinated me with its autobiographical details, the great adventures and yet also the determined step-by-step making of a business, setting up his School of Adventure in the remote north of Scotland, just beneath Cape Wrath. As I was free-lancing at the *Sunday Telegraph*, I suggested to the travel editor that I might write about the place. Privately I thought while I was up there I could usefully look at elver rivers. I contacted Ridgway and it was arranged that I would attend the Businessmen's courses for two weeks that June.

I took the overnight sleeper to Inverness, then the train to Lairg in Sutherland where an instructor met the party that now emerged from various parts of the two remaining carriages, like weevils from a biscuit. A single track road led north for miles beside the thin ribbon of loch Shin then through wild mountain scenery, past the mountains of Ben Stack, Arkle and Foinaven. They were a mixed, interesting bunch of individuals, mostly middle aged, from all walks of life, all a little over-hearty, nervous of what lay ahead. Beyond the Laxford river, we turned down to a sea loch and crossed by boat to the Ardmore peninsula to the Adventure School, tea and reception.

Ridgway was a big man with craggy features, very blue eyes and a broken nose. He had a big presence; meeting him face to face was a bit like

Foinavon ridge from Badna Bay

coming up against a cliff. As we drank tea in the main hut overlooking the loch, he briefed us on the week ahead, starting with the six o'clock early morning run. The man beside me, a director of a large shipping line, turned grey, muttering 'Oh, God, I can't possibly do that.' Suddenly, there was a noise from the kitchen next door where Marie-Christine, John's wife was clearing away.

'John, John, look, down there, look at the loch.' We all piled over to the window.

Below us a titanic underwater battle was in progress: a cormorant had got hold of an enormous eel, which it was trying to swallow. Looking down through the gin-clear water of the loch, we could clearly see as the eel twisted, thrashing, broke free pursued by the bird which swam with its wings underwater, its beak snapping like giant shearing scissors. They would resurface locked in battle until eventually the cormorant managed to toss the eel back, swallowing it head first. There was a great baggy lump in the long black throat, a beating of wings and treading of water with mammoth swallowing; the eel was all gone, just the tip of the tail hung from the beak. Then it must have done something particularly painful for there was a convulsion and it shot from the bird's throat like a spear and the whole chase began again. It was an extraordinary battle, raw drama. At last the cormorant took the eel again with a final gulp and then very slowly, with deliberate, painful effort, like the closing of an overstuffed suitcase, the beak cranked shut. For the rest of the day it sat on a rock offshore, wings outstretched as it digested its monstrous meal.

At the end of a week of sailing, climbing, canoeing and hill walking and before the arrival of another course, I took a day off to explore and was walking back in the afternoon over the Laxford bridge, when I saw gulls on the river below. They were perched on rocks and pecking at the water, eating something I couldn't see. Could it be the elvers that Gavin Maxwell had described? I wondered. Through the trees beside the river I glimpsed the outline of a big house and following the drive down to it, heard voices from the lawn at the front. Two women were sitting having tea. One of them I recognised as the Ridgway's secretary; it was her day off. Her hostess jumped up almost as if she'd been expecting me, and offered me a cup. I had the feeling that conversation had worn a little thin and she welcomed the interruption. She introduced herself as Sandee Mackintosh.

'Yes, we do get elvers,' she replied to my question, 'but my husband is the one who knows all about it, he's the factor for the estate. You'll have to wait till he gets home from work. Have another piece of cake.'

I ended up staying for supper, a memorable meal that lasted for hours. Sinclair Mackintosh had already been factor to Anne, Duchess of Westminster and her estates in this corner of Sutherland for several years. He and his wife Sandee had married the year before and were installed in the beautiful soft timbered house that belonged to the estate, set on the wooded point that looked down the Laxford to the estuary. The evening sun reflected off the river, filling the house with light. It was an idyllic spot.

Sinclair was helpful and interested. Yes, they did get elvers, and that was what the gulls had been eating. And he felt the estate would certainly entertain the possibility of limited elver fishing if it brought in revenue and just so long as it didn't in any way affect the salmon run. Permission would have to be sought from the Duchess, of course. She was not in the north at the moment; he would speak to her when he saw her and then it would be necessary for me to come up and meet her in person, probably in the autumn. Before the meal he took me down to the Laxford, to where it rushed over the rocks below the bridge, the water, soft, peaty and amber-coloured, falling several feet and forming the first natural barrier to migratory fish. This, we agreed, would be the best spot to fish the elvers.

It was after midnight when I left the Mackintoshes but there, in the far north in the middle of summer, it was still light enough to read a book, which made it easy to walk the five miles or so back to Ardmore. It was a beautiful night, not a single vehicle nor artificial light, just a silvery world of mountain, river and loch with a big moon in the sky; no sound as I took to the track that led to Ardmore; just the thump of my boots and the peep of an oystercatcher on the loch below.

On return, I found that my tent was being investigated by a small, fat highland pony, the much-loved pet of John's wife, Marie Christine; he was the enfant terrible of the school, spoiled, stubborn and frequently belligerent. He had evidently decided that the tent was an enemy and anyway stood on the patch of grass he was wishing to nibble. I arrived just as he was extracting the tent pegs with his teeth and chucking them over his shoulder like a man pulling nails from a plank. Even when I shooed him away and replaced the pegs to the sagging tent, he later returned in the night to do battle and a strange scene ensued in which a naked man chased a small pony across a field brandishing a large metal peg and mouthing curses. It was a short night.

★★★★★

A few weeks later I received a writing assignment in Germany. With my flight paid, it was an ideal opportunity once I had done the report to take to the road and look for new markets for elvers. David had given me some money from our communal kitty so I hired a car in northern Bavaria and drove to a succession of fish farms and fisheries I had contacted earlier in the year after Japan had closed its doors. They were mostly located in wonderful out-of-the-way places, far from the autobahn and I drove, enraptured, on little roads with no traffic, over hills, through forests and quiet villages of farms and wooden houses and onion dome church spires. I headed north and to the east of the industrial Ruhr, to the Edersee, one of the three dams breached in the Dam Buster bombing raid of 1943. Herr Seidlitz owned the fishing rights to the lake and stocked it annually with elvers, which matured into the eels that attracted the great numbers of fishermen who descended on it each year.

Eel fishing in Germany was the high point for a fisherman; landing an eel was like catching salmon or sea trout in Britain. Back home, attitudes couldn't have been more different: anglers hated eels, they were a nuisance, they couldn't get the hook out, they got caught up in the line, often it meant cutting the tackle and making a fresh start. In Germany the eel was prized, revered almost; you would keep the eel you had caught, perhaps smoke it later in your backyard, share it with friends. And tell them about the even bigger one that got away.

As I visited one contact after another and parted from each with good intentions of staying in touch for the following season, it was evident that they all bought their elvers from the same source - the Deutsche Fischerei Verband, a government-backed agency charged with the restocking of inland lakes and rivers in Germany. And it seemed to be run by one man whom they all referred to with varying degrees of respect: a Herr Rosen-garten, who was based in Hamburg. The more I travelled, the more I felt I would have wasted my time if I hadn't met him; he was undoubtedly the Mr Big of the German elver market. I looked at the map. Germany was huge: I was roughly in the middle and Hamburg miles away in the north. And I was fast running out of time. I parked the car and jumped on a train.

Rosengarten and I met at Hamburg station. He always remembered the plastic bag I was carrying – my unofficial briefcase – while I remember that he was wearing a suit and, curiously, as if he couldn't find the shoes to go with it - sandals. He was squarely-built with a booming personality and large powerful handshake. My German learned at school but picked up mainly while hitching in the country as a student was conversationally good but rapidly overwhelmed by anything deeper, by the interminable sentences ending with cascades of complex verbs that always totally threw me. Rosengarten didn't do verbs. Through years of dealing with French and Spanish lorry drivers and elver suppliers, he had developed a kind of simplified German that was easy to understand, speaking in phrases like bullet points that could be easily absorbed - that was, until he got carried away.

He'd been born and brought up in East Germany; his father, like Alex Behrendt's, a Fischmeister running a large carp farm in the south east of the country. For all his bluff and bluster of manner, Rosengarten had the East German's old fashioned, traditional values in his business dealings: he was tough in negotiation, firm but always fair, 'immer korekt' as he would have put it. And for over a quarter of a century of doing business with him, he never called me by my Christian name, using instead always Sie – the formal You – and always addressing me 'Herr Brown', until finally the year he retired, we met and he got out a bottle of champagne to celebrate the fact we could now call each other by our first names, and use the familiar Du form of address. 'Ja, Herr Brown,' he paused as if readying himself for the leap, 'Michael, wir können uns jetzt duzen.'

The meeting at the railway station was a turning point. Years later, he would say that even though I had a plastic bag as a briefcase, the fact of going out to meet him in Hamburg showed him I was serious. It was agreed: he would buy from us. He had his main French suppliers but he would be interested in taking air freight deliveries from the UK, though he made it clear that I would have to accompany the first shipment so that we could both agree on the quality and any losses. It was arranged that I should contact him as soon as the season started the following spring.

In between these travels and work in London, I went home to Devon and caught up with my parents, filling them in on the chain of events. All along they were hugely supportive, excited as I was at developments and eager to know how things were going, although I sensed my father – who had spent all his working life in the teak forests of Burma - viewed the elvering with some suspicion, 'a get rich quick scheme' that would not last. They lived on the northern edge of Dartmoor looking across to the sweep of the moor. My father had retired at the age of fifty from the tropical heat of the jungles and with the need to keep earning, he grew Christmas trees in the fields around the house. Looking back on it, for all his inherent caution, this had been a bold and a risky step for him to take, returning from overseas to launch into a business about which he knew little. But it was a magical place in which to grow up. In the school holidays in summer, my brother and I would cycle onto the moors with a picnic and swim in the freezing cold, soft, peaty water of the moorland streams. We spent hours diving with masks and snorkels, fascinated by the small brown trout that hovered in dark places under boulder and waterfall. Occasionally there were much larger fish, a salmon once, and then, a long thin snake-like fish, coiling through the stones, terrifying to me – my first sight of an adult eel.

Later on, as I grew older, I'd drive down from London for the weekend after work, arriving late; all noise of traffic dropped away, and there was just the hush of wind in the pines that grew around the house. It was this experience of childhood in Devon that drew me to the idea of making a life not in town or city but in the country, and it was why the possibility of the business based on elvers was so attractive.

By the autumn, David Forrest confirmed that he wished to step back from the elvering to do a Business MBA and leave me to take it on. We had already set up a provisional partnership under Brown and Forrest; now that we were parting, I asked him if I could retain his name on the notepaper. Brown's Elvers or Michael's Eel – there was already a Mick's Eels in London – sounded decidedly slippery whereas the two surnames had a certain balance, a resonance. Besides, David was now the author of Eel Capture, Culture and Marketing, an excellent study of the then-current trends in the industry. Retaining his name, I thought, might lend marked credibility - gravitas - to the fledgling business. To this, he readily agreed. He also promised for the forthcoming season the use of his VW camper van, which he'd acquired to carry out the research for his book. This was a friend indeed.

That October I received word from Sinclair Mackintosh that if I wished to come up, the Duchess could see me at her house in Sutherland to discuss permission to fish the Laxford for elvers. I travelled north by train to Inverness and north again, and was met at Lairg station by Hector Morrison, the Duchess's chauffeur, 43 years on the estate. He wore a battered chauffeur's uniform and peaked hat and drove an old Ford Zephyr with crates of stores in the back. His wife Peggy ran the post office in the estate village of Achfary. We headed north along Loch Shin, steely grey, the same road I'd followed to the Ridgway's back in the summer. Hector spoke in that quiet, soft highland accent, almost Irish in its lilt. I told him I was nervous about meeting the Duchess, but he reassured me, saying she was 'very nice, very friendly' and when I asked him what I should call her, told me that the best way was simply to address her as 'Your Grace'.

Lochmore Lodge was a gracious house of granite stone and grey roofs built under the hill and set amongst pines, with fine gardens sloping down to high rhododendron hedges and the loch below. I was met by Sinclair and ushered in to meet the Duchess who was standing with her back to the fire, feet planted well apart, a woman in her early sixties, comfortably dressed, with fine wide set eyes, a broad smile and commanding presence. She had the richest gravelly voice I'd ever heard.

She was Anne, Duchess of Westminster – I had been briefed by Sinclair – the fourth and last wife of Duke Bendor, Second Duke of Westminster who in 1924 had purchased the Reay Forest estates – a mere 48,000 hectares – as this part of Sutherland was called, land that his predecessors, the Grosvenor family had had a long association with, having leased it for years. The Duchess's home was in Chester but her real spiritual home was there in Sutherland where she spent most of her summer and autumn salmon fishing and stalking – it was said she was an excellent shot.

We talked for a while then moved into lunch, with Sinclair and one other guest. I was placed next to the Duchess, and while conversation went back and forth with Sinclair mostly on general estate matters, I scrabbled in my mind for something to say, too preoccupied even to taste the flavour of the smoked salmon served as a first course. At a suitable moment, I leaned forward to enquire about her race horses, Arkle and Foinavon, which had both won Grand Nationals, (Arkle three times), and whether she had any other promising ones coming through.

'And when they retire from racing, your Grace, I suppose they are much sought-after and you are able to put them out to stud?'

'Ah, no, Mr Brown,' she smiled a little condescendingly, 'unfortunately, you see, as they are horses that go over the jumps, those huge fences, their equipment has to be removed in case they do themselves damage…' and she flashed me a smile. I winced and nodded in vigorous understanding.

Up to that point no mention had been made of the elvers; then, as we served ourselves to a delicious shepherd's pie from the sideboard, she turned to the subject. Her main concern, it was evident, was not how much the estate made out of the project, but any possible adverse effect that the taking of elvers might have on the salmon fishing and the river Laxford, which she proudly described as 'the best salmon river in Britain.' I assured her that there was no conflict, that the elvers came close to the bank and near the surface and that we fished with hand-held nets. Sinclair backed me, saying he had spoken to Billy Scobie, the head gillie, who agreed there could be no possible harm. She seemed reassured. She was also concerned that I should not lose any money invested, if after a trial year, the estate decided against the venture.

Later, I joined Sinclair in Achfary, the little estate village a mile down the road. On the crags of rock above the valley, the stags, heavy in rut, were roaring into the winter sky, deep bellied roars that seemed to come from their very depths. I was introduced to Billy Scobie, a big, gentle, quiet spoken man with greying hair, clad in a working tweed suit who said that from the first frosts of the year when the hinds came on heat, the stags would roar all night through September and October, keeping them all awake.

Together we looked at the river and Scobie identified the falls below Laxford bridge as the best spot to fish the elvers, which, from his annual records, came around the third week in May – this tied in with Gavin Maxwell's observations. We then went on to the salmon hatchery, his pride and joy, 'the most modern in Europe' he proudly called it, where the estate had built up a lively restocking business sending eyed ova from their own wild fish to rivers overseas. They also hatched and raised salmon fry for release back into the Laxford river. The hatchery was a long low building set on a side stream above Achfary. Inside, it was dark and cool; down one side was a row of wooden box tanks fed by the burn, the water cascading down from one to another. This was where we would store the elvers we caught. It was a perfect holding site.

Sinclair wrote a short time later to confirm that the Duchess had given her permission to fish the Laxford. He looked forward to seeing us up there the following year. With Somerset and Scotland as two sources of supply, and having secured a market in Germany, things were coming together well. I now needed to find somewhere to live in Somerset near the Lang's farm and the holding tanks. I felt if I was to make a real go of the elvering, it was absolutely necessary to live in the area. It was not a business that could be properly managed by weekly or fortnightly visits from afar. Besides, living in the country was its main attraction.

In December 1974, in the search for somewhere suitable to rent, I was fortunate to be able to stay with old friends of my parents in the village of Buckland St Mary up on the Blackdown Hills, about half an hour's drive from the elver tanks. My first visit was to my future landlord, Anthony Lang, to finalise the terms of our agreement: I would run the elver business independently of him using the facilities already in place, the holding tanks and the storage barn, and for this I would pay him a percentage of the turnover. It was a figure that seemed high but I sensed that Anthony had had enough of elver dealers; if I could make it work, fine, if not, that was the end of it. That suited me well; it was just the freedom and independence I wanted.

Having settled the tenancy with Anthony, I then started to explore the surrounding country for somewhere to live. It needed to be as close as possible to the elvers, somewhere I could park a van, a place where I could come and go, often at night, without disturbing neighbours. As I explored, I came across beautiful stone villages with towered churches, and was excited by the thought that this was where I was coming to live. But for the money I could afford, there seemed nothing that was suitable; the best I found was a cramped, second floor flat with no parking in the middle of a small nearby town.

Each evening I went back to my hosts, David and Margaret Norton and reported on progress, or lack of it. They lived in a huge rambling Victorian manor house that they'd bought for a song just after the war. It was dark and shabby and gloriously comfortable, like an old well-worn coat. Over the years various bits of it had been closed off, like the ballroom to one side of the entrance, 'one room less to heat', where the smooth boards of the dance floor had begun to curl like autumn leaves. David was a big florid man who grew Christmas trees in the fields around the house and whose passion was tennis: he played twice weekly, to a high standard on a hard court in the grounds; this was followed always by a huge tea, magnificent fruit cakes you'd want to take on any expedition and tea that came in cups the size of buckets, all provided by his wife, Margaret who never joined the tea party. She had once been a ward matron and ran the household and her numerous family with strict efficiency and with the assistance of a large watch pinned permanently to her chest and a clipboard of lists under one arm.

She was a sweet shy person, always wore a slightly distrait air as if she was permanently running to catch up. At meals in the kitchen we sat amongst piles of books and papers, neatly stacked in ordered profusion, surrounded by more lists with reading glasses attached and baskets, several of them, all packed. Baskets of mending, baskets for shopping, baskets for the vegetable garden. Over all this ordered chaos, a kitchen clock ticked and a big dog creaked in its basket. On my last morning, over bacon and eggs, I was expressing frustration and despair over my house hunting, when David asked me if I would consider somewhere as far from the elvers as their village. Originally I had thought it far too long a journey, but the lack of anything suitable now shrunk the half hour drive, making it feel distinctly possible.

'My daughter has a cottage here which she can't sell. I could have a word with her; she might be prepared to let it, keep it warm until a buyer comes along. We'll have a look at it after breakfast if you like.'

I fell in love with Skye Cottage as soon as I saw it. It was at the lower end of the village, at the top of a tiny lane that led down to an old mill. Settled into the side of the hill, it looked over the wooded valley to fields and hills; it had cob walls painted soft pink, and it sat in its own small garden with a lawn and apple tree, bounded by a wall with the field beyond. At the top of the garden, where there was room for a veg patch, stood a garage, which could be used as a workshop and storage for elver kit. Inside the cottage were three tiny upstairs bedrooms above a large living room and kitchen fired by an ancient rayburn that burned anything. A thin corridor tacked on to the back as an afterthought led down the side of the house to a bathroom. It was fitted with the smallest bath I'd ever seen, a tiny tub on splayed feet. The whole place was perfect.

A few days later I spoke to David Norton's daughter and it was arranged that I could rent Skye Cottage for five pounds a month, starting from the beginning of January 1975 and until such time as a buyer was found. Even with my limited means it was well within the budget.

That Christmas I wrote the usual cards to family and friends, including one to a lady in Australia. Her name was Utta, she'd been born in Germany but her family had emigrated when she was small. She'd become a psychiatric nurse and I'd met her in London a few years before in 1971 when I'd still been with ICI and she had been travelling over in Europe, taking a break from her job back home. She had an infectious zest for life and she was the only person I'd ever met who, when eating an apple or a pear, ate the whole thing, core and all, leaving only the stalk. Very cheap to run, I thought. We had kept vaguely in touch - well enough to know her current address. Scribbling a bit of news, I told her about the elvering and the cottage with its tiny bath, and ended with the throwaway line, 'Why not come and see it!' And posted the card.

An old bridge on the Somerset moor

Chapter Two

As soon as I moved in to Skye Cottage on the Blackdown Hills of Somerset in early January 1975, I began preparations for the coming elver season that would start in the spring. With equipment to make, nets and the trays for the fishermen, tanks to repair, markets to contact, airfreight to arrange, there was a sense of purpose that I'd never felt before and though there was much to do, I revelled in slowly working my way through it; building the new business, steadily putting it together piece by piece. There was the challenge too of having to be inventive, having to make do because for income I had only some tiny savings and the odd payment, usually months late, from the writing. All the while I was free, entirely my own master, in a place of my own in country that was as beautiful and varied as any I'd seen. I felt I'd arrived.

Most days I drove over to the elver site, down off the Blackdown hills to the little village of Hambridge on the edge of West Moor and the Levels. The holding tanks were located in the courtyard of Bowdens Farm at the furthest end of the Lang's property and about a mile from their main farmhouse outside Curry Rivel. The system depended on spring water drawn from a borehole some seventy feet down in a corner of the yard. This fed a small reservoir from which it was then pumped to the tanks. Over the years, the site had been neglected, briefly used during each season and then abandoned. Equipment lay around quietly decaying, the tanks leaked, nettles and brambles invaded the pump house. It all needed a little care and attention. Down one side of the courtyard stood a row of barns, which included a granary, tractor shed and a larger barn with a fine stone flag floor, once used to store cider apples. This was the one that would be my storage shed and workshop.

Across the courtyard was the farmhouse occupied by the farm shepherd, Ernie Woods, who was to become friend and support over the years on all things, including elvers and eels. Ernie looked after the secondary flock of sheep. Unlike the prize breeding Dorset Downs, kept 'up top farm', these were crossbreds reared for their lambs. Away from his boss and the main farm, he was largely left to his own devices, which suited his independent nature. There was nothing hurried about Ern. He walked with a slow, swinging stride as if covering long distances, always dressed in blue overalls and 'wellitons'. The pitch of his voice was a low rumble and he spoke in a deep, burred Somerset accent. He had dark, watchful eyes and a broad, malleable mouth that would break into a great grin or laugh. For his work, he drove a battered little grey tractor, manoeuvring it expertly with a swagger, often one handed and standing up like a Scythian charioteer as he headed up the drive at speed to the shed where it was kept. There at the threshold, he'd squeal to a halt, just in time to disconnect the vertical exhaust pipe, which would otherwise have carried the roof away.

To Anthony Lang, his boss, he was a good, reliable shepherd, but with a difficult, truculent streak, and easily offended. The cause of trouble lay in the simmering rivalry between Ern and the main shepherd, Bill, or Shep, as he was called, a thin, wiry man of few words, dressed in gaiters and hobnail boots and an old army coat tied with string. Ern resented the way Anthony thought the world of Shep, whose word on the Dorsets was law. Shep had been a shepherd all his life, knew his flock like a family, poured his whole life into them, administering to every one of their needs. When you saw the Dorset Down rams clipped ready for a show, they had that smug groomed look of gentlemen off to their club. Under Shep, they won some of the top breeder prizes.

Ernie was a loyal man, with deep respect for his boss, but he found all the attention on the Dorsets hard to bear. He'd come into the barn where I was working, full of grumble and resentment after some particular incident,

'Tid'n right, Mike,' he'd grumble, 'they got all of they there up top farm to do his bliddy job and alls there is down yere is oi. Boss said this morning, he sed, what a good job Shep done, back along at that there show – well, maybe he ave but he got all they to elp en. Tidn right.' And I'd listen and nod sympathetically as he rumbled away.

But it never got him down for long. He'd chew on his grump for a while like a dog with a bone then brighten up. Ernie loved to talk; on the farm, he was known as 'yakker Woods' and he could talk for England.

Working so much on his own, he missed company, loved to come into the barn if I was making nets or trays and pass the time of day. When this first happened, I would stand for half an hour with a hammer or a piece of wood in my hand politely waiting for him to finish but I soon discovered that if I was to get anything done, I had to work and talk – or listen - at the same time.

Geographically his world was on a plane that had a definite tilt: with Ern you went 'up Curry,' and 'up top farm' but always, 'down Taunton,' where he went shopping on Fridays with Norah, his wife. And of course you always went elvering 'down on the moor'. He had only once been out of Somerset; that had been when Anthony, 'the boss' had sent him to collect a piece of equipment from Newport, south Wales. It was also the first time he'd ever driven on a motorway. Feeling hungry around lunchtime, he'd pulled over on the hard shoulder to have his sandwiches. 'Course, when I told the missus I done that, she were mad at me, but oi told her I didn know you couldn.'

Ern had grown up in the 1930s down on the moor in Duck Cottage, by the river Parrett, just a few miles away. It was very different down there, the houses poorer, thin and bony, swaying walls propped up by buttresses, with withy boilers in the garden. It was a world of tight-knit communities where people travelled little and where the local accents, rich and varied, could distinguish a man from this village or that, from 'up Curry' or 'down Aller', by the way he spoke. It had been a hard, poor upbringing during the Depression years. His father had worked as an agricultural labourer on the farms around, often being paid in kind, usually in cider for a day's work – not much good if you were trying to feed a family. Ern could remember him coming home, passed out, slumped unconscious in the cart: the little pony always knew her way back and she'd go right into the shed and park up, wait for someone to unhitch her and remove her passenger.

They'd lived on the moor and they'd lived off the moor, true hunter-gatherers. 'Years ago before the war,' Ernie used to say, 'I've et everything that moved down on thet there moor, fish, eels, elvers, swan, duck, rabbit, crow; you name en, I've ad en.'

As a small boy he went eeling with a spear. It was a fearsome instrument with five prongs like a Greek trident fixed on a long handle. The prongs were flattened like blades and had a barbed notch to prevent the

eels wriggling free. They were a common item and
could be bought at any of the blacksmiths round the
edge of the moor. Ern would walk the rhines – the
ditches around his house, plunging the spear into
the dark peaty waters. He couldn't see the eels, but
they were abundant and sooner or later the spear
would connect and bring one up writhing between

*Ernie's
eel spear*

the prongs. He'd skin them and take them round the village in a wicker
basket for sale. In the spring when the elvers came past the cottage on the
big tides, the family simply cut a trench in the bank and allowed them to
swim right into the garden. 'The ducks, cor they loved them. We did too.
And mother used to cook em in a duck egg omelette. Though I could
never eat too many. They were rich mind, you could'n eve too many.'

It was this local knowledge and a life brought up on the river that
gave him his special prowess as a fisherman and had helped him make
the biggest catch of elvers that had ever been seen, one that had passed
into local legend by the time I arrived. It had happened years before,
when Hancock had still been working the site for Anthony. Ern had been
fishing about a mile below Langport, where the river rounded a long
bend and the elvers were forced to bunch tight as they caught the current.
It was the perfect spot. He'd filled all his trays and buckets, and an SOS
had gone out for help. When it came, his net was so full it had taken two
strong men to lift it out, over a hundredweight in one dip. All in all he'd
caught over 200lb that night – it was all in lbs in those days – and he
earned himself a small fortune, nearly fifteen pounds. It had been the talk
of the river bank for years.

As Ern talked he would always keep a watchful eye on what I was
doing, breaking off sometimes to say,

'Yere, Mike,' as I constructed another wonky-looking elver tray,
'be better is if you made a jig for them trays, then they all comes out the
same size, rather than making they one by one.' (I took his advice and tray
production and quality soared.) Then after a time perhaps his conscience
or his internal clock would get the better of him, and he'd address himself
in a fatherly tone with a note of self admonishment,

'Well, Ern, old son, better get on and do a bit more to these yere
sheep,' though it was sometimes a little unclear whether he'd actually
done anything to start with. Or he'd ask me the time - he rarely carried

a watch, 'One o' clock is it, already,' with mild surprise, 'cor; time to ave me dinner.' And he'd roll off across the yard, stopping to rub the mud off his boots in one of the puddles by the hedge.

Ern had a ritual of daily meals with names and quantities that I found confusing at first. There was his 'breffest' which was often late, taken at around nine thirty, when he'd done all the sheep, a good hearty meal. Then there was 'me dinner' around one, usually bread and cheese and perhaps a few leftovers, then much later, with all the family, 'me tea,' a much more substantial meal, followed by a sort of evensong of bread and cheese just to make sure he didn't get peckish in the night.

I loved working at Bowdens; there was always an atmosphere of deep peace back from the road and overlooking the moor. It was a wonderful place for wildlife. At that time of year when the ground was often hard with the frost, which stayed all day and stiffened the clumps of grass in the orchard, the barn owls would hunt by daylight beyond the tanks; beautiful birds, with white faces like some order of medieval monk, flying low on soundless wings over the tussocky grass, hunting for mice and voles. While in the granary, next door to my barn, little flocks of birds, sparrows and later the yellowhammers came in to feed on the grain dust off the floor, rising in a shower of colour and whirr of wings whenever you entered.

Each night I drove back to Skye Cottage on the Blackdown hills and lit a fire from the wood I'd gathered in and cooked a meal. I was beginning to find that keeping warm was full time work. David Norton had allowed me to forage in his beech woods; most of the timber was damp and though really too late in the year to start a woodpile, by stacking it in the outhouse I managed to get it dry. Almost. To begin with, it lay in the fireplace and hissed dolefully before forcibly drying out. From Ken and Vera Gready who had the farm next door I bought potatoes, milk, and the eggs from their athletic brown hens. These creatures were so truly free range you found them happily scratching about in fields miles away from the farmhouse. I made my own bread and experimented with recipes. It was a good time, a wholesome interlude. I knew that I was playing at the good life, that things would be very different when the elvers came but for the moment it was a time of deep contentment.

★★★★★

28

It was about three weeks into my new life at Skye Cottage when the telegram arrived. I was having an office day, working at the kitchen table, when I heard the noise of a motorbike outside and was handed a cable that read,

'Coming to share your bath. Flight details follow. Utta.'

Back home in Sydney she'd been working for nearly three years in a psychiatric clinic, rewarding work but after a length of time she felt she'd reached a cross-roads and needed a change of direction. And then my Christmas card had arrived and had made her wonder. One night duty, she and two friends, urging each other on, made life-changing plans. In decisive fashion they decided to throw it all in, follow their instincts and see where it took them. For Utta, there were thoughts of career change but first there was unfinished business; she needed to see for one more time the person she'd met in London, just to see where things might lead.

Some two weeks later at the end of January 1975, I stood in the arrivals hall of a Heathrow Terminal, scanning the tired faces of passengers from the long haul flights.

They came in streams, then ones and twos, then another sudden wave. It had been three years since I'd seen Utta last and I wasn't actually sure if I'd recognize her straightaway. My heart was beating, senses hair-triggered. Another wave of passengers and there, amongst them - was it - a familiar face, I couldn't be sure: a suntanned lady with long legs, in jeans and a fur coat, was coming towards me. No, that couldn't be her; Utta wasn't into fur coats. But the figure came on and I moved forward hesitating. She slowed and looked and lights of recognition went on and it was her, and we hugged. And somewhere a voice inside me said, 'Why the hell didn't you do this before.' And she said of the fur coat, 'A girlfriend lent it to me against the cold.'

We talked hard all the way home to Somerset. I introduced her to Skye Cottage and the midget bath and we went for a long walk. It was the perfect introduction to rural England, almost as if it had been stage managed for her: a beautiful, clear, winter afternoon. In the valley below the cottage, we tucked into the hedge and watched as a hunt was working the wood; the huntsman's horn, a ripple of red coats through the trees and the braying of hounds. Above the valley, the village of Buckland St Mary trickled down the hillside, pegged firm by the tower of the church and the crown of trees. A thin moon rose in the sky.

The next few weeks spun by. Utta was enraptured by Skye Cottage and with a few touches, a vase of flowers, a table moved, a picture hung, transformed it from a holiday cottage into a real home. Early on I introduced her to the river. It happened to be low tide and she was much amused, having imagined something the size of the Murray-Darling, not this thin stream between muddy banks. Most days we went over to the holding tanks at Bowdens to carry on preparations for the coming season. The first of the tides when the elvers were expected was only a few weeks away. Ernie was our guide in everything, a word here, a suggestion there, quietly given, resolving difficulties. He was intrigued and impressed by my new companion and paid frequent visits to the barn to see how things were getting on,

'Got company then, Mike,' he said in one aside, 'yea, she seems very nice, very friendly like, but woz er called – I could'n catch en when she said?'

They liked each other from the start but had great difficulty understanding each other's accents and I'd be called upon to interpret and translate Australian-isms into Somerset or vice versa. He was also very diplomatic about offering her advice,

'Yere, Mike,' he'd say, 'the maid, you know er's making they there ilver trays, well she idn doing it quite right, but I didn' know whether I ought to say anything 'bout it, like.'

At last, by the end of February, everything was ready, there were stacks of nets and trays for the fishermen, the tanks were cleaned and repaired and the whole place sparkled. Anthony came down to inspect and was impressed,

'Looks jolly good, Michael: all you need now are some elvers.'

They came on the first big tide in March, small steady catches, and soon we had fifty kilos in the tanks. Not enough to make a shipment but I had agreed with Rosengarten that we would be in touch as soon as we started to catch. I just assumed it was a matter of a phone call and he would place an order. But from Rosengarten there was no reply. He wasn't even there, his office said, he was in France, collecting elvers with the lorry, away to the end of the week. I couldn't believe it. I'd pictured him waiting by the phone for our call. I tried my other contacts in Holland and south Germany, but they weren't interested either: later, try later. I was beginning to panic. Without a market, I was half inclined to put a brake on the catching or stop it altogether. After several days I finally managed to get through to Rosengarten. Yes, he'd take up to 200 kgs, for the following week and I would have to fly out with them as agreed.

For about ten minutes Utta and I were ecstatic - it was our first order - and then came reality: the sudden realization that we had caught only a small part of it. We needed at least another hundred kilos to make up the shipment.

It was a foul weekend of weather, pouring with rain. All week the elvers had worked their way up river to Langport, still tidal in those days, and some fourteen miles inland from the estuary. Now sensing they were nearly at the end of their migration they put in a last great effort, streaming against the current, a dark weaving band a yard wide. There must have been about fifty fishermen, mostly Hancock's men, fishing either side of the old town bridge, where the Romans had once forded the river. We managed to find a good spot above, on a bend where the current bunched the elvers together. French friends, Robin and Christine, teachers from London, were staying with us for the weekend, and willingly came to our help. In the pouring rain with only their motorbike leathers to keep them dry they were soon like a couple of drowned rats. Together we fished half the night, with the stack of trayed elvers growing steadily behind us until finally the run slackened and stopped.

Hancock's lorry must have taken a good tonne off the river that night. But even the four of us had not done badly. Weighing in our catch back at the tanks we found we had almost enough to fulfil the order with some of our fishermen still to clock in.

A few days later I stood at baggage collection in Hamburg airport, waiting for my overnight bag. It had been a busy night: with the help of Anthony and Ern we had packed the elvers, starting at one in the morning, a kilo at a time into the polystyrene containers with ice and water, driven them up to Heathrow, offloaded them in the cargo area by six, then dashed round to the passenger terminal so that I could join the same flight. I had also checked our funds the day before leaving: we had just twenty pounds left in the kitty.

Two hours later, standing in a daze beside a smartly dressed couple by the carousel at Hamburg airport, I suddenly spotted something. There, on an immaculate leather suitcase just passing was a wriggling elver. It was alive and well and seemed very perky and pleased to be out of its box.

My first thought was, 'Oh good, they are still alive,' – and then, 'Oh my god, disaster, they've all tipped over,' for I could now see more elvers, ones and twos on baggage and cases as they trundled past. There was a general stirring amongst passengers, sensing something wrong. Mutterings, heads bent foFrward to examine these alien creatures, 'Was ist denn das;' I heard someone say, 'Würmen!' Worms! And the refrain was taken up. Thankfully I spotted my bag, grabbed it and fled.

Rosengarten was waiting and together we went to Customs and Freight to extract the shipment. I waited, fearing the worst. Then there they were, a pile of white boxes. All looked well but as we loaded them onto Rosengarten's truck I could see there had been a few escapees, no major damage but one box in particular had elvers squeezing through the lid, a sure sign it had been knocked hard.

We drove to the Aalversandstelle, making polite conversation. I was still very tense. I knew the elvers were alive but I had no idea how they had fared from the flight or how they would look in his tanks. I had been expecting a rural setting like our own, a holding site somewhere out in the fields by a river. Instead we drove to a large warehouse on a modern industrial estate about half an hour from Hamburg airport. It gave nothing away; for all the world it might have been a tyre depot or paint factory. But behind the roller doors it had the peaceful dim lit gloom of an aquarium, somewhere subterranean. Two huge fish transport trucks and their trailers filled the main area, while all round the walls were fibre glass tanks; water jetted in from perforated pipes that sucked in air so each tank was a mass of tiny bubbles, like a jacuzzi, to revive tired elvers and fish brought in from all over the continent. It was so spotlessly clean, you could have eaten off the floor; everything had its place, all tools, each piece of equipment went back after use to its clip on the wall. I thought of the chaotic muddle of our barn back at Bowdens where hours could be spent looking for the hammer or tape measure.

Some thirty elver boxes were placed by each tank ready for immersion, but first the lids were removed and water splashed over them to equalize temperatures. Then as each box was gently tipped, the elvers swam away, fanning out like spears, looking strong and healthy. Rosengarten watched them through expert eyes then turned to me and said,

'Ja Herr Brown, alles gut, gute Qualität; Sie können jetzt ausruhen.' You can relax now. But there was still one more test. It had been agreed that I should stay overnight and we would look at them together in the morning. From long experience, he knew that you always got a truer picture after twelve hours.

When we returned the next day the elvers were lying resting in a thick mat at the bottom of each tank, little heads like upturned faces in a crowd, swaying slightly as if to the hidden sound of music. Rosengarten was pleased and gave the order for their loading, for now they were off on the fish transporter for delivery to various fishing clubs far away to the south.

It was over: the weight was good, the fish were good, 'alles korrekt, Herr Brown'. He took me to his office and wrote a cheque, handing it to me with a flourish. Looking back we were so fortunate to have found this man as our main customer for he was open and honest and, above all, he paid on the nail. Cash flow, the speed with which the money returns to a business, large or small, is its oxygen for survival, especially when it's starting out. Had we got into the wily grasp of some of the dealers we were to come across later, we would probably never have survived that first year. And no-one starting a business ever forgets their first payment, that first cheque, because it means that the whole thing, the project they've planned and nurtured, actually works and becomes real. I flew home to Utta, like Chamberlain from Munich with his piece of paper, but this was not a treaty, this was a cheque for over eight hundred pounds, more money than I'd ever received in one go in all my life. And Rosengarten had placed another order for the following tide.

The days passed at bewildering speed, a time of intense activity, snatched meals, short sleep. Time flew, we were always running to catch up. By day we processed the catch from the day before, moving the elvers to clean tanks, removing dead or damaged fish, the 'whites' as they were called. By night, we would prepare the site for the evening's tide, rush down to the river to fish, hurrying back to weigh in the fishermen. We made the second shipment to Rosengarten – I didn't have to accompany it now – and good as his word, payment arrived by post within days. At night we yawned our way back to Skye Cottage, bone weary. At that hour we were often cold and ravenously hungry. To save time we huddled in the midget bath in boiling water with a saucepan of stew, eaten straight from the pot with a spoon, passing it back and forth like survivors in a boat.

33

Then suddenly it was the end of the tide, the tanks empty, the fish despatched; there would be a break for a few days, a coming up for air. In those early days of elvering, when the height of the tide dropped below a certain level, it was generally thought that it wasn't worth the effort of fishing, so buyers and fishermen alike went home and took the week off. Life returned to normal. Friends would come down to stay, there'd be family to catch up with; it was a time to repair kit, and take stock, plan for the next tide.

After all the drama and intensity we awoke to the sounds and smells of the coming spring. Back at Skye Cottage on the hills, we'd stand and sniff the night air, soft with its scent of grass and things in bud. By day, the sun warmed the hedges full of primroses that led down to the old mill. There were drifts of wild daffodils in the wood and everywhere the sound of lambs.

Over at Bowdens, Ernie had transformed the big Dutch barn into a series of holding pens for lambing down the ewes, with a wall of bales to shelter them from the wind and a thick bedding of straw. At night when we came in from the river we'd go down to see how they were doing. It was like a huge maternity ward, a peaceful place under soft light with just the rustle of hooves on straw; muffled noises, the odd cough or grunt; and a sense of the ewes' common concern for one another. When one of them went into labour, lying on her side, panting, the others would gather round as if to give support. But Ernie was always there. Sometimes he'd call us over to hold an animal while he manoeuvred a breached lamb or difficult birth. Deftly reaching inside, great powerful wrists and forearm deep inside the ewe, ever so gently turning the lamb round. It would slither out at last like a wet package and he'd blow in its nostrils with a piece of straw to clear the airways and get it breathing. In a moment it was up on its feet, swaying on little knock-kneed legs like pipe cleaners. There'd be an almost audible, collective sigh of relief from the watching mothers.

Curiously at this time of year, our neighbour, Ken Gready was making the last of his cider. All the big producers pressed their apples in the autumn and winter but Ken, probably using up some late growers stored in a corner, finished up in the early spring. We were first alerted to it at night when we got back to Skye Cottage from elvering and heard a faint trickle coming from his barn by the road where we parked. Following the sound we tracked it to an ancient cider press next to his milking parlour where the last juices were being squeezed into a container. The sharp, slightly vinegary, aroma of the crushed apple filled the air.

We had tried some of the local ciders and, though they were strong, they were nothing like Ken's. His was powerful stuff, dry and unsweetened, a pale straw colour; real rocket fuel: you could surely have run a tractor on it. We once tried a glass and passed out for several hours in front of the fire. Sunday mornings around making time drew a steady stream of visitors to Ken's woodshed in his garden to sample the new brew. They'd stoop through the low door into the secret darkness of barrels for serious tasting of different qualities and vintages. Gradually as the numbers grew, they spilled out and sat around on upturned logs outside with much guffawing and stumbling about until with fond farewells they swayed off unsteady of foot in the general direction of home.

★★★★★

The first two tides of the season had been our apprenticeship. Ernie always said that when the daffodils were fully out, that's when the elvers would really come. Added to that was the fact that we were now approaching the spring equinoxes of March and April, when the sun and the moon pulled in the same direction creating huge high tides, eighteen feet above mean sea level, the second-biggest tides in the world. Great shoals of elvers would be borne up the Bristol Channel, itself a perfectly-shaped net, formed by the converging coasts of Cornwall and South Wales, throttling back into the narrow gullet of the Severn estuary and Gloucester.

Elvers entered every stream and every river, but what made the Parrett so special was its estuary: the hooked shape of its mouth as it met the sea was a curved upper jaw that seemed to snag the shoals of fish as they passed. Then, like the Severn, it had a tidal bore: such a huge volume of water forced into the narrow mouth of the estuary on the high tides that it created a wall of water, two to three feet high, powering its way upriver for several miles. For centuries the river traffic, barges laden with coal and Bridgwater bricks, made full use of it – just like the elvers – hitching a free ride up to Langport, miles inland. But perhaps, for the elvers, it was something else. Perhaps, embedded deep in their communal conscience and programmed into their migration, was the memory of the ancient watery world of the Somerset wetlands and marshes, eely heaven, that had

35

drawn them back year after year over thousands of years. Whatever the reasons, the Parrett, insignificant in size, received a disproportionate share of the elver shoals. And the fishermen were not complaining.

There was something unique about a big tide. It started with the news that fish had been caught. Word would get around, spreading like wildfire.

Ern would call by at the barn.

'Yer, Mike, did you ere? They been catching down low; one of Hancock's men told oi last night; 'ee said ther a lot more to come.'

For all those involved, all day in offices, factories, houses, farms within reach of the river, elver fever took hold and everywhere the vital question, 'What time's the tide?' along with much consulting of the Tide Table for the Port of Bridgwater - our bible for the season. You couldn't think of anything else: men would be glancing at watches, wondering if they could get off early; minds half on the job, agonising over where to go on the river, the best spot to catch. They'd dash home, change, grab a meal, scrabble to pack the kit, trays, lamps, sandwiches, baccy, thermos. From all around, vehicles driven at speed, nets clamped to the roof like snails with strange shells, converged on the river.

Like gold prospecting, it helped enormously if you had a sniff of where the action was. The basic rule was to position yourself somewhere above where they'd been caught the previous night so that as the shoal rose from its resting place on the river bed you'd be there for it. But finding a place to fish was a bit like arriving for a concert without a ticket; the spot you wanted lined with cars. What about the orchard, might just squeeze in there. No, not a chance. Full up. Often you worked in pairs, so if your mate got off earlier – or better still, was on holiday – he'd be able to stake your claim: together you could command forty or fifty yards of bank and see off any intruders.

At Bowdens, if Ern wasn't lambing, the whole family, Norah and the two boys, joined the migration down to the river: gobbled their tea, squeezed themselves and all their gear into their tiny car. It fitted around them so tightly they almost seemed to be wearing it. As it had no roof rack, Ern lashed their nets directly onto the roof with expert knots and bailer twine fed through the windows. They'd bump off down the track, the nets would slither loose, hanging off the side like giant earmuffs until retied, then off they'd roar.

We'd follow, down to the moor, along the river past a straggle of cottages and small-holdings, ancient wheel-less vehicles, overgrown and full of chickens, down to our favourite spot at Stathe where a long bend in the river was good for fishing. We hastily set up, pegging the nets into the bank to stake our claim and unloading the trays and buckets. Many of the fishermen lit Tilley lamps to cast a soft glow on the water to attract the elvers and provide light for working. They guttered and hissed and the smell of paraffin wafted on the air mingling with the tarry smoke from the withy yard by the bridge.

Before the action, little groups of fishermen up and down the banks – a smattering of ours, but mostly Hancock's – drank last cups of tea and chatted as they watched the river rush by upstream, creeping up the banks, huge and bloated. Gradually, almost at the top of the bank, it slowed, stopped, hung motionless, pausing for breath, before plunging back in reverse. A near full moon eased into the sky and climbed slowly over the scene. From lower down came the thonk-thonk, thonk-thonk of the great pumps, deliberately started to introduce the sweet water from the moor into the briny river to lure the elvers into the side to the waiting nets; the pump keeper's perk, highly illegal, but all was fair in love and war - and elvering.

The nets were in now. A critical moment as doubt crept in: was it the right spot, would the shoal come; there was still just time to pack and move, find somewhere better. But no-one moved. Some instinct told us, they would come. We could feel it. A dip; just one or two now. Another dip: more this time. About thirty. A tiny whispering sound in the bottom of the net. From lower down, the first faint clack of wood, which meant someone spreading elvers onto trays, so someone catching. The next dip took your breath away: a ball of elvers in the bottom of the net, at least half a kilo. A sound like chips in deep fry, a sizzling. Into the bucket, the elvers still running, coiling and coiling around the inside. When that was full, we'd scrabble to spread them onto the trays, and quick, because there were more coming. It was fully dark now, getting colder, but all of us stripped to shirtsleeves as we scrabbled up and down steep muddy banks; hot work, feverish stuff. No chat now. A few minutes between lifting the net; just three dips and the bucket was full. Stacks of trays grew higher. From all round now the clacking sound of wood on wood as trays were slapped one on top of another and filled with elvers. That sound, like stacking deck chairs, always meant a good night. There'd be frantic calls for more trays.

'Yere, Mike, you got any more? We run out. I told the missus to put more on the van but she reckinned they waddun going to run.'

Shining a torch on the water showed a band of elvers two feet wide, a foot deep, swimming up river, countless millions of them. That was an elver run, the spring migration of the young eel upriver. That was the official definition. But when you put your hand in the water, felt the tiny points of their noses as they prinkled your skin, you felt their urgency, their straining to get up river against the current. It was what drove them all. In all the frenzy of catching, there was always a sense of awe at their collective energy and their sheer numbers.

Past midnight, the moon climbed, radiant over the moor, silvering the grass and banks. The run had lasted three hours or so and was beginning to wane. The river dropped. Catching was more tricky now as you followed it down, careful not to get stuck in the glutinous mud. Fishermen were packing up. Noises of cars, shouts, farewells. 'Wot time's tide tomorrow? I'll give ee ring then. Cheers 'en.' The drama was over, the audience gone. Perhaps one lone fisherman left who would fish on till dawn; the river exhausted now, just a winding rivulet between sculpted banks of mud, as the moon rode on alone, serene.

Back at the tanks it was weighing-in time. Utta and I would rush to get there first. Our fishermen, often coats tied with baler twine, would arrive in mud-spattered vehicles, nets tethered to the roof. Spilling out of cars and vans, caked in mud, often incongruously wearing bedroom slippers - wellies discarded for driving - and before bothering to unload, they'd head straight for the old set of scales that hung like a clock from the gantry. Trays and elvers were weighed together, then, after the fish had been tipped into reception tanks, the empty trays subtracted to give the true weight of catch. It was a crude rough system, and it meant that we bought all sorts of by-catch: sticks, stones, sticklebacks, shrimp, slime, and mud by the bucketful. To the side of the gantry was a small blackboard to record the names of the fishermen and their catch. It was the centre of all attention; round it they gathered to swap tales, compare catches, get in our way and relive the magic of the evening.

'Oi never seed anythun like it. I were stripped to me waist nearly runnin up and down that there bank trayin up for missus.'

'Cor, do you see that, Ronny, ee got twelve kilo. Ee done well then.'

'Probably why we weren't catchin, ee were roight in front of us. And cor, look, Len, he got eighteen. I told ee we shoulda gone there.'

Often there'd be one big one, a mystery catch, no-one quite knew where. Like a rich seam, glinting future prospects.

'Cor, look at that then, Bruce, twenty two, cor ee done well. Where was ee then?' A silence: no-one knew or if they knew they weren't saying. Such information gave vital coordinates for the following night. Like gold prospecting, anything where the stakes were high, counter-intelligence lurked.

They'd turn to a late arrival. 'How did ee get on then?'

'Oh, juss a few, we couldn' get in anywhere. We missed em.'

But the speaker would hang back, wait till the crowd had gone, then proudly unload a stack of trays from the boot of his car. He'd fished a different spot to the rest, just on the off-chance, and it had paid off. 'Don't tell anyone, Mike, or they'll all be there tomorrow.'

When they were all gone, a debris of kit left behind: an old boot, a slipper, flask of tea or a bucket lying in the yard. And mud, lots of river mud, it was part of elvering: it caked your hands, parched the skin, cracked the tips of the fingers; and its smell - of river and rhine and of dark, still water off the moor - hung in our nostrils through the season.

Not every night produced big catches, far from it. A flood, or a dry cold wind could halt the elvers in their tracks and on most nights catches were moderate, unspectacular, just two or three kilos. You needed skill and dedication to keep catching well. But it was those big tides, those were the nights we would all remember when the season was over and we'd hung up our nets. And it wasn't just the catches; it was witnessing the migration itself. Something stirs in all of us when we see creatures in vast numbers. And so it was with the elvers but with them there was something more: it was their straining, their longing to reach their goal, that touched something deep within us all, perhaps from long, long ago when we were nomadic people moving over the face of the earth drawn, too, by the moon and the stars.

★★★★★

On those big spring tides I first experienced the mixture of feelings, part relief, part panic, I came to know so well over the years. Half of me welcomed the elvers because they were so obviously essential to the business, but part of me knotted in panic as we ran out of tanks to hold them or frantically searched for a market to sell them. In that first year, with eight tanks, we could only hold around 400 kilos safely. You could put more fish in the tanks, get away with it if it was cold because cold water held more oxygen, but the key was to find a market fast, better still have it ready and waiting, and get rid of them quick. The biggest elver tides had a curious habit of coinciding with a weekend or the Easter Bank Holiday: no possibility of cargo flights for three days; the tanks already full and more big nights to come. It was at times like these, as I watched our entire combined assets, such as they were, swimming round the tanks, losing weight, that I wanted to creep into a quiet place and hide. At such times too I used to envy Hancock, my opposition on the river, who could hold eight tonnes in clear stream water, gravity fed, and who had a collection by truck almost weekly from the continent.

Friends to whom I confided my worries would say, well, the most obvious decision would be to stop buying. But only in the most dire circumstances did you ever do that because it broke the trust in you. It showed weakness. And it was part of elver lore that any catch the fishermen weighed in was then yours, to be paid for at the end of the tide – later, even at the end of the season. Effectively you were as trusted as a bank: if there was the slightest whiff of anxiety about your ability to pay, fishermen would melt away like snow on a roof. You had to keep smiling, maintain the face of confidence, express forced delight as yet another catcher unloaded tray after tray of elvers to weigh in, while inwardly you groaned, desperate for them to have missed out.

Anthony had been through it all before, and stowing elvers wasn't all that different from finding space for grain during busy harvests. He'd come down to the tanks in the evening before the catches came in from the river. He had an infectious calming effect; whistling softly under his breath, as if there was not a care in the world, he'd survey the tanks like a general on the battlefield. He was expert at tweaking the system, fitting in a few more here and there, 'Oh they'll be fine, Michael, you can easily fit another ten, even twenty kilo in each of those; we used to load them way beyond.' His breezy confidence would wind up my flagging morale like a clock, ready to survive another night, another battle.

Between the tides that first season, I had had a chance to think around the restrictions of air freight: the most we could ever send to Hamburg by regular airline was 200kgs at a time. Not much use if the elvers were coming in at a rate of 300kgs a night. It was like shovelling sand. With the big tides looming, what we needed was a bigger lift. I had heard of a small company near Biggin Hill in Kent that hired aircraft for private flights and went to see them. They had a fourteen seater, a de Havilland Riley Dove, an ancient beaten-up old bird but with the seats stripped out I calculated that she could hold perhaps four or five hundred kilos of elvers in their boxes. And it was cheap. I booked it provisionally and spoke to Rosengarten who was hesitant at first, but yes, that would be fine if, as before, I would accompany the first shipment so that we could look at the quality of the fish together.

So it was that, early one morning, part-way through the big tide, having packed the fish in the night, we drove down to Exeter, our nearest airport. We were met by two young pilots. They were casually dressed and looked rather as if they'd just come out of the pub. The first thing they wanted was a cheque. Half up front, half on completion. I wasn't quite sure if this reflected doubts about my ability to pay or the aircraft's ability to complete the journey. However, with this small formality out of the way, we were then able to drive straight onto the tarmac runway and load the aircraft, safely and carefully. I was impressed: this was surely the way to go; much better than consigning our precious cargo of baby eels to some loader who drove his fork-lift like a maniac. We filled the whole fuselage with the boxes. There was just room for me to sit in the single seat wedged behind the door to the cockpit. Just before take-off, the pilot asked what temperature I'd like the cargo to be held at during the flight. No heat, I said firmly: the elvers had to be kept cold.

With that we trundled down the runway and struggled into the sky.

The Dove was old and weary and aptly named; with the combined weight of elvers, water, ice and boxes, she must have been at the very limits of her lift capacity. She used the whole length of the runway and almost had to flap at the end to get off the ground, struggling to become airborne. At last as she clawed her way into the sky, with a massive creaking and chittering from the polystyrene boxes rubbing together, I could see Utta and a helper from the farm, two tiny figures, waving from the perimeter.

After about half an hour of flying time, I began to feel numb with cold, but such a cold I'd never felt before; it was entering my body core, leaking into me like ice. I was well wrapped up but strapped in, I couldn't move to keep warm. I began to think that after a three hour flight I'd arrive as stiff as a frozen turkey. With chattering teeth, I managed to lean forward and tap on the cockpit door, vaguely wondering if there was anyone in there. To my relief it flipped open emanating snug warmth. They were having coffee from a flask and one of them was reading the paper.

'Wonder if I could have a little heat. I'm freezing back here,' I screamed above the noise.

'No problem, sure, of course,' came the cheery answer. And the door flipped shut. Almost immediately I felt a reassuring glow of warmth. The heating system on the aircraft seemed very efficient, better than its take-off abilities. What I didn't know and was to discover later was that the hot air was provided by two simple pipes at floor level down either side of the fuselage. These became so hot that they actually melted the polystyrene and cooked the elvers inside. We flew on blissfully unaware of these happenings.

Rosengarten was waiting for us, very excited, with a large pick-up truck at Hamburg airport. As the Dove was on a tight schedule, aiming for a quick turnaround, there was no time to accompany him to his site at the Aalversandstelle to unload so we agreed to do an on-site check. He opened several boxes at random and scrutinised the contents. In each one the elvers were in perfect condition, moving dreamily in their ice and water. By sheer chance he picked the boxes from the top of the stack in the hold. It was only later when he got back to his tanks that he discovered the cooked boxes that had lain on the floor against the hot pipes, and by then I was half way back across the Channel.

'Gute Qualität,' he said rumbling with contentment. Then and there he wrote me a cheque for the shipment. 'I pay you straight away so you can pay your fishermen. You see, I know, I understand all these things.' He did, he was a good man to do business with. For both of us, the ability to ship this quantity of elvers in one go was a real breakthrough, a huge saving of time and energy. And it had seemed to work so smoothly. He was really excited, 'Herr Brown, do you want to send another shipment like this?'

'How about the day after tomorrow, ' I replied, thinking of the several still-full tanks of elvers back at Bowdens. I checked with the pilots. They beamed happily.

The next morning there was a phone call from Rosengarten. I could tell instantly from his tone of voice that all was not well. Overall quality and weight good, he reported, but there had been losses, always coming from the boxes where the polystyrene had melted. It wasn't difficult to piece together what had happened. On the Rosengarten Richter scale this was sombre feedback, delivered in his must-do-better-next-time voice. The next shipment was still on but I would ensure that there would be no heating.

Everything went smoothly as before. Again we loaded the old Dove at Exeter airport – we were beginning to feel rather fond of her by now – and waved her into the skies. I had made it clear that there was to be no heating in the hold.

We had cleared the tanks at Bowdens, not an elver remained, and the tide was over. That evening we were sitting having a celebratory meal at Skye Cottage when the phone rang.

'Katastrophe,' a voice bellowed. It could only be Rosengarten and this time we were at the top end of the Richter scale. A disaster, a total disaster. The fish had arrived frozen, even the ice hadn't melted. I listened, my heart in my boots. The losses were huge, it was a disaster. 'Katastrophe,' he bawled again. A huge let-down for his customers. And so on. And so on. Gradually the great blast waves of his voice subsided by degree into more reasoned considerations. It was not our fault, he knew that. It was the plane. The lack of control. He was bitterly disappointed; it could have been the perfect system, so easy. And yet, now, never again. There was one last bellow of 'Katastrophe,' like departing thunder. He would call me in the morning when the fish had had a chance to recuperate and let me know the worst.

We waited, sleepless, full of dread. His call came the next afternoon. It was like the calm after the storm. A different man, a different voice; sombre yet level; they had just shipped the fish out; the losses hadn't been as bad as he'd first thought. Apparently we'd been generous with the weight and that had made up for the losses. He was sending a cheque that day. 'But, Herr Brown, no more private aircraft.' A useful experiment but it was too risky. It was back to the Heathrow run.

It was late April now and the season nearing its end, the catches dwindling, many of the fishermen had stopped. We sold the fish from the last tide to a company in Gloucester who came to collect them. The price was reasonable and it cleared the site. It was our first contact with the Gloucester buyers. We liked this particular company. They were also starting up; they were called Bristol Channel Fisheries and we felt we might do business with them in the future.

Since her arrival in England, Utta had worked all hours, shared in all the highs and lows of the season, been a huge support, and such good company. We made a good team, and we were very happy together. I could think of no-one else I could more enjoyably spend a life with. One evening at supper, plucking up courage, I asked her to marry me. She was so surprised, she asked for more time to think it over.

The following day she accepted.

And then before we knew it, the season in Somerset came to a close, the elver migration was over; the fishermen had lost interest. The show was over. It was time now to head north; we were off to Scotland in the van to seek our fortunes on the river Laxford. But no fishermen this time; just us.

Kingsbury Church across the moor

Chapter Three

We packed as if preparing for a polar journey away from civilization with stores of food and clothing, the van stuffed with fishing gear, nets and trays. It was a beautiful day. Skye Cottage looked ravishing and we were almost reluctant to leave.

From the Blackdown Hills in Somerset to our destination, the little fishing port of Kinlochbervie, just south of Cape Wrath in the far north of Sutherland, it was over seven hundred miles - about the distance from London to Berlin or south west France.

North of Inverness, beyond Lairg, the road became single track, with tufts of grass down the middle. If you met a vehicle, particularly a fish lorry, you dived into one of the lay-bys created for your survival. Over the years we learned that you never messed with a fish lorry. They were like the road trains on the desert tracks in Australia: totally unstoppable; they had one speed which was full on and woe betide you if you expected them to slow or back up; they didn't appear to have a reverse gear. The odd rusting vehicle carcass, wheels poking out of the heather alongside the road attested to the foolishness of those who'd tried.

As we travelled north up the side of Loch Shin, a long grey loch, thin as a blade, the scenery became more barren with low bleak hills, brown heather and scraggy clumps of firs by the odd cluster of houses. Gone were the green sweeping hills, the majesty of Perthshire further south. I looked at Utta, wondering what she made of it. Ever since she'd arrived, I'd never stopped telling her how beautiful Sutherland was and how she would love it. She was looking thoughtful. We stopped the van to stretch our legs. The wash of the engine stilled. We breathed in the pure air and stood listening to the lap of water from the edge of the loch. And silence.

Then, past Overscaig, the road crossed a divide and dropped down into the grandeur of the Reay Forest estate and the Laxford, a beautiful river, gleaming and sparkling in sunlight. It was only about eight miles long, flowing out of Loch More through Loch Stack beneath the mountains, before it swept and swung for four miles, through deep pools where salmon lay, over shingle shores, heather banked, tumbling down through wood and boulders to the estuary and its meeting with the sea. It could change in an instant: one moment so low, it rattled on the pebbles, the next, swollen from countless streams and burns off the mountains, as it raced and roared down the valley. It had been, still was, one of the best salmon and seatrout rivers in Scotland. Even the ancient Norsemen had known it, fixing it forever with the name of 'lax' meaning salmon. And this was where we were coming to fish for elvers.

Sinclair Mackintosh, factor to the Duchess, had arranged for us to stay for a peppercorn rent at a property belonging to the estate in Kinlochbervie known as the Colt House. From the outside it looked like a large packing case plonked down on the water's edge. Approached by a precipitous gravel track it had parking on a grassy level just above the shore. Inside, most of the front of the house was one large living room with huge picture windows. One way, you looked out onto the life of the small harbour with its cluster of trawlers; on the other side, up the loch to the mountains of Foinavon and Arkle. It was the most stunning location. We just couldn't believe our good fortune. It was to be our home for the next six weeks.

Though this was my third visit to Sutherland, I'd never been to Kinlochbervie before and it was not at all what I had expected. I had imagined a small fishing community with narrow cobbled streets and old houses winding down to a harbour. But not at all. At first encounter Kinlochbervie looked oddly bald and impermanent. Old low stone white-washed houses did still exist but neat rows of pebble dash modern homes had sprung up alongside to accommodate a population working in and around the fishing industry that then, in 1975, was just starting to expand and prosper. The rich fishing grounds north west of Cape Wrath were yielding consistently good catches; the market for sea fish was growing fast. Iced down, in wooden boxes, the fish were trucked south each night to the bigger market centres at Aberdeen and Edinburgh. To cater for the surge in traffic, the old road down the hill into the village had been widened: half a mile out of town, it switched triumphantly from single track to an expansive breadth of tarmac that swept past the Colt House gate on its way down to the harbour where it came to an abrupt end.

The harbour was the heart and soul of the place, its main focus. At any time of the day from the windows of the Colt House we watched across the water the comings and goings of harbour life. A trawler unloading or fork lifts, scurrying like beetles, moving stacks of fish boxes. Sounds of repairs, mighty bangs from metal plates, noises of welding, drilling, echoed across the water. And the seals, like the gulls, were always scouting, waiting for bits thrown from the boats. Their big broad heads with wide-set dark eyes followed you, watchful, inquisitive, then they'd snort and blow and vanish without a sound.

In those days the fleet of trawlers, mostly small and from up and down the coast, would head out on Sunday evenings, away from the shelter of Loch Inchard, often heading north and west beyond Cape Wrath. As the string of boats emerged from the loch and met the open sea, they looked like the classic picture postcard, so happy and carefree through the visitor's eye, but when you focussed the binoculars on them, you saw the heave and roll of the deck as they met the swell; you could feel seasick just looking at them. One of the sons of Mr Morrison, the postmaster opposite, had shown us round his trawler – the Loch Inchard – and it helped to visualize life aboard: eating and sleeping in a small, cramped space with the reek of diesel oil, fish and cooking; a dark night, in a big sea with a force eight gale brewing, up on deck trying to get nets in, amongst the clutter of ropes and gear and winches. And there were very few days when they didn't go out. It was a hard, perilous way to make a living, but the landings were good, so the money was good - and getting better. And earning a living from the sea was part of the way of life of these small tight-knit coastal communities.

The boats were usually back by Thursday evening or Friday, but if there'd been a good catch and they were full up, they'd be in much earlier. Then they'd quickly unload, take on fresh ice and boxes, turn and run back out to sea. When they did that, it reminded us of the elver fishermen down south: that same sense of urgency, feverishly off loading to get into the rich seam of catching again.

Only at the weekend did it all stop. Then all was quiet, all the noise and bustle gone. Trawlers hugged the pier, tethered, peaceful, waiting. No-one moved down there.

As soon as we'd settled in, we set off to explore the mouth of the Laxford. Below the looping stone arch of Laxford Bridge, a path ran down one side of the river, down to the estuary where the river widened and deepened as it met the sea. There we peered under stones at the water's edge for the first signs of elvers but there was nothing, nor any of the tell-tale activity - gulls converging, pecking the water - that I'd seen the year before.

We were not really at all surprised. It was only the beginning of May and all the indications were that the elvers came at the end of the month, just as Billie Scobie, head keeper on the estate, had recorded. By arriving early in Sutherland, we had an ideal opportunity to do some amateur research and find the extent, the beginning and the end, of the Laxford migration: if it lasted nearly three months down south, then why not in Scotland? Maybe Scobie's records were evidence of the one main run, but overlooked others?

Checking the river was to become almost a daily ritual: along this stretch of estuary where the sweet river water met the salt, we looked most days for early signs of the elvers. We never tired of going there. From the bridge the path ran through a little wood of silver birch and rowan strewn with mossy boulders and clumps of primrose; the river rustled below, the air sweet with the scent of spring. Further on, as the tide rose and fell, it exposed banks of seaweed and beds of fat mussels - delicious eating. At low tide, sheep grazed the thrift-knotted grass at the edge of the pebbly shore where heron fished. In the middle of the river families of eiders bobbed and cooed whilst oystercatchers peeped and gathered on the green lichened rocks at the point where the waters from Badna Bay emptied into the main estuary.

Near this point stood a tiny single-roomed cottage, with its own pier and landing stage and with a wooden paling fence, built as a picnic place – well chosen - for Queen Victoria in 1868 in anticipation of a visit that had never happened. From this spot we'd sometimes see otters, whiskery heads drawing a long V, rippling the water. Once, a mother with her cub emerged onto the shore, a large spider crab in her mouth and we watched as she gave her young a master class in how best to deal with its armour plating, crunching it as effortlessly as if she was eating crisps.

On these visits to the river, we often called in for coffee and a natter with Sandee Mackintosh, wife of Sinclair, whom I'd met the previous year. She was a lovely lady, great fun, bright eyed, with a soft Scots accent and an irreverent sense of humour. She'd be cooking, busy preparing meals for the seasonal stream of visitors connected with the estate, people up to see the Duchess or to see Sinclair, accountants or officials from the Grosvenor offices in London. She would have news of the estate, of who was up visiting, news of the Ridgways at Ardmore and stories about the businessmen or the instructors. And she was inquisitive, wanting to know what we were up to, if we'd seen any elvers yet, what it was that we looked for. Over the years, Sandee, from her vantage point over the Laxford, was to become our unofficial watcher of the river, providing us with the first news and sightings of an elver run, a role vital to us so far away in the south.

Soon after our arrival, we also set up the salmon hatchery in readiness for holding the elvers, if and when they came. It was located in the tiny estate village of Achfary that lay in the shadow of Ben Stack, a single gravel side street of estate cottages with the factor's office, a school and a black and white phone box with coat of arms fronting the main road. The hatchery lay across a small river that flowed off the hill and was reached by a stout wooden bridge that gave a hollow clonk as you crossed. We would get to know it well - along with the crushed coconut scent of the yellow gorse that grew on the banks.

The hatchery was a long stone shed, fed by a small burn, perfect for holding elvers: in the cool darkness they could rest peacefully and recover from the trauma of being caught. We set about connecting up the holding tanks, long rectangular boxes, that we were allowed to use. Like boats after a season out of water, they leaked badly and needed time for the wood to swell. Painted pitch black, they descended a series of stepped levels so the air was full of the splash of water as it cascaded from one tank to another, damp and dark as a cave.

From the hill behind, the burn tumbled down through spindly pines, flowed through a set of header tanks before being piped down to the hatchery. It seemed such a safe, reliable system, a gravity-fed supply of pure water and there'd be no need for pumps.

But this happy little stream, I was to learn, could be highly temperamental. In the course of an hour, winds and heavy rain could transform it into a rushing torrent that swept down cartloads of pine needles that blocked the pipes into the reservoir tanks, throttling the precious supply of water. Equally, in dry spells, the volume of water reduced to a pathetic trickle, which was why, I was to realize, the header tanks had been constructed in the first place to provide a buffer of safety. In fact it needed constant watching and vigilance. Sometimes I longed for the reliability of the old electric pumps and the borehole back in Somerset.

Setting up the hatchery, it wasn't long before we met Willie Jones. Or rather he met us, coming over to introduce himself: he could see the hatchery from his house and he was bursting with curiosity to know what we were up to. Willie was a stalker on the estate but for the rest of the time worked wherever he was needed, jack of all trades, in the estate sawmill or in the forestry or doing maintenance jobs. Unlike many who had worked for the Duchess all their lives, Willie was a relative newcomer to the region, a Glaswegian, speaking at machine-gun speed, almost unintelligible to us at times; he had a ready, easy laugh, husky from cigarettes and whisky, and a wicked eye and sense of humour. Married with a pretty wife who worked in the estate lodges, his fair-haired freckly children went to the school in Achfary. Over the years, when he learned of our problems with the hatchery, he was to become invaluable, keeping an eye on the water supply from the temperamental burn.

At that time of year, in early May, we'd see the men 'cutting the peats' in the long black trenches beside the road. As one man cut, the other would toss the black sods onto the heather to dry for a time before they were stacked in loose mounds, like old bee hives on either side of the road from Achfary to Scourie and up to Durness. One evening on our way home, we stopped to talk to Billie Scobie, head stalker, who was stacking the peat he'd cut. He was a great naturalist and our oracle in matters of bird watching: yes, he confirmed, they were black throated divers nesting on the little island on Loch Stack, and yes, that would have been the red throated diver whose uncanny scream we'd heard from a high loch we'd passed on our walk. Immaculate as ever in his tweed trousers, shirt and tie, hair brushed back, only his hands were dirty, black with the peat. He looked slightly out of place, surprised, as if it was an occupation, like washing up, that he'd been asked to help with but didn't normally do.

As seasonal visitors, we loved the stacks by the road, the scent of peat fires in the air as we walked up through Achfary, but cutting, drying and gathering was hard work, a seasonal chore, much more romantic to the beholder than being engaged in its back-aching work. Each household burned well over a tonne of the fuel and there was a sense of primal satisfaction, relief as it was squirreled away under cover: Mrs Morrison, the postmistress at Kinlochbervie told us with deep satisfaction that her whole shed at the back was 'full for the winter'. And it was free. But when the estate went over to oil fired heating in the late eighties you could sense the relief. No more of the grind, and for the women, no more dust and grime in the house, 'it were messy stuff' they'd say.

At this time of year, too, the mussel fishermen came. They had ancient rights to fish the river and did not need to seek permission from the estate, though I think they told Sinclair they were coming. Suddenly they were there, like swallows returning, an old van parked in a lay-by. They'd wade down the river with glass-bottomed buckets that enabled them to spot the big black freshwater mussels, swinging the glass through the water from side to side with rhythmic sweeping motion like gold prospectors. When they'd collected a bagful, they'd light a fire on the bank and boil them just long enough to open. What they were after was not the meat, it was the prospect of a pearl, rare and much prized. Some, it was said, had adorned the necklace of Mary Queen of Scots and the most rare, of greatest value, we were told, were the black pearls. We never knew if they'd found any and before you could ask, they were gone, leaving behind great piles of shells.

As we passed the row of cottages in Achfary on visits to the hatchery, we got to know other members of the estate. Many of them in those days had lived and worked on it all their lives, in fact it was their life in an almost feudal sense. And the estate looked after them. Next door to Willie, lived Nita, now in her eighties, who'd been the cook in the village school while her husband had been chauffeur to the Duke. Well educated - she still did the Times crossword every day – and a stickler for old fashioned values, she lamented the decline in modern standards. And made the most amazing teas. We huddled in her kitchen, by the peat-burning stove, with hot tea, tucking into her superb shortbread. Its flavour burst like a 'star shell' before melting in your mouth. I found my hand wandering of its own accord to the plate for another piece. It went perfectly with the scalding tea.

She could remember the visits before the war of Duke Bendor, the Duchess's husband, a great socialite with a vast fortune – he owned most of Belgravia - and an entertainer on a grand scale, passionate about stalking and fishing. After the First World War he had bought a destroyer off the Navy, his own royal yacht, to take parties of friends over to Norway to fish the great salmon rivers there. It had been moored in the Kylesku inlet, on the southern edge of the estate, and to charge its batteries the Duke had had a hydro-electric generator installed running off a burn that cascaded down the mountain. It was still there. Utta and I walked over to look at it by the old post road from the south that ran over the hills. The machinery was still in operation after all those years, and now supplying electricity to the nearby community. 'But those people,' Nita observed in a matter-of-fact way, 'they were very nice, but didn't live in the real world. They had no idea what life was really like.'

★★★★★

As the days passed, we checked the river but still there was no sign of the elvers, not even the odd early arrival, forerunners of the main shoal. The thought began to gnaw at us: could they have come early that year, could we have missed them completely? The timing of the seasons varied from year to year. With the milder spring perhaps they'd come and gone. We waited, eyes strained. And there was help: Sandee by the Laxford kept watch for signs of the gulls on the river; the instructors, often out in small boats or canoes up and down the coast, kept a look out too. News came back one day that they'd seen shoals of small fish near the mouth of the Laxford. We hurried down to the estuary but there was nothing, not an elver to be seen. Perhaps it'd been a shoal of sand eels or fry of some kind.

While we waited, it was a gifted opportunity to explore and get to know such a unique landscape. And it wasn't all about walking and exploring outdoors. There were days during those weeks when the weather closed in and it was a delicious excuse to sit by the fire in the Colt House all day and read from the pile of books we'd brought with us. The estate provided coal for heating but mostly we gathered driftwood from beach or loch when on our walks. Old fish boxes made the best kindling. In those days the trawlers used wooden fish boxes stencilled with the letters 'K.F.C.' which stood for the Kinlochbervie Fishselling Company. They washed up everywhere along the coast, jammed between rocks or littering the tide line on remote beaches. They were the ultimate re-usable box: driftwood for the fire, cutting board for the sandwiches, sledges for hauling wood; stacked up on their side they formed windbreaks. The locals used them for growing vegetables, blocking gaps in walls. If we'd lived up there all year, we vowed we'd make shelves and furniture out of them. Over the years there would be a gradual transformation of the fish box as it broke down, splintered by the Atlantic waves. The pine grew smoother, the edges rounder, whitened like bone by the salt. Starting life as something functional the fractured pieces became objects of beauty shaped by the sea and the tide. Almost too fine to burn.

Sometimes I could just manage to tear myself away from reading in order to catch up on the accounts. My father had given me a huge old ledger he'd once used, the size of a door. Having had not the slightest interest in any form of book-keeping before, now that we had our own business, I found that I rather enjoyed the satisfaction, like completing a crossword, when all the separate totals in the double entry at the bottom of the page balanced with that of the main column. It would sometimes take hours, accompanied by much muttering and swearing, to find the error that prevented me from turning the page. I did not possess a calculator then, so worked with pencil and a rubber – a most useful tool. My brain groaned, stiff from lack of exercise and needed buckets of tea to keep it oiled. What was sobering was to see how rapidly the small overheads, quite apart from the big items like elvers and air freight, eroded the sales income that had seemed so meaty, so substantial at the time. It was like watching ice melting in the sun.

The weather changes all the time off the north west corner of Scotland and often a foul morning would turn into a sparkling afternoon. A mile or two beyond Kinlochbervie was the little settlement of Oldshoremore, cottages tucked into the hill, like gulls on a ledge, the odd ruin of a turf-roofed croft, a dilapidated caravan used as chicken shed, all overlooking the sweep of the most beautiful beach that curved round to an island at the far end. On the way the path led up past a small cemetery ringed by a wall, an ideal setting for the souls of the dead to slumber in peace. We would walk to the far end to a sheltered spot amongst the rocks and brew smoky tea over a driftwood fire in a blackened whistling kettle. It became a special place and along with the river at Laxford, the first that we would return to year after year.

For a community that lived off the sea, it was remarkably difficult actually to find any fresh fish to buy. The few local stores kept packs of frozen fish fingers, tins of sardines, but nothing else. The entire catch seemed to be sucked immediately into the wholesale chain and to vanish south. The only thing to do was to wander over to the harbour quay where the auctions took place at the end of the day, armed with a plastic bag. Inside the fish house noise, shouts, smells assaulted the senses. From the trawlers stacks of boxes of fish were being winched out of holds, dripping melting ice, grabbed by porters and dragged across the floor, arranged in neat lines. Each box sorted and sized into separate species. At the end of the rows were fish that didn't fit in boxes, halibut the size of rowing boats and dogfish like sharks, and creatures of the deep you never knew existed. It seemed in those heady days, and for the years that followed, a world of endless plenty – just like the elvers - a boundless harvest worked from the sea, unhindered by quotas or size restrictions. No thought of it ever coming to an end. If you spoke to a local bystander, and asked if you could buy some fish, without a word, they'd pluck a few herring, or plaice the size of soup plates and fill your bag, refusing to take any money. It meant that you didn't ask often, but the fish were the best we'd ever tasted, the flavour and tang of the sea still fresh within them.

Down south it was the beginning of summer but there, in the far north, Sutherland was a good month behind. Trees were just coming into leaf. Behind the Colt House little posses of lambs bounced on the hill, racing up and down in sheer exuberance, rushing back to feed, butting their mothers as they sucked greedily, tails wiggling in pleasure. On warm days, small families of them sunbathed on the edge of the road, even causing the fish lorries to slow. Everywhere the ewes moulted wool, leaving long strands of it clinging to every wire and fence. With the arrival of spring and longer days people emerged, blinking like moles as if from a winter hibernation sustained by telly and whisky.

Stumbling past our window each morning the figure of Alastair Corbett, the local crab fishermen, made his unsteady way down to his

An old stone wall
at Oldshoremore

small boat, where he pottered for hours painting and slowly making it seaworthy for the new season. Every now and then he'd walk down to the water's edge and wipe his hands clean on a great wad of seaweed. At times it all seemed too much for him and he would sit on the thwart of the boat and stare into space in a dream. He was a bachelor, living on his own in a croft above us. A lonely soul, shy and hesitant, he would come in for cups of tea and a chat and stay for what seemed like hours for he had no sense of time. Often at the weekend we'd see him sprawled by the side of the road out of the village, passed out in a drunken stupor after a night at the Rhiconich. It was sad, such a waste of a good man. When he was well enough to work his boat, he would come back loaded with crab. Sometimes, there'd be a knock on the door and there'd be a sack full of what he called, 'the toes,' the big claws. They were delicious, full of sweet meat.

Then, suddenly, in the middle of the month, a storm blew in with several days of heavy rain. Every burn was full, springs and waterfalls sprouted off the hills; the Laxford swirled dark and swollen. Surely this would bring the elvers, we thought. But there was nothing. 'Don't worry,' Scobie reassured us, 'They'll come, they always do.'

★★★★★

Soon after our arrival we made contact with the Ridgway's School of Adventure at Ardmore. John and Marie-Christine were flat out running courses but would sometimes drop in to the Colt House for a cuppa on their way to join one of the activities or to pick up something from the chandlers. Business was thriving, the courses fully booked. They were a good team. John was the front man; people came to meet the legend, the man who'd rowed the Atlantic. He had a steely determination yet an unexpected modesty and interest in other people; he asked questions. Behind him, strong in support, was Marie-Christine, a remarkable lady in her own right, beautiful in looks and with a deep quiet strength, a real anchor to the business.

As the days and weeks passed and we waited for the elvers, we saw a lot of the instructors from the Ridgway School of Adventure. Some of them I'd already met the year before. They would often visit us on their days off or all come round for an evening. They were great company, full of energy and buzz, full of tales of their adventures and travels, climbs and expeditions, or hilarious anecdotes about the things that had happened on the courses, the most recent being the saga of Marie Christine's pony - he who had taken a dislike to my tent the previous year. Apparently he had wandered into the shed where the course lunches had been temporarily stowed. The door had swung shut behind him. To while away the time he'd thoughtfully consumed over twenty picnic lunches as well as much of their wrapping. This had had an immediate and explosive effect on his digestive system. He was in disgrace. Judgement was pending.

The instructors were not permanent staff, they worked flat out at the Adventure School for six to eight months during the season, fed and housed and paid a small sum; their reward was the wealth of experience gained under John as well as the contacts they might make instructing often top personnel in the business world. At the end of the season they'd take off like swallows to join the Armed Forces, to travel, study, even to set up their own adventure schools, while some stayed on to accompany John and Marie Christine on one of their out-of-season expeditions, sailing to some remote part of the southern hemisphere to explore wild places.

When they came for a meal, while more sedate guests might have sat round making polite conversation and nibbling peanuts, the instructors spotted the small granite cliff behind the Colt House, about thirty feet high, which made a perfect practice climbing wall. They swarmed over it like baboons, before coming in to eat vast quantities of food. They thought nothing of walking the five or six miles back to Ardmore after the meal.

One of them was Staff Morse, a young Australian, whom I'd met the year before. He was from a farm in northern New South Wales. With a shock of wiry hair and a bushy beard, Staff was always positive, cheery, and tough as nails. Nothing fazed him, he was a 'No worries' man, totally self-reliant, able to fix anything. He had a gift of enabling you to push yourself and stretch your limits. We used to go running together and he gave us our first and only steps in climbing which confirmed my belief, as I dangled off a cliff shouting, 'Staff, I'm stuck, where do I go next?' that this was not my favourite sport and that I preferred to have my feet firmly on the ground. With him, too, we abseiled eighty feet down a funnel in the cliff into the sea cave known as Smoo, near Durness, landing on a tiny ledge. From there, it being high tide, the only exit was to swim out of the cave into the sea, so cold that Utta barely touched the water, almost aquaplaning, in her haste to escape.

A few years later, while climbing in the Himalayas, Staff was tragically killed by an avalanche. We were very sad; he had been such a radiant soul, it was hard to believe he was no longer there.

★★★★★

To feed ourselves, and visitors to the Colt House, we found shopping for food in any bulk a little difficult. The nearest stores of any size were in Lairg, an hour south. In those days Kinlochbervie had hardly any shops apart from the chandlers and a hardware store attached to the garage. For food supplies, we relied heavily on Mrs Mackay and her London Stores that stood at the crest of the climb just before the village. Few shops could have had a more impressive view. It looked down onto Loch Inchard and away to the mountains. Inside it was like a cave set in the side of the hill, stacked floor to ceiling with every conceivable item you could think of. And very expensive.

Mrs Mackay was a tiny Canadian, with an accent almost as soft as a highlander. She was always cheerful and welcoming. In the confusion and gloom of her shop it was difficult to find what you were looking for so she did the gathering for you. 'Peaches, oh, yes.' She knew exactly where they were and would work her way down the side of the shop, often hidden from sight, stepping over boxes and unpacked deliveries, to a canyon of tins where, in between asking you how long you were up for and wasn't the weather just awful, she'd swipe at the top row where the peaches roosted with a well aimed whack of a walking stick. At this, the whole pile would collapse like a rock-fall but somehow, like a conjuror, she'd emerge holding the can she wanted. At the end of several forays there was utter devastation, like bomb damage, the floor littered with a rubble of cans that she stepped over as nonchalantly as if she was crossing the beach.

It must have taken hours to stack everything up again and we always wondered who did it. Probably her son who lurked next-door in an even darker cave where he put together local orders, muttering to himself and surrounded by a chaos of boxes, loading them onto an ancient green delivery van that did the rounds.

When it came to settling up, 'Is that all then?' Mrs Mackay would ask and she'd run it through the till. You had no idea what anything cost and the bill was always astronomical, so we'd have to have an ice cream to soothe our nerves.

From time to time there'd be a visit from Rory in the hope of a bit of bread and a wee dram. He was the local tramp, homeless, sleeping rough on the hill, sheltering in bothies. At a glance, with his boots and red rucksack, he might have been a tourist, a hiker, until you saw his rough hands and his eyes and nose. Rory ran on whisky. He'd lurch up to the door of the shop and try and cajole a visitor into buying him a drink. Mrs Mackay never raised her voice or stopped what she was doing, very matter of fact as if dealing with a naughty boy. 'Now Rory, you're making a nuisance of yourself. Just sit there and wait outside and I'll come to you in a while.' Meekly, in anticipation, he would obey, sitting on the little bench outside like a small boy waiting for a treat.

★★★★★

As we waited for the elvers, there was another concern: the later it got, the more difficult it became to find a market for them. Rosengarten had made it clear that his quota had been fulfilled. Besides, shipping direct to Hamburg from the north of Scotland was nearly impossible. Instead I had made tentative arrangements to sell to Rosengarten's counterpart in Holland, Mr Zumke of the O.V.B., responsible for restocking the country's inland waters and whom I'd met at a Fish Farming conference organised by Alex Behrendt the previous autumn. There was a direct flight from Aberdeen Dyce airport to Holland. But if things dragged on too long, his interest would also wane. And shipping elvers as the weather warmed up was not easy: the fish were more active, needed more oxygen, the likelihood of losses more likely.

From a business point of view, it would be a major disappointment if the elvers never came or if we'd missed them altogether because we were hoping Scotland might become our trump card, allowing us to offer a supply long after the big boys down south and on the continent had hung up their gear and shut down. But at the same time we told ourselves, if it all came to nought, it had been worth every minute, just to get to know this part of the world.

Sometimes with Staff, but often on our own, we walked all day from the Colt House north up the coast to Sandwood Bay, a remote beach with abandoned crofts. Sometimes we took the old post road south from Achfary over the top to the Kylesku inlet passing the tumble of ruins where the post horses once stabled. Every day there were discoveries, sightings: ptarmigan, still partially in white plumage on the slopes of Arkle, tiny orchids in the peat bogs or wild flowers growing on the mountain tops, the nest of a greenshank, a glimpse of an osprey on the river. At the end of the day we'd spend hours with our noses stuck in reference books trying to identify what we'd seen.

Mostly we explored the mountains that dominated the landscape, Stack and Arkle and Foinavan, all just under three thousand feet. Foinavon was perhaps the most spectacular with its winding ridge, a spine nearly eight miles long and a few feet wide. From up high you caught the essence of Sutherland and its bleak loveliness. Slopes of rock and scree fell away into desolate empty valleys; bony fingers of land, pitted and flecked with a thousand lochs and tarns stretched out to the sea, to where earth and water merged into one. It was a wild landscape, totally indifferent to man, ancient beyond measure, ground down and scoured by glacier and weather and bared to the bone. A world of rock and water, of light and sea that captured the spirit.

A spur off Foinavon ridge

Then, just as we were beginning to wonder whether they would ever come, we spotted the first elvers: it was the third week of May, just as Billy Scobie had predicted. There had been a big spring tide, we were down on the estuary and suddenly under every pebble, stone and rock there was a squiggle of movement, an elver hiding. They were bigger, stronger than their early cousins in Somerset, already pigmented, a lustrous black with a hint of silver. Seeing them at the lower end of the river, we thought we'd start to catch that night but there was nothing at the falls. The elvers knew exactly what they were doing. They wouldn't attack the climb until they'd gathered the numbers to do so. Over the next days, we watched the shoal, still augmented daily by new arrivals from the sea, creep nearer to the waterfall beneath Laxford Bridge. The gulls had spotted them too, big black-backs stabbing the water, gorging on this seasonal delicacy. The ducks joined in the orgy. The elvers came on, steadily, undeterred, up both banks of the river, working their way up to the foot of the falls. In daylight, through the amber water, we could see them resting down amongst the rocks, their tiny heads crowded tight, like throngs of people looking upwards, swaying together in the music of the current. They filled every crevice, every nook and cranny of the river bed.

They were like an army amassing, not ready to move until its troops were in place. A communal consciousness, knowledge learned over millennia, seemed to hold them in place, awaiting the moment to act as one, for the assault on the falls to begin.

At last after the third night, as light thickened, they emerged from their hiding places from either side of the river and streamed towards to the rapids, not attacking them head-on as the salmon or seatrout, but clinging to the edge of rock, to the line of least resistance, working their way round until they met the full force of the current. Here they formed a column, intertwining themselves, like climbers roped together for greater strength on some perilous slope. It seemed inconceivable that any creature of their size could make its way past this first booming torrent of water, yet somehow, smeared flat against the glistening rocks, just above the water line, clinging to any shreds of moss or ledge that gave them purchase, they edged their way round and up to a higher level of the falls. Frequent splashes of water, irregular pulses of current, would flick them off the rock and they'd be swept back – Sisyphus-like - to have to start all over again. Over the course of the night, some would make it to the relative safety of the upper river, a climb of some six feet up through twenty metres of rapids. The key to their success was their inter-dependence, working together to mount the river. It was almost humbling to watch their striving, so heroic, and the migratory force that drove them on.

It seemed cruel to catch them but, we consoled ourselves with the knowledge that they were only going to be redistributed: caught and released in other waters. It took us a little while to work out the best places to fish. I found a spur of rock that projected into the river, a spot they had to pass on their way to the climb. Utta took up position on the other side of the rapids. With the boom and rush of water, we couldn't hear each other so we flashed our torches to communicate. As I held the mouth of the net tight against the rock, a great band of elvers began to stream into it against the current. After some time I shone the torch and gasped half in wonder, half in excitement for it was a seething mass of black and when I tried to lift the net to empty it I had to heave and drag it out of the water, such was the weight of elvers; they completely filled the two buckets balanced on the rock beside me. Making my way up to the road where the van was parked I spread them onto the holding trays. They were more docile than their Somerset cousins, also bigger, blacker with a greenish tinge, for they had begun to feed on minute zooplankton. But just like their Somerset cousins, they swirled round the bucket like a moving rope desperate to continue their migration.

All night, we fished in our own worlds, alone with our thoughts, the darkness full of the roar and rush of the river, the smell of water pounded by the falls, the scent of trees in early leaf. Sometimes there'd be the odd plop or splash as seatrout rose and gobbled elvers. The breeze was soft and there was a near full moon in the sky visible through the graceful arch of Laxford Bridge. There were no haggling fishermen, no-one pushing onto our spot. It was bliss - except on windless nights when the midges descended en masse and devoured us. At the end of that first encounter our faces and hands were covered in round pink spots like circus clowns. We itched furiously. Only a heavy application of insect repellent – available of course from Mrs Mackay's shop at great expense – would hold them at bay and for a limited period. Then they came and hovered over us in clouds, ready to pounce as soon as the repellent wore off. But as soon as a breeze sprang up, they were gone. They were our predators; it was only fair, we figured, to have to suffer a little as we fished.

As the first silvery light stole into the sky around two or three in the morning, the march of the elvers on the falls began to wane, their energy exhausted, and they would drop down to the floor of the river to rest for another day. Dog-tired, we packed up, loaded the trays of elvers into the back of the van and drove slowly up the valley to Achfary and the hatchery. It was a magic time, the valley growing light, sounds very sharp and clear. We drifted along, the windows down. Once, a big stag was leading his harem of red deer down to the river to a shallow crossing. We heard the clink of hooves on rock, the rustle and splash of water as they crossed. At this hour, the world belonged to them. We waited in silence by the road, watching. A curlew's cry echoed up the valley. In the back the elvers whispered on their trays.

We stowed them in the hatchery, carrying the trays down over the wooden bridge, releasing them into the dark wooden box-tanks. We could see that there were virtually no losses. They were beautiful fish and they settled almost at once. That first night our catch was perhaps thirty kilos, already impressive, but as we worked out how best to fish the river, it increased the following night to nearer fifty and the hatchery was rapidly beginning to fill. I contacted Zumke from the O.V.B. in Holland and arranged a shipment for the week ahead. Like Rosengarten, he made it clear that I should travel with them so that we could both witness and agree their quality on arrival.

When it came to packing the elvers, we had already had our polystyrene boxes transported north so it was just ice that we needed. I went with several large fish boxes to the harbour master at Kinlochbervie who directed me to a tall rusty corrugated iron structure on the edge of the quay. This was the ice house, a massive machine that delivered chip ice direct to the hold of the trawlers, blowing it down through an enormous pipe like an elephant's trunk. 'Put yer boxes there,' shouted the operator and vanished into the workings of the giant. There was a great rushing sound as if I was inside a washing machine and then suddenly the giant pipe began to blow an avalanche of ice chips, thin and white as scales. Within seconds my puny boxes were full, so too were my boots and my head and shoulders covered. 'That's enough, okay, that's it!' I yelled as the deluge continued and I was in danger of being completely buried. All of a sudden it came to an abrupt halt. Descending from an iron ladder the boots of the operator appeared,

'Will that do ya all right?' he bawled above the noise. I thanked him profusely and asked him what I owed, expecting some astronomical sum matching the price we paid in Somerset.

'Three pounds for the lot,' he said.

We packed at midnight, helped by the tireless Staff, weighing out nearly two hundred kilos of elvers. The flight was at eight in the morning and there was a four hour drive to Aberdeen Dyce airport. It was a tiny plane, a Fokker Friendship. Security was wonderfully informal after

Heathrow and we were able to drive alongside and help load. There was no cavernous underbelly for cargo. What didn't fit in the baggage area at the back, went into a cupboard in the cabin and the final three boxes were placed on the seat beside me with their own seat belt. I felt like a proud parent travelling with a small child and was personally able to monitor them all the way. It occurred to me that if we ditched in the sea, they would undoubtedly have had the best chance of survival. On arrival, Zumke, a friendly, avuncular figure whom I liked from the outset, took me and the shipment straight to a holding station where the elvers were gently immersed into tanks to rest. Zumke was pleased with them, 'ferry goot quality, ferry strong fish, goot for restocking,' he pronounced. They were due to be released into one of the big inland lakes to recharge the eel population for commercial fishing.

It was all over. The shoal was gone. The whole thing had run like clockwork. It was time to head home. We began to pack our belongings. Tidying the Colt House, we decided to burn all our waste paper in the grate, feeding the flames with the usual crop of old jottings, envelopes, bits of cardboard that had accrued. All of a sudden the fire changed note and there came a deep and terrifying roar from the chimney. The innocent friendly grate in front of which we'd spent many cosy hours with our books, was transformed into the seat of a furnace, glowing white hot. It was quite clear the chimney was on fire. And as the Colt House was an entirely wooden construction, like a packing case, built around the support of the chimney, it wasn't going to be long before the whole house was on fire. I imagined informing Sinclair, and the Duchess's reaction. Panicking, I raced up the track to the Morrison's post office opposite our gate.

'We've got a bit of a problem,' I gasped.

'Ay, your chimney's on fire, we've been watching it.' Mr Morrison observed matter-of-factly. It wasn't hard to miss. Looking down on the Colt House below, an exhaust of black smoke belched from its chimney straight up into the sky.

Mr Morrison had the complexion of one who has been sitting too close to the fire for a long time and was obviously something of an expert in these matters. 'Dunna bother, it's just the soot. It'll give the chumney a good clean, it's a good way to do it but if you want to be sure, you could just give the Fire Service a call.' Tearing back to the Colt House, I followed his advice and dialled 999.

A voice far away said, 'Inverness.' Breathless, I gave them details. 'How quickly can you get here,' I screamed.

'Oh, about three hours.'

'Three hours,' I gasped, horrified. We could have burned to the ground by then; there'd be nothing more than a heap of rubble.

'Ah, yes, the fire service has to come all the way from Inverness. But you can contact your local Fire Officer in Kinlochbervie.' Relieved that help was so close, I took the number and dialled it immediately.

'Harbourmaster,'

'Oh hello, I wonder if you could help, I wanted the Fire Officer.'

'That's me.'

I explained the situation. He sounded very interested; this was definitely the most interesting thing that had happened all week, possible longer. We stood outside waiting for the red fire truck. Smoke still poured from the Colt House chimney. After some time, an old banger rumbled down the drive and a large man heaved himself out, leaving the car door open, and lurched towards us. As we moved to greet him, his car, having discharged its driver, began to roll down the slope to the rocks that lay below, gathering speed as it went. I managed to dive through its open door and yank on the handbrake to bring it to a halt before it toppled over the edge.

'Ah, thank you,' he said, as if it happened all the time. He examined the fire with expert eyes. 'Sand is what you need. We pour sand down the chimney. That'll stop it.' He was in no fit state to climb a ladder, sober or otherwise. Fortunately he had brought no ladder, and we had no sand. 'Och, it's dying down now anyway. You're over the worst of it. Just leave it. It's given it a good clean. Got rid of all the soot.' He left some while later after several cups of tea and casting wistful glances for something stronger.

We were just congratulating ourselves that the estate need never hear anything about this little embarrassment, when there were noises outside and a tiny red fire engine, late 1920's, polished and shining like a dinkey toy, appeared with an excited crew led by Willie Jones. It was the Duchess's Auxiliary Fire Engine, stored by her house at Lochmore Lodge for just such an emergency. They did have a ladder and they did have sand. Willie went up on the roof and poured buckets of it down the chimney until the fire was declared dead. There were more cups of tea, more wistful glances for something stronger, and farewells.

As we headed south the next day, the van packed, and crossed the Laxford, we saw in disbelief from the gull activity on the river that another shoal of elvers had arrived. Stopping to look, it seemed just as large as the one we'd fished. We hesitated: should we unpack, start again? But would we find a market? And if we did, would they survive? It was well into June,

the weather very hot. We stopped to see Sinclair at the estate office in Achfary. He was, unusually, wearing a kilt and he was in high spirits, 'This is summer,' he said, 'don't miss it. It might be over by tomorrow.' He'd seen the elvers too. No, we decided together, interesting as it was to know that the migration could come in more than one shoal, enough was enough; leave them be. And we bid our farewells and carried on.

Slopes of rock and scree on Ben Stack

We returned to Somerset. The season was over, quickly forgotten. Skye Cottage basked on the side of the hill. Grass shimmered in the fields; it was a perfect summer. Friends came and went. We were married in September. For our honeymoon we walked with Staff and his girlfriend Sheenagh across the island of Corsica. It had been a momentous year bringing a wife and much happiness, a business and a sense of purpose. We had sold just over two tonnes of elvers, a quarter of which we had caught ourselves. We had made a small profit; there was some money in the bank. For the coming year, the next season, we had high hopes.

Chapter Four

The first year of the business had been blessed with beginner's luck. We were about to learn that no two elver seasons were ever the same. And that a livelihood based on a natural harvest from land or sea is never a certain one.

Yet the season started with high hopes. And new helpers. In the previous autumn, while Utta worked in a local pub, I'd helped David Norton – whose family owned our cottage - with the harvesting of his Christmas trees. It was there, crawling along the rows, bow saw in hand, that I'd met Pen Beauchamp, a bespectacled, grey-haired character who lived on the edge of the village. With the look of a retired schoolmaster, he was in fact an airline pilot, recently retired from British Airways, formerly BOAC. As we cut and hauled Christmas trees, I learned that he was a keen handyman and enlisted him into preparations for the approaching elver season: we needed a new pump house, windows for our storage barn, more tanks, nets and trays, the list was endless.

When it came to maintenance and repair work my mentor so far had been Ernie, a very tolerant guide. 'Ee'll be alright,' he'd say as we peered hopefully at the lopsided bubble in the sprit level, 'tidn a million mile out.' But not Pen. He was a perfectionist, he liked accuracy and he wasn't happy until all the levels and the uprights were spot on before he went any further; precision had been part of his life as a pilot. 'We need to offer it up,' he'd say, 'just to make sure it fits.' He had an ease of manner, a way of working, that never made you feel anything other than his equal. Though he was old enough to be my father, his youthfulness of spirit and his openness made him more like an older brother. And unusual for someone of his generation, he was totally classless, always took people on merit whoever they were.

Over picnic lunches in the barn I'd sometimes get him to talk about his time in Bomber Command during the war. He had been highly decorated, risen to Squadron Leader, not that he told me himself, and, incredibly, had flown over a hundred sorties, well over three times the normal number. He must have led a charmed life in a service that had suffered the most terrible losses. The worst part of a raid, he recalled, apart from the flak over the target, was waiting to take off at dusk out on the runway, the nerves, the time to think, the loneliest time; best was getting back, to the family he was billeted with, farmers in East Anglia, to a cooked breakfast or to a glass of whisky by his bed when he got in. 'And stockings, silk stockings,' Pen remembered,' our girls couldn't get hold of them but we could. Through the American airmen. You could ask for almost anything if you could promise a pair of silk stockings,' he remembered, 'Anything at all with two pairs.'

★★★★★

One of the things we had identified, looking back on the previous season, was the need for more holding capacity. What dictated the size of an elver holding unit, I was to learn, was not so much the volume of elvers bought and sold, but the speed with which they could be shifted: if you had a buyer who came every night or every few days to empty you out, then there was no need for massive holding facilities but if you were dependent on overseas markets as we were, then you needed space to hold fish while you found the market, confirmed the sale, arranged air freight, organised the pack; it all took time and time was space. If we were going to buy in more elvers to increase production, then we would need more tanks. The plan was for another row of four to add to the eight that existed already.

    I'd never built tanks before, in fact I'd never built anything. After deep consultation with Ernie, it was decided that, rather than use concrete blocks, it would be much quicker and easier to pour concrete into a mould I would make that would then do for all the tanks, 'Then you kin probably get away without sand, which is spensive,' said Ern, 'you kin use scalpings instead; get they from Morris's, ask fer a quarter to dust, and use the PTO off of the back of the tractor which you kin hook up to matey's cement mixer. I asked en t'other day. Ee said you kin borrow en, ee idn needen en right now.'

    The plywood mould for tanks with its inner and outer skin to form the walls took shape over the next few days, six foot square and three feet high. Ernie looked it over, 'Well, ee looks alright, Moik, ee should do the job.' It might have looked impressive but I was totally unaware of the weight of concrete.

Pen Beauchamp was away at the time, unable to give me a hand. Instead, Utta's brother-in-law, Tony, and her sister, Barbara, along with their two-month-old baby were visiting from Australia, staying with us for a part of the elver season. Just out of art school, Tony was experimenting with performance art: this meant he didn't paint pictures, he did things, often with a camera and after much intense contemplation and muttering. He had just won a prestigious award, which came with a year's sabbatical that they had decided to spend in Europe, starting with us. He very much looked the part, the Bohemian artist with shoulder-length hair and a great beard. He had a wonderful quirky sense of humour and quick wit. He and Ernie, though almost unintelligible to one another, got on famously. 'Cor, ee's a card, that there Tony, idn ee,' Ern would chortle.

Tony and I mixed the concrete, shovelling it into the mould. The liquid was pink from the dust in the gravel scalpings as we tamped it down between the wooden ply walls of the mould. As the level rose inside there were ominous creaks as it took the strain. The outer skin began to belly out at the base under the sheer weight. When finally we reached the top, the wooden structure had lost its neat, pristine precision. Splattered with concrete, it looked battered and exhausted, and very worried. With a final apologetic groan, as if to say, 'Sorry, just can't hang on any longer,' there was a wrenching sound and one wall developed a huge bulge like a serious hernia. Covering it with sacks against the frost, we left it in intensive care overnight.

The next day we popped the mould, carefully removing the shuttering like a bandage, eager to see what lay underneath. And there it was: a sort of tank, very pink and naked. There wasn't a single straight line anywhere. It had a molten, organic, natural look like pottery unfired or an earth fort somewhere in the mountains of Central Asia. In parts the surface was pocked and pitted as if struck by cannon fire where the tamping hadn't worked. It appealed greatly to Tony's artistic nature. It could almost have been a piece of his performance art, 'I think it looks great. I think we gotta call it the red fort.' And so it became. It was to last nearly twenty years. Over the next few weeks, tank production improved. The mould was discarded and block work tanks formed up in a line alongside the red fort, rendered to make them smooth and waterproof, and new pipe work and pump installed to link them into the system. We were ready for the season.

★★★★★

February was bitterly cold. We went down to the river, but there were more fishermen than elvers. 'Nothin' about,' they said standing around in clusters, drinking tea and chatting, sharing memories mostly of the previous year. It had been a good one for everyone. 'Me son-in-law and I, we caught one point one tonnes,' pronounced Wilfie Cousins, one of Hancock's fishermen, a good catcher. Wilfie, who'd been a regular soldier, always brought a spade and cut neat steps down the bank to where he was fishing, with another step to rest his bucket on. At the end of a night's elvering, while the rest of us would be lathered in mud, Wilfie was always immaculate. His Tilley lamp always worked first time; Ernie's usually brewed black smoke or blew up completely. It was always fascinating to me that at a time when everyone still used pounds and ounces in daily life, fishermen would recall their catch in metric, in kilos, because they were paid in kilos, and because their buyers, ourselves and the Hancocks, were selling to the continent in kilos; metrification had already reached deep into the lanes of Somerset. It made me think too that if Wilfie and his mate had caught over a tonne on their own, just how much was Hancock hauling off the river when he had hundreds of fishermen: perhaps thirty or forty tonnes. There was no way of knowing but I realised that we were just bystanders, very small fry in a very much bigger game; no wonder he didn't seem too bothered by us.

As we stood round chatting, Colin Dyer, a fishermen who used to catch eels on the moors when the elver season was over, told us he'd been reading up about the eel, 'And do you know,' he addressed a group of us idly watching the river, 'when they adult eels get ready for migration back to the Sargasso, they change, see, their skin gets thicker, and their nose goes all pointed, sharp-like.' We listened, vaguely interested. 'And then it stops eatin', see, and its gut and its anus – its back passage – blocks up like, and its eyes go all huge and round, enlarged like; tis just bleddy marvellous when you think about it.' I was intrigued, but the rest were not much impressed. Quick as a flash, someone said, 'Well, Col, tis just

69

normal really: if your back passage were all blocked up, your eyes would be bliddy bulging too.' Delivering such pearls of scientific information could be a thankless task on the river bank.

But he was well-informed; that was exactly what happened, I was to learn, in the adult migration of the eel.

The tides came and went. It stayed cold and dank with very little being caught. I was beginning to worry. Our funds had almost run out. Here we were in late February: the last cheque paid into the business had been the previous June from Zumke for the Scottish elvers. Through odd-jobbing and casual work, we had survived the year mostly without dipping into the business. Now however with all the work at Bowdens preparing for the season, as well as feeding extra mouths, our reserves were melting away like snow on a roof. We desperately needed to start selling elvers.

Eventually, after what was supposed to have been one of the first good elver tides, when big catches had been expected, we had scraped together barely eighty kilos. At least it was a start. I rang Rosengarten to firm up a sale. He was all right for the moment, thank you; France were doing well and his lorry was going down almost fortnightly to collect. 'Viele Arbeit, very busy,' he bellowed. His voice was distant, not interested in our predicament; eighty kilos was hardly tempting, more of an irrelevance really, and the fish were already a week old. I tried Zumke in Holland: no go, too early, try later. I tried Haas in southern Germany. He was cautiously interested. How many had I got. No, not for eighty kilos, it just wasn't worth going all the way up to Munich airport for such a small quantity. I hesitated, then plunged in, 'We can deliver them, we'll drive them out to you.'

'Und wann? It'll have to be soon, I am expecting a lorry load...'

'We can leave tomorrow. We'll see you on Monday.'

I heard what could have been a little chuckle on the line; 'Also, bis Montag, Herr Brown.' I think Haas knew he was dealing with a desperate man.

I set about booking a ferry, across the Channel via the Dover–Calais route. This was 1976, long before all the trade barriers and tariffs came down. We'd only ever used airfreight before, where all documentation was prepared for us by the airline and I was therefore a bit hazy about the paperwork needed for road freight. Our nearest customs offices in Bristol were closed for the weekend anyway so we decided, to hell with it, we'd go without papers and just cover the elver boxes with sleeping bags in the back of the van and hope for the best. Desperation made things very simple at times.

We had been joined at this stage by an old friend from Devon, Christopher Vlasto, Chippy to all who knew him. He'd dropped out of university and after some years of wanderings had joined L'Arche, Jean Vanier's centre in France for the care of the severely handicapped. He'd been working at one of its satellite homes in south Wales. Exhausted and needing a break, he had come to stay and give us a hand for a month or two. Chippy was an innately spiritual soul but with a wicked twinkle in his eye. And definitely in the hirsute phase of his life; with shoulder-length hair and a beard to match, there was something of a biblical look about him.

We gathered our kit and packed the elvers, stacking them in their polystyrene boxes in the back of the kombi van. We left from Skye Cottage to fond farewells from Utta and Barbara having loaded the food they'd prepared for the journey: thirty rounds of sandwiches. We were very excited by this; Utta's sandwiches were legendary and she'd mentioned cold lamb and chutney. As we drove up the A303 and it got somewhere near lunch, Chippy who was in the back and had an appetite almost as keen as mine, said, 'Let's break out the picnic. Just try one of those sandwiches.'

There was the sound of rummaging in the back. Tony and I salivated in anticipation.

'That's odd,' came a voice from the back.

'What?'

'There's nothing in the sandwich. We've just got bread and butter.'

'Oh, I know, they'll have put the filling in a separate container to keep them fresher.' We were relieved. Of course that was it. In a separate tin, very good idea. There was another long pause, then the voice from the back said, 'No, nothing here. All we've got is sixty slices of bread, and two large apple crumbles'. For a while murderous thoughts assailed us, then,

'Oh well, let's have the pud.' Apple crumble is delicious but loses its appeal somewhat when eaten cold with a spoon from the bowl.

The crossing from Dover was short and uneventful. It was dark and windy as we got into Calais. The polystyrene boxes in the back had been casually strewn with sleeping bags. We were just three guys, off on holiday in a camper van. As we drove off the ferry through Customs, expecting just a nod and a wave, our hearts stopped. There must have been a tip-off, an alert for something: they were searching every single vehicle.

'Oh God, this is it chaps,' I said. What more obvious target was there: three goons in the front, wool hats pulled down over their ears, two of them hairy as orang-utans. We froze like rabbits in a headlight. An officer in a greatcoat had just finished rummaging in the vehicle ahead, bullying the passengers. He straightened up and fixed his gaze on us like a bull in a field. 'Oh, shit,' said Tony. 'Here we go.' For a moment the officer surveyed the occupants of the kombi van and then to our utter astonishment waved us through. Perhaps he'd done his quota for the night, it was bitterly cold, and thought what the hell. Or perhaps the gods just smiled. Whatever, we were through and on the road.

We drove non-stop, taking it in turns, while one of us lay in the back between the stacks of boxes and remains of apple crumble, trying to get some sleep. Reaching the German border, tension rose again but the weather was foul, with flurries of snow; the customs officer didn't even get out of his cabin, just waved us through. Now it was just plain sailing, follow the autobahn all the way down to Munich, then on again to Haas's place at Koenigsee on the Austrian border. With foot flat down, urging the VW on, we couldn't help noticing that she seemed to be getting slower. Cars, even lorries flashed past us. 'Just tired, I expect,' Tony suggested.

As dawn broke over southern Germany we cheered as we passed the turn-offs for Augsburg and Ulm and headed south for Munich. Nearly there. But elation was short-lived. From the map, Haas's place looked a long way south still and there was no doubt about it: the van was definitely slowing. A sort of chugging sound like a paddle steamer was coming from the rear engine and occasionally she backfired and for a second almost stopped before staggering on. We nursed her, willing her to keep going. It was beginning to get very tense and very cold; the heating was off to keep the elvers as chilled as possible. 'Bloody 'ell,' said Chip, 'I can see why he didn't want to come to the airport just for this little lot.'

'How long can elvers last?' asked Tony. About twenty four hours. I calculated that was how long we'd been going.

'Have a look at them, Tony, would you.' He removed the bands on one of the boxes and peered in. 'Yup, they're fine. No worries. They look great.' He was wonderfully reassuring. Or a bloody good actor.

Eventually we limped into Koenigsee and found the sign saying, 'Alois Haas, Fischzuchtkoenigsee'. It was four in the afternoon; we'd left Skye Cottage twenty seven hours ago. The arrival of a camper van with three bleary eyed creatures seemed to cause no concern. A team appeared from nowhere, the van was unloaded and we were led away like sheep to a huge purpose-built wash house. Under steaming hot showers came a sense of delicious relief. I'd just had time to glimpse the first boxes of elvers being released into the holding tanks and they had looked fine. We were off duty. It was one of the best showers I've ever had. We were famished and quite keen not to eat any more slices of rye bread or apple crumble. Haas led us over the road to a guest house where we were installed at his expense and given a huge meal before collapsing into bed and a deep sleep.

Besides rearing trout and running a sizable smokery, a large part of Haas's business seemed to derive from dealing in live fish for restocking, supplying the surrounding lakes and angling clubs with what they required. Trucks rumbled in day and night from the Iron curtain countries, Hungary and Czechoslovakia, huge lorries with tanks full of fish and trailers on behind, bringing with them the exotic flavour of distant lands as to a modern caravanserai. The second night, I discovered Tony outside, enjoying goulash stew cooked over a primus stove and drinking vodka with one of the drivers. When Tony had enquired how the man knew when the stew was ready, he replied simply, 'Ven dere's no vodka left.' It looked delicious, a lot more appealing than the carp Chippy and I had just shared with Haas and his wife. It'd had bones like umbrella spokes and looked suspiciously like one of the dead fish we'd noticed lying belly up in the ponds surrounding the house; we'd felt a certain unease about its freshness and provenance.

Restored by the family's generosity, it was time to settle up and head home. They had weighed the elvers, they were already on their way to a lake in Austria, 'Das Gewicht war gut und die Qualität auch,' Haas said, 'So, now, do you have your paperwork and we can settle up with you.' I had been dreading this. I explained that we'd left in such a hurry, there been no time for such things. Haas and his wife, a round and comfortable lady who did the accounts, listened wide-eyed in silence. Just as I thought there was going to be a major bureaucratic hitch and refusal to pay up without proper paperwork, they both burst out laughing. There was a muttered confab.

'Wir können denn bar bezahlen. We'll pay you in cash.' They drew me into the office and locked the door; from a safe in the wall they counted out what was due from a great wad of deutschmarks. It formed a comforting thickness in my pocket.

We waved our farewells and climbed into the kombi. But it wouldn't start. Other vehicles were brought alongside and jump leads attached; the engine turned but it would not fire. Ignominiously, we were towed to the VW dealer in the nearby town. There was a rapid diagnosis: a blown gasket, she was only running on two cylinders, and something else had dropped off, I couldn't understand the rest. But in record time the repairs were finished and I was relieved of a substantial part of the wad of notes leaving a much thinner feel to my pocket. The van ran perfectly all the way home and continued to do so for the rest of the year. Back at Skye Cottage there was much rejoicing and recounting of tales, and yes, the girls had discovered – and much enjoyed - the fillings for thirty sandwiches.

★★★★★

The income from the sale of the elvers to Haas gave some small temporary relief to our diminishing funds. This was a season however that was beginning to show us up for what we were: naïve beginners who'd had a lucky start. Our production was too small to attract the bigger buyers who would collect from us, as they did with Hancock; and our knowledge of the market was so limited that if turned down by Rosengarten, Haas or the Dutch, we had nowhere else to go. Then, at the end of March, it looked as if our fortunes might change. The weather warmed, the daffodils appeared and with them came the elvers. Suddenly we were catching and the tanks including the new ones began to fill. I made the usual phone calls to the continent, but they were saturated by French supplies, and I was politely told to try again in April. Anthony Lang came to the rescue with the name of the buyer in Gloucester he and Hancock had used when they had worked together on the elvers.

Dr Grunseid was Austrian, with fish farming interests near Vienna, amongst them the lucrative contract to stock with elvers two of Europe's largest lakes: Neusiedler See that lay across the border with Hungary and Lake Balaton deep within that country. To fulfil these orders he arrived in Gloucester each spring like a swallow from his native country, to spend the season buying and dispatching elvers from his holding unit beside the pub at Epney on the bank of river Severn, a couple of miles below the city. He must have been in his fifties then and known by his henchman and his fishermen as 'the Doctor,' though no-one quite knew what his doctorate was in. He was a wily old bird. When I spoke to him, he was charming, yes, of course, bring the fish up, any day would do, he was there all the time. The price was not dazzling but then, I thought, there was no freight, no running up to London, none of the worry involved in finding a market.

His elver tanks were behind the pub and I found him in a tiny office playing chess with his helper, a fellow countryman. Both were in lederhosen, there was a wooden clock and alpine scenes on the wall, a plate of black bread and sausage and the smell of good coffee: an incongruous piece of Austria on the banks of the river Severn. He waved me grandly to a chair while they finished the game. Eventually we unloaded and he professed himself satisfied with the delivery. He would send me a cheque in the next day or so as soon as the fish had been rested and then weighed. It all seemed to have gone well, I reflected, as I drove home.

In the days that followed I waited eagerly for the cheque. Nothing came. Anxious, I began to phone him. Each time there was more criticism of the fish, the weight was not good, less than I had said, and there were several kilos of dead, which, of course, he'd have to subtract from the total. I'd seen our losses, often barely a cupful, when delivering to Rosengarten or Haas; I began to grow very suspicious. The phrase, 'as slippery as an eel' came to mind. At last payment arrived, an amount so much reduced that we'd barely covered the purchase of the fish, let alone made a profit. We decided that dealing with the good doctor any further was not going to be good for our health.

It had however opened our eyes a little to the extraordinary intense, closed world of intrigue that existed there in Gloucester, along the Severn. Grunseid was just one of several buyers on the river who vied for a share of the great elver migration that came each spring. Just a few hundred yards down the road from Grunseid's operation was the Elver Station Epney, run by the Clarke family with strong links to the East End of London. Further upriver in Gloucester, Peter Wood and fellow vet, Glynn Wright, along with the help of Jim Milne, had positioned holding tanks on an old trawler to create a floating site on the canal in the city. On the other side of the Severn, at Minsterworth, Horace Cook, a farmer and fish merchant, had gradually drifted into selling elvers, first to the locals to eat, and then to the Spanish market, the frozen trade..

They all fought like rats in a trap. At the beginning of each season all was sweetness and light, there would be professions of good faith, agreements not to drive the price so that everyone could make a bit. But by the end of the first tide these promises had usually all gone out of the window and open warfare raged. It was often high volume, low margin business.

Each station had its core of loyal fishermen, often bound by tradition or family ties. 'I've always fished for Ted, I've known ee for years.' Up there, they called the teams of fishermen 'crews'; some of the top crews were wooed like star players, able to command the highest price over and above what smaller catchers were paid. Secret deals were struck, the crews sworn to an omerta-like silence – until approached by a rival buyer. Having a top crew fish for you meant you could bank on a tonne or two of elvers, a huge boost if you had a large order on your books, until suddenly in the middle of the season they might melt away and be found fishing for the competition.

It was all on a massive scale that dwarfed Somerset: where the river Parrett yielded perhaps twenty to thirty tonnes a year, the Severn and Wye would net around five times that amount, a hundred and fifty tonnes, much more in a good year. What characterized the elver fishing - and it was the same in France and Spain where the combined seasonal catch might have clocked nearer a thousand to fifteen hundred tonnes - was the shadowy nature of it all, the complete lack of accurate information: no one ever knew for certain what the total catches were, they could only guess.

Of course every dealer knew what he himself had purchased, but like poker players, none was ever going to declare that vital information and display his weakness or strength. Besides, this was a nocturnal world of black money, 'argent noir' or 'liquide' as the French called it, money paid in cash to the fishermen, greatly interesting to the taxman if he could get hold of how much and to whom. Ever more reason not to publicize the statistics.

★★★★★

To add to worries about the survival of the business was the uncertainty of our own future at Skye Cottage. It was on the market and we were obliged to show round potential buyers. Although highlighting the damp and the freezing draughts, there was nothing we could say that could deflect the peace and loveliness of its setting, nestled into the side of the hill overlooking a wooded valley. We loved the place, felt very possessive of it. We'd even been to a mortgage company to see if we could raise the money to buy it but when we described how we earned a living their eyes glazed over. Very nearly, though, one bitterly cold night in March, we almost lost everything, ourselves and the cottage together.

It had been so cold that we had given Barbara and Tony an old electric blanket to lie on. They had pushed their beds together so they could huddle together for warmth, unwittingly crimping the electric blanket, causing it to short. It had ignited, burned down into the bed, smouldering very slowly like a cigar, filling the room with smoke. What woke them was the crying of their baby daughter, Nova, who slept snug as a bug on a sheep skin fleece in the half open drawer at the bottom of the dresser. As Tony got up to find the source of the smoke and opened the window to peer outside, the smouldering fire, greedy for oxygen, burst into flame.

I was woken in the middle of the night by Barbara's scream outside our door, 'Michael, Michael, there's a fire!' Their room was thick with smoke. But even the effect of opening the door fanned the flames, licking the bed with a devilish glow. It was like a time bomb waiting to explode. We slammed the door shut and tumbled downstairs. This was much more serious than our chimney fire at the Colt House. Tony and I grabbed the fire extinguisher, very small, about the size of a wine bottle but in our paroxysm of fumbling the instructions seemed written in a foreign language. We flipped it back and forth with trembling hands like some mad game of pass-the-parcel with lots of 'Here let me try'. Finally it burst into life, showing off with a wild ejaculation, blowing foam in all directions through a thin rubber pipe. By the time we'd raced upstairs and pointed it at the fire its moment of glory had passed and it could only manage a feeble dribble.

The firemen arrived and donned breathing apparatus; the cottage was full of giant figures, the hiss of breathing and the thunk of helmets colliding with low beams and soon the fire was under control. Earlier pacing up and down in the lane outside, waiting for them to arrive, I had suddenly been aware that I had nothing on but a pair of wellies and an old sweater.

★★★★★

By the standards of those days, 1976 was a poor season all over Europe. We kept waiting for the big tide – and the orders were beginning to appear now as buyers found themselves short – but it never came. There was just one memorable night's catch that stood out like a beacon amidst the gloom. Anthony Lang had always said that it was worth checking the weirs upriver above Langport, as the elvers would collect there before climbing them and moving on.

One night between tides, remembering his advice, I drove to Pibsbury lock on the Yeo about two miles above the town. It was the Easter weekend and we were desperate for elvers to make up a shipment. The lock and all the ground around it was private land and beautifully kept by the lock-keeper, Dick Champion, a stout, florid-faced man with a fiery temper. I parked quietly, slipped over the fence. As soon as I shone my torch in the water, I felt the thrill of the prospector sighting gold. A thick band of elvers was working its way upriver and massing below the step of the weir. They had found a route up one side of the wall where it was moist and they could just find purchase to climb and reach the upper level of the river.

A weir upriver

I found a spot to fish and with each lift of the net came the frying sound of elvers en masse. Soon I settled into a rhythm of catching, traying up, carrying the full trays back to the van. To get over the fence the way led over a stretch of gravel past Champions house. I had to place each foot down flat, very gently and creep by. Once there was a cough from a bedroom inside and I froze with the tray held out like a waiter delivering room service. But all was quiet. Each time I unlocked the van, the noise of the side door sliding open was deafening. In the end I just left it open. By the time I got back to my net, it was full again.

It was a beautiful spring night. A soft breeze stirred the poplars. An old moon had climbed into the sky. You could feel the earth stirring. Below the weir in the rhythmic boom of the fall, the breath of the river carried on the air, wafts of damp earth, mud, moss, musty yet sweet, a cocktail of scents stirred by the tumble of water.

Gradually as the night wore on, the run slackened until with the first light of dawn the elvers dropped out of sight. I packed up my kit, careful to erase all signs of my presence and left for Bowdens to put the elvers to bed. I'd caught about 40 kilos, a substantial boost to the order for Holland, which could now go ahead that week. As the sun came up, I drove back to Skye Cottage on the Blackdowns just as the others were stirring and cooked a triumphal breakfast of bacon and eggs.

It was decided that we should all go that night. Alasdair and Christine, friends of Staff, were over from Australia to help us for a few weeks, and keen to come with me. We parked in the same spot, made our way noiselessly over the fence. We'd just put our nets in the water when I was pinned by a blinding light and a voice shouting, 'What are you doing here. This is private property.' Mr Champion was exultant at his catch. 'I knew some bugger been yere; I seed where you'd been trayin up. And I could follow where you went.' He wasn't one to waste words. 'Now you bugger off and don't come back again or I'll call the cops.'

Muttering apologies we withdrew with minimal fuss. I got to know Champion in later years, bought elvers off him, met him at the odd social gathering. We never mentioned the incident. It was quietly buried. Looking back, what really riled him was the fact that he hadn't been out to catch the elvers himself. But then he'd made up for it: he'd caught me instead. We were quits.

★★★★★

79

The season drizzled on. Everything seemed to go wrong. A large shipment to Haas, by air this time, arrived safely, but in the frenzy of packing the elvers in the night we under weighed and could have sent many more, at the very time when we had both the fish and a market. There were more problems with the airlines: a shipment to Holland was left on the tarmac all day and suffered heavy losses. In Scotland we were desperate to make up lost ground. We caught well but, during a storm, the water supply to the hatchery choked with pine needles and we lost half our precious catch. It was the last throw of the dice, the end of a disastrous season. Our total production was just over a tonne, half the previous season. Even from rough workings on the back of an envelope, it was obvious that we had done little more than break even and the coffers were very low. Returning to Somerset we learned that Skye Cottage had been sold and we were to be out by the end of June.

My head was full of doubts and self-examination. Should I chuck it all in and get a proper job, or try again, give it one more go. My parents were never judgmental, always supportive but I couldn't help but sense their disappointment and wistful thinking, 'If only he'd stayed with the company, the salary, the pension.' Perhaps I was wrong, perhaps it was more in my own head. Friends, contemporaries, meanwhile, seemed to be doing so well, being promoted, looking affluent. They'd ask, 'What will you do now, after the elver season, where will you live?' I fumbled to fabricate answers, trying to sound relaxed and full of resolve. Inside I felt grey and probably looked it. And while I scribbled and crossed out 'Plans for the Future' on scraps of paper, groaned and lolled about like a wilting weed, Utta by contrast was sunny and positive; she had an unshakeable conviction that we'd get by. 'I'll just go out and get a job.' And she did. Very soon she was keeping us afloat, doing three nights a week in a nursing home for the elderly while I made efforts to resurrect my travel writing contacts – a little difficult when we weren't travelling.

Meanwhile we stored our belongings in the elver barn and lived in the camper van. By day we scoured the surrounding villages for a place to rent. By night we parked on a wide grassy verge on a lane near Bowdens beneath a big oak tree, drawn by its sense of friendly shelter. Anthony lent us an empty cottage on the farm for a week. We camped on the floor and kept up the hunt for somewhere to live. One day, asking around the village of Drayton, we heard of a landlady whose tenants had just done a midnight flit. She was Betty Parks and the property in question had been the gardener's cottage. It was grandly called the Lodge, more substantial than Skye Cottage and though it hadn't the view or the setting, it had a welcoming feel. Beyond the overgrown garden at the back were several acres of ancient orchard. Inside, beside an enormous open fireplace, a rickety wooden staircase led to three bedrooms upstairs that opened in friendly fashion, one into the other.

It was perfect. Rent was agreed at the large sum of fifteen pounds a month – more than Skye but still very reasonable. Perhaps its greatest asset was that it was only five minutes from Bowdens and the elver tanks. It was unfurnished except for one bed upstairs. We moved our few belongings in and Utta bought a carpet for a pound in the Langport market. Within hours it had become our new home. And it was to be so for the next six years.

★★★★★

I was just looking for some part time teaching work, when Anthony called me up to the farm to meet a Belgian industrialist he'd met at the Bath and West Show; he was a hobby farmer keen to buy some Dorset Down sheep, but he also had several restaurants and was looking for a supply of live eel. Long before David Forrest or I appeared on the scene, Anthony in partnership with Hancock had used the holding tanks at Bowdens, once the elver season was over, to buy in adult eels and had traded some eighteen tonnes in their last year of co-operation. Somerset was full of eels, Anthony told the Belgian, and Michael was just the man to supply him. 'Just one small problem,' I told them, 'I've never caught an eel in my life. Only elvers.'

'Ah, but that is not at all a problem,' the Belgian replied, 'I have an old friend, a Dutchman, he knows all there is to know about eels. He's fishing in Ireland at the moment but he'll come here after that and teach you.'

Pieter van der Schluwys turned up one evening at the end of July in that long hot summer of '76. It was typical of him to arrive unannounced. We'd been away for the weekend and found him waiting on the doorstep. He was probably in his early sixties, neat in appearance with greying swept-back hair, a big man with a great broad chest and powerful arms.

81

An arthritic leg gave him a lumpy awkwardness about the place until he was on the water; there, he was in his element. His great bulk filled his little rowing boat, weighed it down perilously but he rowed with power and natural ease, could hold the boat midstream, manoeuvring it deftly, oars like antennae sensing the current, stroking the water, moving a fraction to left or right to work the nets or survey a potential site.

His name defined him. Translated from the Dutch it meant literally Pieter of the Sluices. And that's what he was, a man of the water, a fisherman, and his family for generations before him. He'd been brought up in a fishing community beside one of the great inland lakes in Holland. A professional fisherman all his life, he had fished for eel all over Europe from the Camargue in southern France to the marshes of the Guadalquivir in southern Spain to the lakes and rivers of Ireland. His only interest and conversation was of eels. In his broken English he'd recall the incredible catches he'd made and his eyes lit up as he described nets bulging, the tonnes of eel he'd caught. And yet, it seemed, there'd always been a snag: the nets had carried away, or a villain had stolen the boat, or the transporter hadn't turned up to collect and they had all died. Nothing had ever quite worked out. And sensing perhaps his time was running out, he was driven, always looking for the next big catch, like the prospector for the seam of gold that would set him up for ever. Even then, when he came to us, he seemed to be travelling constantly in a sort of nomadic desperation. There was brief mention of a daughter and family but essentially he was a lonely, restless soul.

We didn't warm to him. It annoyed us that he seemed to assume that he was staying with us. There was no 'would it be alright if,' or 'until I find somewhere else'. He just moved in and that was that. The other irritation was that he wouldn't eat the meals we prepared. He'd peer suspiciously at the plate and then push it away, serving himself instead from his supply of raw vegetables and jars of pickled fish. It was like having a pelican in the house. There was no sense of sharing, it set him apart and with his vast bulk shuffling about the cottage we were forever bumping into each other. He reminded me of Toad taking up residence in the home of Mrs Tittlemouse. As nothing had been properly settled with the Belgian as to how long he was staying or where, or who was paying for his accommodation (a lesson from which we were to learn), we began to have nightmares about how long he'd be with us. Fortunately we were rescued by Betty, a bright and friendly lady, who lived on her own over the road; she had a spare room and we breathed a sigh of relief as Pieter moved out.

As soon as I showed Pieter the Somerset Levels, he became intensely excited. He stood on the bank of one of the great rhines, where I first took him, the Kings Sedgemoor, a ruler of water bisecting the moor. He tapped the side of his nose. 'Ya, here is eels. I can smell dem.' To test the waters he used very small fyke nets that he could set rapidly from the bank without using his boat. The fyke is one of the main methods of catching eel. In simple terms, it looks like a windsock attached to a tennis net. The eel, feeding on the bottom of the river, encounters the upright curtain of the tennis net, the leader as it's called, and is guided to the mouth of the windsock net, held open by a series of hoops. Ever curious and with a fondness for going inside confined spaces, the eels eases forward through the several throats of the net that prevent its return until arriving in the final chamber, the cod end, the final jail from where it cannot escape.

Pieter showed me how to weight the cod end and sling it out into the water, pulling it back so that the net was held rigid and the leader upright before staking it into the side of the bank. He handled them with easy familiarity, his hands working the knots without even having to look what he was doing. On exploratory forays he'd shoot a dozen nets in the evening in different places then go back early next morning to pick them up. Despite my gloom and despondency, I couldn't help feeling the thrill of pulling in a net, to see what we'd caught, to feel the tug and thrash of live eel in the cod end. And there were eels. Lots of them but very varied in size. From living in the peaty waters of the moor they were dark brown and olive. Their distinguishing features were the broad, rounded heads and thin lanky bodies, a sign, Pieter said, of their immaturity and nutrition. I could see him looking at them closely, assessing their value. They weren't the best quality, but they'd do for cooking, they'd do for the Belgian's restaurants.

With its wide-open skies and landscape, broken only by the willows lining the rhines, nothing happens on the levels without someone spotting you and seeing what you're doing. Within days I was reliably informed by a fisherman who had no idea I was involved that 'a Dutch guy was over 'ere with hundreds of nets and they were takin' all the eels.' Nor was it long before it came to the attention of the water authorities: they pounced on us one morning as we were lifting the nets on the moor near Othery, north of Langport. Pieter, perhaps not for the first time in his life, made a hasty escape in his car – a wise move no doubt as it would have been impounded – leaving me to face them. I was read the riot act: we needed a licence for the nets and we had no right to fish in angling club waters. They left, taking all the nets with them.

Banned from fishing on the moor, Pieter, undeterred, and with more nets in the boot of his car, turned his attention to the coast and estuarine waters where restrictions were lighter. It was then, on one of our forays to Burnham-on-Sea, just beyond the mouth of the Parrett estuary, that we met Les. He spotted us unloading nets and offered to help. He and his wife were from 'up north' but had come to a dream retirement by the sea, the bungalow, walks on the promenade in the sun, fishing off the boat for Les. But leaving friends and roots far behind had left them bored and lonely. He was dying to play and he was a useful man, knew the local tides, had a small boat of his own which he was happy for us to use. Very quickly Pieter co-opted him into our ventures and I found I had a mate. Les had a wonderful, perky sense of humour, the only person I ever saw who could make Pieter laugh, and as we wrestled with nets and hauled boats, much of which Pieter was too lame to do, we grumbled together, cracked murderous jokes like two old lags under the gimlet eye of their warder.

Les took us to the mouth of the Brue, his local river. I could see Pieter's eyes open wide with interest, his nostrils scenting eel. Immediately

Eel fyke nets drying

from the boot of the car he produced a big double fyke, a single leader with a cod end net at each end, which we set across the river by the tidal gates. When we picked it up in the morning it was heaving with eels, so heavy we could hardly lift each cod end. They were beautiful fish, quite different from their cousins on the moors; they were silvery, plumper and mostly they had sharp noses, the result of better diet, Pieter said, good for smoking. He was very excited, his plans accelerating like fire spreading through straw. He'd

84

get more nets, we'd set them here, all up and down the river, he'd get a boat and set more down the estuary. We'd all make lots of money. A little crowd of curious onlookers was beginning to gather. Les and I were trying to hustle him away, when the lock keeper appeared, 'You can't use they here,' he bawled at us, 'It's illegal within fifty metres of the gates. Now bugger off.' I remembered I'd heard that phrase once before that year.

Pieter wasn't finished. He'd seen the promised land; there were the eels out there in the estuarine waters off Burnham. To save the long trek from our house in Drayton, it wasn't long before he was leaving the gear at Les's house, breakfasting there before we lifted the nets; not long before Pieter was beginning to talk of moving in, taking over the spare room, it would save him miles of driving, he'd be right there on the spot. Caught up with it all, Les was like a small boy, as excited as Pieter. 'Aye and then we could put up tanks in the garage for keeping the eels, sort of holding place like Mike's.' Les's wife said nothing but she was deeply suspicious. She'd seen the likes of Pieter before, could spot them a mile off; she also knew that her man could get a bit overheated. With Les on a firm leash there would be overnight discussions and he would greet us in the morning, looking shifty and uncomfortable, 'Er, missus says she dusn't think it's a very good idea if you stay here.' He was embarrassed.

'And she dusn't like the idea of us using the garage.' Pieter would snort like a bull and swat away the objections as if he would bring his will to prevail. But he'd met his match. No meant no with 'er indoors.'

But Pieter would not give up. Goaded by that catch, by the glimpse of eels that swam beneath the muddy waters of the estuary, he had to try again. It was like watching someone obsessed, trying to prise open a treasure chest. From Anthony we borrowed a boat with an outboard motor, towed behind the farm land rover. The aim was to set a string of double fykes across the lower tidal estuary. Pieter got carried away with the outboard throttle and Les and I nearly vanished over the side as we paid them out. In the night the fierce tide rolled them over and over, rendering them useless and the catch was minimal. When we came to leave, we found the land rover and trailer parked half way down the beach had sunk in the sand, bogged down to their axles. The incoming tide was racing in, licking its lips. A garage near the waterfront obviously specialised in hauling hapless victims off the beach. I wondered if it was their only business, they had a sly, studied indifference to all pleas of poverty or charity.

'We're stuck on the sand and tide's coming in,' I panted.

'Yeah, we been watchin.'

'Can you help us.'

'Oh yeah, we can help all right.' I was greatly relieved, 'But it'll cost ee.'

'How much?'

'Fifty pound.' We balked. It was a king's ransom in those days.

Pieter was explosive. He wouldn't pay, it was extortionate. 'That's up to you then,' unmoved, they turned back to their work. Outside the tide was creeping inexorably up the beach and just beginning to lap around the wheels of the trailer. Reluctantly, fuming, Pieter shelled out the cash. In minutes a tractor had hauled us off the sand to safety.

Over several weeks we tried all sorts of waters for eeling, setting nets in tidal rivers, in inland waters and rhines. Pieter was looking for big steady rhythmic catches day after day but we only caught bits and pieces, patchily, always moving on in restless search. At intervals he would gather up the eels we'd caught and that were held in the tanks at Bowdens and vanish home to Holland to sell them. There'd be a blissful week of peace and then he'd be back again.

Then one day, in early autumn, he gathered the eels and left. And never returned. We never saw him again. He'd had enough. Perhaps somewhere south in Spain, he'd heard, they were catching. Neither Les nor I were ever paid for all the hours, days of work we put in but in a way we'd never expected it. We'd got to know Pieter and it came as no surprise. For Les it was company and escape from the quiet tedium of life by the sea. Utta and I heaved a huge sigh of relief and decided to put the experience behind us. At least, I told myself, there was some consolation: I had learned a new trade. It had been my apprenticeship: now, as well as elvers, I could catch eels.

Chapter Five

That autumn I found a part-time job teaching languages two days a week at a little school, grandly known as a tutorial college, just under an hour away on the south coast near Bridport. From the teaching and Utta's nursing we had just enough to live on and time to plan for the next elver season. I learned years later that a third of small businesses fail in their first three years; if they passed that point, they usually survived. This cheery information probably compiled by banks to boost morale wouldn't at the time have made the slightest difference, for like all those caught up in the elver world we were hooked, ever hopeful of better times to come. We had seen the glint of gold, learnt some painful lessons. Surely it had to get better; we just needed a few more fishermen to give us a more reliable supply of elvers, less dependence on our distant continental customers. And just a bit of luck.

Besides all these considerations, we were increasingly happy at the Lodge. I'd spent most of my childhood on the edge of Dartmoor with few neighbours. Living within a village was a totally new experience for both of us. Drayton was a friendly tight-knit community, alive and busy with three working farms within the village itself, one about a hundred yards down the street. The sound of cattle and tractors passing was part of the daily life. Close by, the tiny post office, not much bigger than a cupboard, was the hub of local information and gossip. At the crossroads, opposite the pub, the soft grey, square-towered church rose, topped by a plump golden cockerel, glinting, visible for miles. Rooks cawed in the beech trees and on practice nights the sound of bells showered the village.

Early on we made good friends, especially with a young couple, David and Ingrid White, living opposite with small children. To those either side of us, our two families must have been the neighbours from hell. The sound of their babies crying and the thud of nightly demolition work as they got rid of various unwanted bits of their house mingled with our own nocturnal comings and goings. Though working as a solicitor with a large law firm in Taunton, David's hobby was his sheep which he kept in the orchard behind the house. Occasionally he would load a few into a home-made trailer like a large pram with sides made out of pallets. He needed these as the sheep were of a particularly lean, athletic variety – no relation to Anthony's well-rounded, comfortable Dorset Downs – and never that keen on a visit to Taunton market. As they neared the point of loading they'd bolt and high jump out of our clutches, leaping gleefully like kangaroos back down to their orchard. At last he would depart with the trailer juddering and swaying from unrestrained internal bedlam. He was very proud one week to get top market price for his girls.

Meanwhile in the orchard behind the Lodge, I had learned from Ernie how to snare rabbits, setting the slip wires in the hedge where they made their runs, anchoring them to the fence wire or to a stake. It was like eeling with fyke nets: set at night, pick up in the morning, the same sense of anticipation to see what had been caught. We skinned and jointed them, making casseroles mostly, often with cider, a delicious addition to our menu until one day I caught a big buck rabbit, so raunchy that no matter how many times I scrubbed my hands I couldn't rid his wild smell, an odour so pungent that it pervaded the stew and made it inedible. We went off rabbit for a while after that.

What we enjoyed the most were our forays to collect wood. Our heating came from a massive old fireplace and, later, a wood burner. Both needed a constant supply of logs. It was the time of Dutch elm disease and Anthony let us remove some of the dead trees about the farm. We spent whole days, cutting and gathering; picnicking in quiet autumn fields, with the caw of rooks and smell of sawn wood. Once one of the elver fisherman delivered a trailer load of great elm stumps; we were touched by his kindness and thanked him gratefully. It was only when I tried to split them, I found why he might actually have been happy to get rid of them: they were so fibrous and knotted they might almost have been knitted by hand. Not even Goliath could have split these cleanly. The axe head sunk into them like glue and you found that you were swinging something the size of a medicine ball above your head. Yet little by little they could be worn down, highly satisfying. Certainly the activity kept you warm. Any male visitors down for the weekend relished the challenge and I'd show them to the pile of stumps; hours later, dripping with sweat, stripped almost to their underpants, they'd come in for lunch, exultant at having conquered one of the hulks while wives or girlfriends would flutter, 'Oh darling, you look so hot,' excited by this resurgence of masculinity.

★★★★★

In those days the main event of the fish farming year was the Two Lakes conference organised by Alex Behrendt and held over three days each October at his fishery near Romsey in Hampshire. It was attended by a mix of those involved in the young industry, many from overseas, from suppliers to farmers and stockists, to river keepers and landowners, in fact anyone making a living from water. I'd been going for a couple of years and it was where I'd met Zumke of the OVB in Holland to whom we sold our Scottish elvers. Never slick or dominated by big brands, the conference mixed amateurs and professionals and the mood was characterised by an eagerness to learn, a willingness to share experience. The lectures were always practical and diverse: farming trout in earth ponds might follow a talk on transporting live fish with oxygen, keeping guard dogs or growing water lilies in a lake for additional income. Though they might not be your subject, there were always useful tips, and information to stow away.

Two Lakes was also where the latest developments in the industry would be aired. That year there were the first whispers about eel farming. We had already been contacted by a scientist, Alan Walker, and supplied a few kilos of elvers for growing trials he was conducting. By taking elvers – baby eels – and growing them on in warm water, it was possible to produce adult, marketable-size eels in the space of two years when in nature it could take anything up to ten, fifteen or even twenty years depending on water conditions. Looked at on paper, it seemed a recipe to make money and it brought a glint to the eyes of accountants and venture capitalists alike. The recipe looked delightfully straightforward: take one kilo of elvers, approximately 3,000 in number, costing at that time around five pounds per kilo, grow them on, fatten them up and at the end of two years you had three thousand eels weighing not one kilo but, at an average of 250gms each, 750 kilos in total or three quarters of a tonne, and worth, at the then-sale price of around £3.50 per kilo, a cool £2,625. Not a bad mark-up. At this point accountants and investors would be licking their lips, wiping the mist off their glasses. Of course these were perfect figures, making no allowance for feed and operating costs, nor for the reality of losses or disasters. But it didn't matter, that was the goal and eel farming looked very interesting indeed.

It counted on two things: a reliable source of warm water from waste heat; and a supply of elvers. Unlike most other fish species where the eggs from the female are simply stripped from the fish in the hatchery and with the use of a feather, mixed with the sperm from the cock fish – love in a bucket as it was known – the eel steadfastly refuses to reproduce in captivity, in laboratory conditions. Eel farming was going to have to depend completely on elver suppliers. On us – if we could get in first. Looking round the conference, I was relieved to see that there was no sign of Mike Hancock or any of the big boys; only Peter Wood's Bristol Channel Fisheries from Gloucester was present and in contention.

Alan Walker who had bought the test sample from us was working for the food giant, Rank Hovis McDougall. In a new venture, they were looking at a pilot project to farm eels using the waste heat from the cooling towers of Drax coal-fired power station in south Yorkshire. In 1977 we made further small sales to Alan and for the first time he bought some Scottish elvers from us.

Nearer to home, we made a small delivery of elvers to Maurice Ingram, a retired submariner, who had set up a pilot project at Hinkley Point nuclear power station to the west of Bridgwater in Somerset. Maurice had been fascinated by the sight of prawn farming while serving with the Navy in the Far East. Fired up by the potential for farming species in warm water, he had left the service and was experimenting with various fish grown in the warm water from the cooling towers, looking in particular at prawns, turbot and elvers. The prawns were the least successful, not liking the high suspension of silt in the muddy waters drawn from the Bristol Channel. The turbot were happier: they lay on top of each other at the bottom of the tank and snoozed like old men in a London club. But it was the elvers that showed the best promise.

The difficulty was getting them onto feed. Maurice experimented with all sorts of diets, trying earthworm, lug worm, and cod's roe, all of which they did well on but which were time-consuming to prepare. In the end he found that the tiny pellet crumb normally fed to trout fry worked perfectly and the elvers took it and thrived. Mixed into a kind of paste with additional oils, it was placed in feeding trays suspended round the edge of the tanks. The elvers, already becoming little eels, would appear in seconds out of the murky water as if from nowhere, massing round the basket like cattle to a feed rack, making tiny sucking sounds as they attacked the paste. In a frenzy of feeding they'd polish it off and be gone in minutes.

But the eel was not easy to farm. There was no tried and tested manual to turn to as there was with, say, trout or carp farming. All the farms were starting from scratch, learning as they went. In the beginning the survival rate of the elvers was often very poor, as low as twenty percent. It was to resolve such problems as these that Maurice - a great communicator and networker – formed an eel producers' group which met regularly to exchange and share information.

The following year, in 1978, the orders from the eel farms grew bigger as the projects were scaled up. I was contacted by an equipment supplier whom I knew from Two Lakes who had just been asked to tender to RHM for a huge number of fibre glass tanks to be installed at Drax for their next phase of development. He'd been told they were going to need substantial quantities of elvers, perhaps two tonnes a year, and he was going to recommend us as a supplier. All this was intensely exciting. And it couldn't come too soon for the '77 and '78 seasons were much better, restoring our faith and confidence in the business. At the height of each season, with an abundance of elvers, we were desperate to get them away to market in order to make space for fresh catches coming in. Suddenly, here was the prospect of a market within the UK, easy to reach and no longer dependent on airfreight.

★★★★★

These were not only better years for elvers but also our team of fishermen was changing, growing in number and strengthening. When I first arrived it had been made up almost entirely by the men on the farm, like Ern and Shep and their families and a few locals and ourselves. A new breed was starting to appear. Word had got around that there was money to be made from this thing called elvering. Young men would turn up at the tanks, wanting 'to have a go', to buy netting and pick up a tide table. They were fellows who could turn their hand to anything: lay patios, erect fences, supply logs, anything that would earn a crust. 'Decided to go self-employed,' they'd say, ''ad enough working in Clarks factory. Couldn't stand it no more.' They were naturals at elvering, made feather-light nets from aluminium, far better than the heavyweight wooden ones I supplied, and quickly picked up how and where to catch. Being free to drop all else, they'd follow the river each night and devote their whole time to fishing. It became a seasonal part of their lives and earnings, and they loved it. For years they were to become our core fishermen, responsible for the bulk of our elvers and though loyal, as competition grew, they became an increasingly powerful force, tuned in to the latest price on the riverbank. And never afraid to ask for more.

In terms of elver catches however, the years of '77 and '78 really belonged to a character called George Cotty. We'd got to know him because he'd done some work for us, plastering the new tanks Tony and I had built the year before. Like Ernie, he'd been catching elvers all his life, and in the Fifties, long before Hancock appeared, he used to put them on the train in sacks at Athelney and send them up to Bristol for the glue factories. It must have been the smelliest of all glue. He'd lived by the river all his life and knew it like the back of his hand. He was a small, dark, swarthy fellow with jet black hair. He'd served in the Navy, he told me, during the War and had been steward to Admiral Somerville in the Far East, 'against they there Japs, when 'ee were commander of the Eastern Fleet.'

Looking at him in his old coat tied up with string like a parcel, peaked wool hat pulled down hard over his eyes, it was hard to imagine. And yet, if he scrubbed up well, there was a hidden gloss; if you squinted, you could just see him in naval uniform with the smile that lit up his face. I never thought he made it up, his memories and anecdotes and the respect he held for Somerville, were just too vivid. Though George did like the dramatic flourish. When I stopped the van to see how he was doing, he'd sidle up and looking round conspiratorially, drop his voice to a rough whisper, 'Theym running hard tonight. I got thirty trays of ilvers out the way in the back of me van - if you want em.' He let the information hang tantalisingly in the air, giving it time to dissolve and be absorbed, and then in a voice so low I had to bend close to hear, 'they say ee's paying one thirty a kilo. That's what they say, though course I adn seen him meself. Ee don't come round yere.' Of course ee' meant Hancock and I used to think it strange at the time that Hancock had not approached him to buy his elvers. He had most of the fishermen in his grip. As the season wore on I was to find out why.

George was potentially a wealthy man, owning several properties along the riverbank, but all in a state of serious decay and he spent much of his time defending them, beating off the thieving vultures, 'they buggers from Bridgwater' who picked them clean of tiles and bricks. He owned one that would have been idyllic, a red brick cottage with outhouses and orchard right beside the river. It was here that George had his special fishing spot, his private gold mine. Beside it, a small brook, more of a conduit, drained excess water from the moor. Like dozens of such outlets up and down the bank, it was controlled by a hinged flap or clapper like a one way valve that swung open at low tide to release the water penned up behind. During high tide the pressure of water forced it shut to prevent the river entering the moor. On a good night when the elvers were running, George would wait until the river had dropped enough for him to reach the clapper and crack it open, just enough to release a flow of what he called 'that there sweet' which drew the elvers in a steady stream like some heady scent, a promise of the watery moors they sought to enter at the end of their long journey.

Hour after hour, crouched over his net, long after the others had gone home, he fished the river down to a thin trickle between the high muddy banks, mining it, squeezing it for its precious cargo. He took great care of his elvers; if there was a frost he stacked them in the back of his van covered with sacks. Each time he opened the doors the reek of fish hit you and nearly bowled you over. Mean as a flint, he'd find every excuse to save petrol and not to bring them up to the tanks at Bowdens: too many trays to fit in his van, his lights weren't working, or the brakes had gone. I'd wait, fretting, dog tired, dying to get home. If I was teaching the next day, there'd be only be two or three hours sleep before I'd have to head off to school. Fortunately the big tides fell in the school holidays, but there were times when I would find

Catching on the crawl

93

myself nodding off in the classroom. Or I corrected homework while I waited for George, handing it back stained with mud and bits of riverbank to puzzled students. I saw now why Hancock had happily passed him on to me.

At last he'd croak, 'theym dropping off now. I spose youm wanting to get on.' My heart would leap, but this was not the end. Far from being able to load his trays and head home, now came the weighing. It was a nightmare, always a battle; it could take at least another hour. Sometimes we'd go back to his house, a mile up the road, or if there was no-one around we weighed on the riverbank. I used a metal tripod from which hung a portable set of scales. We loaded the trays, as many as we could get onto a base plate attached by chains to the scales. Then in the light of our torches we'd both peer at the needle on the dial. It would quiver, hover undecided between two figures. George had a way of angling the beam of his torch so that the shadow of the needle seemed to climb the scale.

'Ee says forty seven kilo'

'No, George, if you look at it straight that is definitely forty five.'

It was like arm wrestling, we'd haggle on until a glimpse of the stack of trays yet to come would drive us to sudden compromise. But that was still not the end. When we finished weighing, the empties had then to be weighed back to give us the true net weight of catch. It was hugely laborious. All this time his ancient Alsatian dog, large and shapeless, inaptly named Lucy, would gobble the elvers. No doubt this was her dinner. If they were from the stack of trays waiting to be weighed, George would shoo her off, 'Get away Lucy, I toldee before, get on with ee.' She would look up and stare at him as if to say, 'oh sorry, wrong pile,' and paddle round to the other stack, which had been weighed, and were therefore mine, and resume her feeding.

By the end we were like prize fighters dead on our feet, stumbling around in the dark. There'd be trays all over the place and lists of figures on damp bits of paper that I'd try to add up. It was hard to believe what he'd caught. Night after night fifty or sixty kilos; over the season of '77, of the three tonnes we bought that year, over a tonne came from George. But caught gently, with care, they were beautiful fish. 'Gute qualität,' Rosengarten would bellow down the phone. He loved them and kept ordering. We seemed forever to be driving to Heathrow in the middle of the night.

To help with the elver season of '77, a friend of Utta's sister and brother-in-law was staying with us. Due to go back to Australia as a teacher but having what would now be called a gap year, Stephen Bowers was a big, quiet, shy man, fascinated by European history and culture, and by wildlife. He drew beautifully in pen and ink, scenes often infused by his sense of humour. As he threw out sketches that he deemed below standard, we'd surreptitiously retrieve them from the waste bin and hang them up when he'd gone. During busy times, Stephen took over the nightly weighing of the fishermen and the marathon sessions with George while we packed elvers for an air freight shipment. Crucially, he looked after the site on the days I was teaching, moving the night's catch to clean tanks, removing damaged fish. With his interest in wildlife there was much for him to observe.

Once the elvers were in the clear water of the tanks, it was easy to see the by-catch that came in with them each night, mainly stickle-backs, fresh water shrimp and sometimes little flounder. The sticklebacks were doughty little fish, bristling with self-importance, glinting green and gold, with armour-plated heads and a spike on their backs, sharp as a thorn, which gave a painful stab if you handled them wrong. This was their main defence against other predators, sticking to the roof of a pike's mouth, forcing them to eject this little morsel. They seemed to be very fertile: frequently their undersides were tinged with pink and red, swollen with eggs. In the confines of the tank they discovered they could catch elvers and try to swallow them. However, unable to deal with their sinuous length, they'd swim round in mild surprise with the elver jammed in their mouths like a Cuban cigar.

It was Stephen, when I was teaching one day, who took the surprise call from Hancock. The German truck was over to collect and was loading the next day; there was some room in the tanks on board for about three hundred kilos. Were we interested? We hesitated. It seemed too good to be true: would this be another Gloucester episode as we'd had with Grunseid? Anthony was very suspicious. 'I wouldn't trust the blighter if I were you,' and Ernie backed him, 'Yea, you be kurful, Moik. You gotta watch en, mind' But the price was good and with no delivery costs, no running up to Heathrow, very attractive. I phoned Hancock and agreed the deal. We loaded the fish onto trays and I met him in a lay-by near his site. He obviously did not want me to meet his German customer, Herr

Klinge from Hamburg. So, here at last, was the enemy face-to-face. I'd seen him on the river of course, a tall, powerfully built figure, with wire framed glasses, but never met him properly. He was a reserved man, didn't say much, but he had a definite presence, a charisma. At times I'd heard he could be blunt and abrupt, and then again he could charm the birds from the trees.

On this occasion he was perfectly friendly as we chatted about the season, bemoaned the amount of mud we seemed to buy from the fishermen, then he loaded our elvers and was gone. He'd put the cheque under our doormat, he said, on his way back from the river that night. Sure enough, to my great relief I found it there, just as he'd promised.

When I spoke to Rosengarten next I was astonished that he knew about the sale to Hancock; furthermore he'd orchestrated it. There was lots of yohoho-ing down the phone, chortling at my bafflement and incredulity. He knew Herr Klinge well; they often worked together. The lorry had already been over several times to Hancock in the past few weeks and gone back full, but this was the end of the tide and he'd known Hancock hadn't enough to make up a full load. Hence the call to us.

Rosengarten was always inventive and resourceful. Sending shipments of elvers by air to him, one kilo per box, I was rapidly running out of boxes. They were expensive, specially made for us and I could never afford to buy too many at the start of the season. Quickly Rosengarten came up with a solution: Klinge, who came over regularly to collect from Hancock, would return them in his empty tanks. It would also save on the high cost of recycling which was already obligatory even then in Germany. I'd get a phone call usually in the early evening and meet the truck at the services on the motorway to collect my boxes. It was always a good chance to gather useful information about the quantities Hancock was catching and compare them with our own: as a rough guide, I reckoned that his take was on average ten times greater than ours.

Meanwhile, I liked Klinge and he promised to do business if we ever became big enough or the occasion arose for him to collect from us directly. His huge Scania lorry and trailer carried sixteen tanks capable of hauling up to 1.6 tonnes of elvers at a time. The size of a battleship, it underlined the sheer volume of catch taken off the Parrett estuary each season, and the size of Hancock's empire.

Then just when we thought the season might go on for ever, the catches would drop, the fishermen drift away, they too had had enough. With the last of the tides in May, life began to return to normal, always about the time the lilac, that grew up the side of the cottage, broke into flower; the scent of its blossom would became forever associated with the relief and euphoria that the season was over. It was like coming up for air, emerging, blinking, from a darkened room. And when the lilac was out, it was time to head north, to Scotland.

My father had a theory that when a young couple started to acquire pets, babies were never far behind. We had been given two extraordinary kittens in need of a home by Betty who lived over the road. One was a classic tabby who would grow into an enormous creature with a ravenous appetite. We had no idea what make the other, Peepoche, was; he had a luxurious fluffy coat of grey, there was definitely a touch of class about him; in one of his nine lives he must have been a French textile magnate or perhaps a Count. He was intrepid and innately curious. And he loved elvers. He'd crawl into the nets that were strapped to the trailer we took to the river and crunch on the dried ones. Then fall asleep. Several times departure to the river was delayed as I'd get as far as the next village where I'd become increasingly aware of a strangled yelling and see him in the rear mirror frantically waving at me to stop. He also liked to sunbathe on the roof of David's car across the road, when he'd be driven part way to Taunton before being returned to base.

But my father was right about animals and babies. During our stay in Scotland, that year of '77, while walking to the top of Cranstackie, a green sweeping mountain to the north of Foinavon, Utta felt uncharacteristically queasy and with a woman's intuition knew instinctively she was pregnant. Our daughter Emily was born the following year in February 1978. On Valentine's Day.

Her arrival into our lives was made even more dramatic as it coincided with the biggest snowstorm since the great blizzards of '63 and '47. It had been bitterly cold for over a month. The ground was like iron and ice lay thick on the moors around us; even the river froze along its edge into a fretwork of ice. I was with Utta in Yeovil hospital for Emily's birth: a tiny, beautiful baby but wearing a distinctive frown as if worried about the weather. I made one further visit the following day before the blizzard hit, engulfing the whole south west of the country. With luck I was able to get home by following a local snowplough. By morning it had stopped but it was up to the windowsills and a great muffled silence lay over the landscape. The road to Yeovil and the hospital had vanished, hidden under waves of snow. We had been told that Utta would spend three or four days on the ward before coming home; instead she was treated to a delicious enforced rest of over a week, looking down with her baby from the windows of the ward on a town reduced to a white landscape and bent figures in the snow like scenes from a Brueghel painting.

From then on, while the elver season swirled around them, Utta gave Emily her regular feeds, an oasis of peace in the midst of chaos. At night when I got back from the river or the tanks, I'd find them in bed in the middle of grub time and my daughter would break off to give me an enormous smile, a drop of milk on the end of her nose, before plunging back to work.

Meanwhile, our helper for the season had arrived. Gina, from California, was just nineteen, recommended to us by a good American friend who'd been her teacher. She was over in Europe to work and travel and was to be with us for the whole of the elver season. She arrived with just two pounds in her pocket and was starving. I sat her down to tea and toast with Utta's home made blackberry jelly. Very shy at first, she gradually revealed a rusty wheeze of a laugh and an infectious sense of humour. She was also quite fearless, setting off on her own to go elver fishing in all conditions. At night she and I took turns sleeping in the loft of the barn at Bowdens in order to weigh in any late fishermen. Once in the dead of night one of them tried unsuccessfully to rouse her,

'I couldn wake her, though I were stood there knocking and hollerin'. So I just weighed meself in and went on 'ome. But oi could hear 'er up in that there loft; she were snoring like a badger, she were.'

★★★★★

It was another good season with increasing catches from our growing team of fishermen. Fortunately Rosengarten took most of what we had. Though used to collecting elvers from France, coming over to England was more daunting and complicated for him, definitely foreign territory. However, in convoy, with Klinge to lead the way, he did make the journey once, and while Klinge loaded at Hancock, Rosengarten's truck came to us. It was a magnificent vehicle with something of the fairground lorry about it, in immaculate condition. He was terribly proud of it. Best of all were the loading steps. With a lot of trucks you just hefted the bin of elvers up to the driver on the rig who dropped them in the tank. Not Rosengarten. He had a massive set of highly polished wooden stairs with rubber treads that clipped onto the side of the vehicle and made loading very dignified. As you walked up them, you almost felt you were off to dinner somewhere. What was striking was the speed and ease of loading a truck, so much quicker than packing a box at a time; we were all done in just over an hour. It gave food for thought; one day perhaps one of those would be very useful.

Unfortunately, the ease of such a collection was a luxury. Most of the time it was airfreight. To arrive at the Heathrow cargo terminals at around 6am for the first flight out, we'd start the elver pack around one in the morning. By now we had an established system with a team of helpers. Anthony would always join us if he could – Jane too sometimes; not many landlords would spend half the night in a packing shed but they were that kind of people. A lean-to attached to the barn was used as the wet area for weighing the elvers. Ernie, who always helped, would fish them out of the tanks; no-one could do it quicker, and he'd cross the yard with two full buckets and the ritual banter,

'Tis all go, Mike, they'm running well tonight.'

'Where you catching Ern?' Anthony would ask.

'Oh I'm down on the bend at Stathe, boss.'

I'd tip the elvers half a bucket at a time into a sieve tray to let them drain then used an old chicken feed scoop to ladle a kilo and a bit into a tub set on an old set of balance scales. It had to be just over the kilo to allow for the water that clung to them. About three thousand elvers to each kilo. From there they were tipped into the polystyrene box, ready with water and ice. As soon as the elvers went in, Anthony would clap on the slotted lid and pass it onto Utta who'd strap the boxes with strong rubber bands. Any delay or fumbling with the lid and the elvers were out over the edge and you couldn't get the lid on properly. Our friend Holly, a young silversmith we'd met in Drayton, was our other mainstay. I'd devised a kind of pallet, a lid and base that held the stacks of boxes together in a bundle so they were more stable, less liable to tip over. Holly and Gina made up the pallets, strapping them together with binder twine.

Ernie checked the knots. As a finishing touch Rosengarten instructed us to write 'Nicht Kippen', meaning 'Do Not Tilt', in large letters on the sides of each pallet; very appropriate, we always thought, for those up and about in the night. Meanwhile, in a corner of the shed, Emily slept in her Moses basket, as snug as a bug, wrapped in blankets on a lambswool fleece, oblivious to all around her.

It was tense work, with not much time for chat as we worked tight against the clock, the deadline half past three for the drive up to Heathrow. Setting off, the first test was the bumps and ruts on Ernie's drive; the pallets would creak and settle, the boxes snickering and squeaking, but if nothing tipped, then the load was safe. At night the road, empty, climbed beyond Mere in Wiltshire onto the swell of the Downs, sheep dotted the hillsides, humped shapes frosted to the grass, while further on, Stonehenge stood alone in the night with its ancient spirits under the moon.

At Heathrow we were using a Pan Am flight that year but it was a stop-over from the States en route to Hamburg, which meant that despite delivering the elvers to cargo, it was never certain that they would actually get away. Passenger baggage had first priority and if the flight was full, there was no room for us. By mid-morning we would learn whether they had been loaded. Rather than hang around at the airport, we used to retire to my sister who lived near Farnham where for two to three hours we luxuriated in a delicious routine of breakfasts and hot baths, even a sleep, before phoning the cargo terminal. Only once that season did we have to go back to collect them.

As always, Rosengarten pushed us. After a shipment that had gone out in the morning, the phone would ring just as we got back to Somerset in the early afternoon.

He'd already have the shipment resting in his tanks, 'Herr Brown, alles gut, gute qualität.' Would we like to send again tomorrow? Over one tide at the end of March, Gina and I made five consecutive trips to Heathrow, shipping out nearly a tonne of elvers. They were lovely fish, well caught, well handled, with virtually no losses, all sold for the restocking of rivers and lakes, to angling clubs and landowners. Rosengarten gurgled in delight and sent his cheques by return. We were all exhausted, stumbling about, reduced to cat-napping in the van on the way back from the airport. Fortunately it was the school holidays so I was free of teaching.

I learned too that fatigue comes in two forms: if everything was going well, no matter how tired you were, it was far easier to keep going, pumped up by adrenalin and success. The real test was when things were falling apart, the situation desperate; that, I was to find out, was when it got much harder.

★★★★★

With two good seasons, each making a small profit, we squirreled away as much as we could, living on our part-time work, in order to start building up a deposit to put down on a house. But we were aware, even then, that elvering might not last, that there could be bad years. There had to be another string to our bow. Now was the time to put into practice what I'd learnt form Pieter the Dutchman. It was time to go eeling. I bought some second-hand fyke nets from one of Hancock's fishermen, a net-maker in Bridport. Keen to stay within the law this time, I got a licence and gained the permission of various farmers out on the moors to cross their land to get to the rhines. I began on the main drain on West Sedgemoor below Curry Rivel, setting the nets by casting the weighted end out as far as I could, pulling the leader back tight into the bank, as Pieter had shown me. Very soon, however, I was reminded that whatever you did on the moor in open daylight could be seen for miles around. I started to lose nets, or found them pulled out of the water and emptied. Then the same fishermen who'd sold me the nets recommended a totally new approach: put on a wet suit and get into the water to set, then you could put them way out of reach, and better still do it at night, so no-one saw you.

I found a wet suit in a sale in Taunton. It came with a hood and boots, was very cheap, the last of its kind on the rack. And a size too small. Made from incredibly thick rubber, getting into it was a wrestling match; by the time Utta had helped squeeze up the final zip I was boiling hot and exhausted. When I tried it out the first time, it was so buoyant I floated on the surface of the water like an enormous rubber sausage. It obviously needed a weight belt. From a diving store, I bought several lead weights and threaded them onto an old leather belt. However, when entering the water the next time wearing the sausage, I sank like a stone and nearly vanished without trace, just managing to haul myself up the bank. After several adjustments, casting off and adding back bits of lead,

I finally found the right balance to be able to work properly in the water and to set the nets.

Throughout that summer I'd set off in the evening after dark, already clad in the wetsuit with overalls over the top, bumping down tracks to one or other of the big rhines that sliced across the moor like small canals. Most of them were five to six feet deep, and I could just about stand. The worst bit was getting into the black peaty water, feeling the glutinous mud and the occasional slither of things beneath my feet. Once submerged in my wetsuit I was a prisoner of its confines. If I wanted to pee there was no way I could prise the thing off so I peed in the suit and found it reassuringly warming. Furthermore, after a good evening meal and squeezed tight by the wet suit, it was a true case of trapped wind, and I found that I farted like a trooper. When I did so, I was intrigued to discover that the wind sought exit either from the cuff of the suit, or from under my neck, either way creating an impressive bubble in the water, like the marsh gas that rose from the mud beneath me.

I tied the nets together, making double ended fykes. I'd anchor one end with a weight, then moving backwards, half-walking, half-bobbing, pay out a whole string of them down the middle of the channel, anchoring the other end with a similar weight. They were now far from the reach of curious hands or prying eyes. With my bare feet I checked the leaders – the tennis net bit between the two catching ends – to see it was upright and not twisted.

There was something magical about being out there all alone. The eel being nocturnal and shy of light meant that I set mainly in the dark phase of the moon. There was a softness on the moor on those summer nights, very still, very quiet with the smell of dew, wet grass and peaty water. Sometimes in the midst of setting I'd stop and listen, taking in the sounds: cattle chomping grass from the field beside me, the cry of a peewit, or an owl from a nearby farm, the occasional plop of a fish, a church clock striking somewhere. The moor was never quite silent, it was as if you could feel it breathing, settling. At times, especially if there was a mist, as I walked backwards with the nets, I'd get too close to swans and there'd be a hiss like a cobra from the cob that scared me rigid. I'd freeze and wait, hoping they'd glide away. Usually they did, if not I'd have to reposition the whole string of nets.

Having carefully marked the spot, the next night I would return to lift the nets. It was always an effort to change and leave the house, especially if we had company. I'd come away with conversations still playing in my head, but gradually the excitement took hold. I'd slide into the water and feel for the nets with my feet. However well I'd marked them, it would often take a minute or two to find them; I couldn't see underwater so I used my feet like antennae to feel the tautness of the fyke or part of the leader. I'd lift them with a foot, then using the net as a rope, pull myself back to the cod end where they were held. You knew at once if you'd caught. The end would start to thump and jerk; a heavy tugging and thrashing that increased as you hauled them out of the water. It was incredibly exciting, that primal thing to see what you'd caught. Sometimes the net was so full I could barely get it up the bank. Often the cattle, young calves, would crowd around, curious, with lots of snorts and heavy breathing. I'd have to shoo them away or they trampled on the kit.

It was hard to believe how many eels would go into a net. These were brown eels, still feeding and growing, not yet mature or ready to migrate back to the sea. They came in all sizes, most around half a pound and about a foot and a half long with the odd monster nearly three feet – the largest I ever caught was over five pounds. Once on dry land, I tipped them into a bin, with a firmly attached lid. For a while they writhed and coiled making loud sucking noises until gradually they'd settle. Even smothered, one on top of the other, they were able to stay alive through their ability to breathe out of water. You could never fill the bins right up or they'd escape in seconds, peeling over the top like live spaghetti and sliding away into the grass. As long as the ground was moist and cool they could travel easily and find their way back to water. It was the thing people always seemed to know about eels. 'They go overland, don't they?' they used to ask. The truth was that they didn't do it for fun – it was not their natural habitat – but they could, in the right conditions, move along ditches or over damp grass to feed elsewhere or find another river.

Trapped and confined in the bins, they were understandably stressed and angry. I was once amazed to see one large eel grab hold of another half way along its body and with jaws like bold cutters simply crunch it in half. Both halves of the poor creature continued to writhe and move as if it was still whole.

I never baited my nets: you didn't need to with fykes, where the leader part of the net did the catching for you, guiding the eel into its throat. But some people did: Anthony was a great advocate of earth worm, crushed and contained in a stocking to spread the scent; others swore by rabbit guts; one old catcher I met who'd fished the Norfolk Broads all his life, used the legs of herons he shot, boiled into a glue. It'd worked like magic, he said.

Looking back it is easy to remember only the good times, the big catches. The reality was different: frequently there might be only one or two good nets and the rest would have nothing at all. Often I'd find the tell-tale hole, ringed with slime, just one weak point, through which all the eels had escaped like prisoners through a window. Back home at the Lodge, to save running the pumps at Bowdens, I stored them in a tank in our landlady's orchard behind the house, oxygenating them with a very fine jet of water. Betty Parks loved eel, cooked in parsley sauce or just fried; if there were any casualties, I dropped them into the water trough in her garden where she'd see them in the morning. Inside the Lodge, Utta would peel me out of the wet suit. I stank of mud and wet rubber and was covered in duckweed that had worked its way down my neck and used to itch like crumbs in a bed. Reward was a hot bath.

If it was warm and to avoid any losses, I'd pick up in the morning just after dawn before anyone was around. Often the moor was covered with a carpet of low mist, just fences and willows and the heads of cattle poking up through. I loved that hour when all the world was your own; every leaf and blade of grass seemed to sparkle in the rising sun. Working in the water up to my neck, surrounded by a jungle of sedge and reed and yellow iris, brought into focus an intimate, self-absorbed world I'd never seen before, teeming with insect and aquatic life. And lining the banks, purple loosestrife, tangles of vetch and the thick musky scent of meadow-sweet. On one occasion, while I was feeling for the nets with my feet, a hare lolloped onto a bridge just yards away, then blissfully unaware of my presence, sat in the sun to wash herself with her paws.

A fyke net drying in the garden

Once in those early days I had set my nets in the river Isle on Anthony's land below Bowdens but on lifting them, found I was missing one. Putting on mask, snorkel and flippers, I set out to search for it, gently drifting down the

104

river over great patches of weed like underwater cabbage, over little shoals of flickering coarse fish, rudd and roach. Then suddenly I saw something, not a net, but a long shape, dark mottled green, lying still as a log in the vegetation; it seemed to go on for ever, until I reached the end and saw I was looking down not on a submerged branch but on the marble eyes and deadly snout of a giant pike. Through the magnifying effect of the mask, it looked as big as a Russian submarine. Seized with panic I burst like a cork onto the bank. I never found my net.

★★★★★

Having gathered a load of eel it was time to get them to market. I had already contacted Billingsgate and spoken to possible buyers. They all seemed part of a Cockney fraternity rooted in the East End, synonymous with jellied eel and eel pie shops. For them, eel was king, eel was currency, their life-blood. They had wonderful names, Tubby Isaacs, Barney's, Manze's, and Lou Hart. They were friendly but non-committal,

'Yeah, we buy eel. Always interested in eels. Ow much you got? What size? Four to the pound – nuffin smaller, that's what we like. Bring up a load and we'll 'ave a look. OK my friend, got to go, 'ear from you later.' The trouble was the cost of getting them there and the uncertainty of getting anything for them. There were no carriers in those days.

From my net supplier, I heard of a much more attractive proposition: a Dutchman came over every fortnight and picked up along the south coast. And paid on the nail. He had various pick-up points, my nearest was just outside Poole in Dorset. With some difficulty, and Ernie's help, I packed them into wooden boxes I found in the barn. Hancock had once used them for transporting eel; each one held some fifty kilos spread on trays inside. Melting ice trickled down through them to keep them cool and moist. After considerable coaxing and rearranging I finally managed to close the lids and nailed them down with a flourish. At least they weren't going to escape.

I set off very early on a perfect summer's morning, the sun just climbing into the sky and I was in good spirits as I drove over the hills to Dorchester and Poole. I was on my way to market, the first sale from a new project. I was about half way there when gradually I became aware that the accelerator pedal seemed rather stiff. Odd that, never had any trouble before. Perhaps I was just imagining it, but no, it did seem to be sticking. I glanced down at the foot well. To my horror I saw a very large eel coiling around the pedals. It could only mean one thing. Break out. I leaned down, grabbed the escapee and tossed it over my shoulder into the back just as two more emerged from under the passenger seat to join me in front. Pulling over, I opened the back and was greeted by a writhing mass. I could see what they'd done: they'd got their tails under the lids that I'd nailed down and prised the planks open, enough to push through. Even as I looked another sinuous shape slid out of the box. There was no way I could get them back in. I slammed the door shut and drove flat out to the pick-up point.

The truck was waiting, a small queue of fishermen ahead of me being weighed in. When they'd finished I introduced myself to the driver, a big burly Dutchman; they always seemed to be called Henk or Willem. This one was in a hurry; I could sense he was running late, keen to get on. No time for small talk.

'You get your eels and we weigh dem here.'

'I'm sorry there are a few escapees. Have you got a net?' We peered into the back of the van where there was now utter free-for-all, a writhing chaos. I saw the look on his face.

'You not jokink,'

Fetching a broad-mouthed net he smoothly recaptured them and within minutes they were in his weighing bins. I could see him looking doubtfully at them, assessing their value. 'These your eels?' he shouted above the noise of the air compressors.

'Yes,' I said, ever the proud producer. 'And what's the price per kilo?'

'Normally for good eels, I pay good price. But not for these.' He gave a figure well below what I'd been expecting. I was aghast. He shrugged.

'Dey no good. Only good for kookink,' he said. When it came to weighing, the scales hung from a metal arm that slid out of the body of the truck, a clever design, but the whole vehicle shook from the vibration of the diesel compressor. The needle on the scales flickered like a nervous twitch over a range of several kilos. This was a Dutch art. Before I could even focus on the figures on the dial, Henk had read it and swung the bin of eels into one of his tanks. 'Wasn't that 33?'

'No, 31,' and it was gone. George Cotty would surely have met his match here.

'So what do you do with the good eels then?' I asked him after he'd settled up.

'Dey go for smokink. But not yours; yours are only good for kookink. Not enough fett in them for smokink.' He couldn't have made it more clear.

As I drove home, I thought about what he'd said. If they weren't good enough for him and for smoking in Holland, then, dammit, I'd try smoking them myself.

Derelict hatches on the moor

Chapter Six

Over thousands of years the elvers had seeded the rivers of Europe. In Somerset, barely touched by commercial fishing, the migrations that Ernie saw each spring as a young man on the Parrett were massive: the river so full of elvers, clogged by their sheer numbers, 'so thick that you could walk across them'.

By our standards, though not on the same scale, the late Seventies and early Eighties were also vintage years. Three of the four seasons that followed were outstanding. The elver run of '81 was prolific, but '79 and '82 were colossal, the stuff of legend, larger than life, ones that anyone involved, here or on the continent, would remember, like all great natural events, like floods or snowfalls. Their sheer weight and numbers were staggering; once the elvers came, they seemed to keep on coming in wave after wave almost as if nature were showing off, demonstrating her boundless supply.

The fact that the eel farms were now fully on stream was perfect timing; if they had not existed, faced with these huge seasons, we would probably never have survived. They were our lifeline, as Rosengarten was. Certainly at the start of the '79 season our order book looked as it had never done before with firm orders for well over two tonnes between RHM and Maurice Ingram at Marine Farm, all of which could be delivered easily without the use of airfreight. On top of this, Rosengarten had booked another half tonne. In fact, the orders looked so good, my main concern at the start of the season was whether we would get the elvers to fulfil them.

The elvers were late that year; spring well underway when the first catches arrived. They were from new fishermen I had met the previous season; from Bridgwater at the mouth of the Parrett river, 'Bridgie' as it was known affectionately by its dwellers. I'd had never bought from the area before and it was the start of a long association. H and G were an unlikely pair, classic contrasts, one big and burly with several teeth missing, the other thin, wiry as a whippet with a roll-up fag clipped to his lip. They arrived at the tanks very early one morning, rattling up the drive with a trailer full of trays. The elvers were beautiful, fresh, the first of the season, not yet pigmented, translucent as glass. Ernie looked at them with me, 'Must be from down low somewhere, cos they got all that there green weed in em.' He was right, the pair had discovered a fresh-water outlet low down on the Parrett controlled by a hinged clapper. By propping it open at low tide they were able to introduce a flow of sweet, fresh water into the river, attracting the elvers as if they were magnetised. For H and G it must have been like discovering a pot of gold.

There were many such fresh water outlets that stoppered rhines and ditches up and down the estuary. Yet theirs was one of the most productive and this new source of supply brought a significant change, for where in the past the flow of fish onto site had ceased as the low tides began, now suddenly we had elvers arriving every day. A huge boost to our production - they regularly brought in 40 or 50 kilos. Hancock had been buying for years off the clapper men, the 'down low' boys but for us it was a revelation and opened our eyes to the sheer quantities of elvers drawn into the Bristol Channel.

To meet the new orders, we were now building a useful team of catchers. Beside newcomers H and G, and George Cotty who was gradually being persuaded to bring his fish to the tanks, there were other new fishermen who had joined us in recent years. Most striking of these were three brothers, big fellows; they filled the doorway of the barn and blocked out the light when they called in for a chat or to buy netting. Whatever they did was larger than life and if they decided they were going to do something, they did it with ruthless intensity. Most fishermen at the start of season bought netting by the yard; the Boys, as we called them, bought it by the roll, paying for it from a fat wad of notes. Their spokesman and leader was into second-hand cars. When they left they'd pile into his latest saloon like a rural mafia. There was never any threat of violence, or venom about the Boys, it was just their combined power, sheer presence that overawed. Like looking at buffalo: you just knew you wouldn't want to meet them on a bad day.

The Boys caught consistently and recognised early on that pooling their catch gave them greater bargaining power. From a buyer's point of view it was always better to have a broad spread of fishermen, all contributing more or less equally, but inevitably every elver station had its top crews. And with them, the threat was always implicit: if you didn't pay enough, they would go elsewhere. The lure of a regular steady supply of elvers blinded me to the danger of becoming over-reliant on them.

Every season, about the middle of the second set of tides, the first bargaining session took place, usually at the end of a night's fishing. I could always spot the signs: an avoidance of eye contact, a certain stiffness. They'd arrive at the tanks in their small army of rattley transits but rather than unload as they normally did, they waited to one side while I weighed in the other fishermen. 'How did you get on?' I'd call over to them, knowing that something was brewing.

'Oh, we got a few.' A studied nonchalance. And then the words that would chill my insides,

'Mike, can we 'ave a word when they all gone.' And I knew it wasn't going to be about the first cuckoo. When the last of the fishermen had left, they stood around me in a semi-circle. Over their heads, a late moon in the sky. I waited for the opening gambit.

'Mike, we got over 'undred kilo in the back on they trays. They'm lovely elvers, mind. They crawled all night.' That was the bait, very tempting: a hundred kilos, instantly my mind was calculating, yes, that would make up the load for the next order very nicely. But they had only started.

'But we feel we're not getting enough.'

'Yeah, we think we're worth more, like,'

'How much did they have, that last lot?' It was a rhetorical question, they knew very well, it was on the scoreboard. 'Eight kilo, thassall, only eight kilo, and the buggers were in the best spot. They adden a clue, bleddy useless.'

'So what are you asking?' I said, playing for time.

The spokesman was always the same, the really big one. His voice lowered, confidential.

'T'other bloke.' they always made great play about not being able to remember Hancock's name, 't'other bloke is paying £1.80.'

'No, he's not,' I tried to sound confident, 'only £1.60'

'Well, when we spoke to Beardie tonight, you know that bloke wot drives the green van, well he says t'other is paying his top fishermen - only his top fishermen mind - £1.80.'

'Yeah, Mike, no word of a lie. Swear to God, tis true. Ee is.'

'Yeah, an I eard it from that other chap, drives that little white van, always got a light on top of is head. Can't stand the fucker meself, but ee said it too.'

It was a chorus now. 'Yeah, it's true Mike. He's paying that to all his top fishermen. We wouldn't lie to you.'

The moon went behind a cloud. A breeze shivered the blossom on Ernie's plum tree. They waited, watching me. Time stood still. My mind was racing, shuffling the options. Was it true? Probably. Would they defect if I refused? Probably. Could we do without their catch? Probably not. It would make a very big hole in our output. We couldn't let the farms down.

'OK, I'll match it.'

In a second, the tension was gone; they were affable, happy, unloading the trays and weighing in. It took me much me longer to settle down. When they left in a posse of trucks and scrunch of tyres, my insides were still churning. I needed to sift it all, assess the impact. Like needing to rub a bruise. I could see the margins slipping away. And how long would the deal last; there was always the danger of peace at any price. Yet, I consoled myself, if pushed there was no doubt the Boys would sell to t'other chap and I needed their catch. Having checked the fish all round, I stood for a while breathing in the night air, soothing, sweet with the scent of spring, then climbed the ladder to the loft in the barn and the sleep of the dead. As I drifted off, I thought to myself, 'Just two months to go to Scotland'.

★★★★★

Both our eel farm customers, Marine Farm at Hinkley Point north of Bridgwater and RHM at Drax, drew warm water to grow their eels from the cooling towers of the power stations alongside. Hinkley was nuclear while Drax was coal fired. As sites they were totally different. Drax was in country I'd never visited before, the flat lands south of York between Selby and Goole, close to the Derwent and Ouse rivers that flowed into the Humber estuary. Its six massive cooling towers dominated the landscape for miles around, belching smoke into the sky. The eel farm was laid out on land opposite the power station with an elver rearing unit beside huge earth lagoons, butyl lined, for growing them on. Like Maurice, the water quality, drawn from the river and passed through the cooling towers, was always cloudy, a chalky grey. It must have made life very difficult as you couldn't actually see what you were farming. It was a grubby farm, expanding so fast, like a gold rush town, it never had time to catch up with itself and settle down. For all that it was to produce nearly two hundred tonnes of eels a year by the end. And it was our main customer for elvers, taking at least two tonnes from us each season.

Maurice Ingram's Marine Farm was, as the crow flies, only about twenty miles away at Hinkley Point in the north of Somerset. Just getting into the farm was a slow and deliberate affair and we learned to allow the best part of the day when we made a delivery to Maurice. Within sight of the great squat bulk of the power station, a rusty sign directed you down winding lanes to the little community of Stolford, more a scattering of houses, built on the edge of the salt marsh and the estuary. There, from a phone box pungent of cats, you called the farm and they came down with a key to shepherd you in. No access was permitted through the power station itself; the only way in to the farm was a spectacular drive of about one and a half miles along the top of the narrow sea wall through a series of strictly locked gates which contained the sheep that grazed the marshes.

It had long been a fishing community and in the salt wind the scattering of low white painted houses and sheds, nets strung up to dry, had a kind of harsh desolation. At low tide the sea receded, revealing the vast expanse of mud flats of Bridgwater Bay, ribbed and channelled, stippled by lines of old posts, like rusty nails, set into the ooze by past generations of fishermen. As we waited for one of the team from the farm – and the key – to arrive, we'd often see Brendan Sellick, a remarkable character who made his living as a fishermen from the fixed nets out in the bay. His voice was always a rasping shout, worn hoarse, as if having to carry above the sound of the wind and sea. To reach his nets, he used a mud sledge: a contraption like a small table set on wooden skis. Dressed in shorts and gym shoes – wellies were no good - and a thin top, he pushed the sledge across the treacherous mud, often a good half mile out from the shore, to empty them. They were not dissimilar to my fyke nets but much more firmly anchored. They'd catch anything that was passing as the sea tore up the Bristol Channel and filled the bay. A great lucky dip. Shrimps and prawns were his stand-by, but there might be bass and cod, salmon and flatfish, and eels, that we were to buy from him later. It was hard, gruelling work, winter and summer, and treacherous. You had to keep moving; the mud only bore your weight for twenty seconds before it gave way and sucked you down. Small wonder that other families around had given up. Brendan was the last of the sledge fishermen.

It would sometimes take half an hour or more for either David Ogilvie or Richard Berry to arrive from the farm with the key to open the many gates along the seawall. And their patience had to be admired for they would have had to stop what they were doing to fetch us; it seemed such a waste of their time and energy but they knew to accept it as part of the running of the farm. I wasn't the only one to observe that as landlords, in return for their rent, the power station might easily have put in an access road to Maurice round the station's perimeter that would have saved all this trouble. Instead we followed the narrow sea wall. Bad enough for a car or van, it was very tense the first time you took anything wider, like a truck loaded with tanks, especially when after a big storm large chunks of concrete track had fallen away making it even narrower. Yet, on a fine day, it was a stunning place, the light reflected off sea and marsh and a haven for birds; great flocks of shelduck, goose-like birds, white plumage with beautiful chestnut and black markings, migrated there in the spring to feed in the estuary and on the marsh, whilst waders of every kind, curlew, whimbrel, red and greenshank skittered and probed the foreshore, just yards away in front of the farm buildings. Binoculars lay on the windowsill ready to spot or identify. Maurice once told me that they'd identified over 160 species of birds.

There was always a welcome at Marine Farm from Maurice and his team; after offloading the elvers, always a cuppa and chat in the office, Maurice at his desk in one corner, wreathed in pipe smoke, the level of which intensified to smokescreen proportions if Utta had come with me and happened to be breast-feeding Emily. By then, in '79, he was already making his first proper sales of marketable eel and had made contact with an old established firm in Holland, the Dil brothers, who were specialist eel smokers. The Dutch market was well suited to his operation for they liked smaller eels, from 150gm to 250gm. The Germans favoured a much bigger eel from 400gm upwards to get their teeth into. Having a market for smaller fish was ideal for him as they reached market size quicker and provided much-needed cash flow.

I happened to be there at the farm on the occasion that Henry Dil made his first visit to see for himself the quality of the farmed eel. Up to then he'd only bought wild stock and he was perhaps understandably sceptical that farmed eel could be as good. Richard Berry drained down one of the big tanks: as the water emptied away the whole floor, twelve metres across, was a mass of writhing eel, some of them large. I watched Dil's face, saw the look of anticipation sharpen into a gleam of excitement as he saw what were in effect perfect silver eel, sharp nosed, firm bodied, and full of fat for smoking. He was to become Maurice's main customer, taking all the tonnage he produced. They were indeed superb eels for smoking, I was to discover, fully on a level with the best of the wild. Perhaps it was due to the fact that they were grown in salt water that gave them such flavour.

However it was always a struggle for Maurice. The water in which the elvers were fattened into eels and which came from the cooling towers was drawn direct from the Bristol Channel and contained very high levels of sediment. Maurice, in a lecture at Two Lakes, once said it was like farming fish in sandpaper and, worse still, the water was so cloudy, they were farming blind, unable to monitor and spot problems early. Salt water too was particularly hard and corrosive on pumps and equipment. But the greatest problem was water temperature: to get good growth, the farm needed a steady temperature of twenty degrees or more from the cooling towers. In winter the sea temperature sank to ten degrees onto which the power station could only ever add four or five degrees at most, creating uneven periods of growth or no growth at all and often leading in turn to stress and disease. It was an uphill battle, with constant setbacks; it needed deep pockets and it consumed money. In the best years the farm produced the tonnage needed but it could never be sustained. Yet, having started with a number of individual backers – Brendan Sellick had been an early investor - Maurice somehow always managed to find fresh financial support. His natural charm, his conviction and passion for what he was trying to achieve - and indeed had achieved in a completely new field of fish farming – coupled with a good accountant, continued to bring him backing to the very end.

Every year I placed an advert in one of the International Fish Farming magazines, which brought interest and orders from home and overseas. At about this time we were contacted by a government agency in Czechoslovakia charged with restocking waters and lakes. The phone rang in the barn and a Mrs Horacek, a very determined lady speaking excellent but plain English, placed a sizable and worthwhile order for elvers.

She was evidently in some hurry, maybe to make use of state funding while it still remained, for, while I struggled to arrange air freight and get the shipment together, she rang the barn most mornings with the plaintive cry: 'But Mister Brown, what are you doing; please send them soon, the people of Sarvas are waiting.'

It was said with such passion and yearning, I could see the people of Sarvas standing out on the hills and fields scanning the skies for the aircraft to appear and the elvers to rain down upon them like some wartime supply drop. The delivery was a success and she rang to thank me from 'the people of Sarvas.' Although I'd been a little nervous about dealing entirely on trust with an Iron Curtain country, with an organisation I'd never heard of, payment came almost immediately. The cry was to become part of our family lexicon, if you were waiting a long time, 'the people of Sarvas…'

★★★★★

For the first month or so of the season we managed to keep up with the inflow of elvers, delivering regularly to the farms, and air freighting to Germany. It was like sailing in strong winds, heeled over, just within our limits. But we had a good crew.

In fact '79 brought a wave of new helpers who were to appear and reappear over the next few years and remain life-long friends, not only with us but with each other. Andrew, a family friend, joined us from Devon; Roddy, the brother-in-law of David Forrest helped in his Easter student vacation. And then there was Annabelle from New South Wales, Australia who arrived like Mary Poppins and landed in our midst in April. We met first of all on the phone.

'Hello, is that Michael? I'm Staff's cousin, you know the Staff that worked at Ridgways that you met in Scotland. He gave me your phone number and said you might need a hand. I'm in Bristol.'

'When would you like to come?' I asked, expecting some date in the distant future.

'Tomorrow, if that's all right. Just for one or two nights.' She was to stay for two months.

'Sounds good,' said Utta when I came off the phone, 'but do you think she paints her toe nails?' It was our code for assessing would-be helpers: aspiring female applicants who took the trouble to paint their toenails, we had found, were usually not too keen on wellies and squeamish when it came to handling elvers. A languid lady from California with beautiful feet and painted toes had come earlier in the season and lasted only a couple of days before deciding to reshape her travel plans. Annabelle's feet had clearly never seen nail varnish, indeed it looked as if a fair bit of her life had been spent bare foot. She was a warm sunny personality with an infectious laugh. Brought up on a farm in New South Wales, she was strong, capable, never minded what she did, one of the best helpers we ever had. And a wonderful person to have on board in a time of crisis.

At the beginning of April, the week of big spring tides produced an avalanche of fish. The catches were huge, coming in far faster than we could get them away to market. The only alternative was to stop buying but that was suicide, a sign of weakness and we might never get our fishermen back.

'Bet you'm happy,' they said, then looking at the tanks full of elvers, 'Hope you got plenty of markets.'

Behind my forced smile, the pretence of being in control, I was desperate. At the start of each night I surveyed the tanks, try to work out where I was going to hold the night's catch. Then came an even bigger night of catching. By dawn, having weighed fishermen in all through the hours of dark, we had taken over 700 kgs and every tank was full. We were now perilously close to going under. Everywhere it was the same: in Gloucester, that night Peter Wood took three tonnes, Hancock probably more. With Anthony's help we doubled up the tanks to create space, then doubled again. The system was at full stretch, beginning to creak.

'You've got to get these away, Michael. As quick as you can.' The irony was that the market was there with orders to the farms still to fulfil; in fact, we were only half way through the RHM order. What held things up was the time needed between deliveries to bed down the new elvers, start getting them onto feed. There was only so much they could absorb in one go and they weren't yet ready for another load.

I was dead on my feet, at the stage when clear thinking becomes difficult. David Forrest happened to be staying and helping; he spelled it out clearly.

'Just get on the phone to RHM and tell them they've got to take delivery now. Otherwise you're stuffed!'

I rang them the following morning. Their new farm manager, Rob Clement, was very understanding. When I explained the situation and asked him if he could take half a tonne of elvers the following morning - and the day after as well - there was a sharp intake of breath, a moment of consideration. Then, 'Yes, OK. What time?'

We were saved. Fortunately the tides were getting later, the fishermen weighing in from midnight onwards. We started packing as they began to arrive in order to free up tank space for their incoming catch. It was all hands to the deck as we packed most of the night. Anthony and Jane Lang, our landlords, came down to help, along with David Forrest and anyone else I was able to lasso. Utta brought Emily, just over a year old, carrying her in a backpack. Utta was 'on lids' which meant clapping the slatted lid with air vents onto the weighed box of elvers. From her position on her mother's back, Emily passed lids from the stack behind her and handed them to her Mum. She took it very seriously, frowning with concentration. At fourteen months, unpaid, this was, I think, the ultimate in child labour.

We had got out of jail but only just. In doing so, however, we had used up our credit with the farms; the RHM order was now almost fulfilled and Maurice too. We urgently needed another bulk order and quickly. It came through Peter Wood at Gloucester. He was becoming a great ally; it was hugely reassuring to talk to another elver station, hear the same tiredness in the voice, share the problems and the disasters, to know that we weren't the only ones suffering. They too had been inundated with elvers and were as desperate as we were. His Bristol Channel Fisheries was far bigger than us. They too were supplying the eel farms: Tomatin, a whisky producer near Inverness that used waste heat from the distillation process to grow elvers to eels and Coats Paton, the textile giant, who'd set up a venture at the Hunterston power station on the coast south west of Glasgow. Peter was also big enough to attract the continental buyers if needed to load direct from his site. A firm from Hendaye, on the Spanish border in the Basque region of south west France, was loading that very day and had space for more fish. He'd send them down to us and we could add some of ours.

The truck that turned up at the tanks was vast, quite unlike anything we'd seen before. Enclosed like a massive horsebox, it contained not a row of tanks but a sort of swimming pool with the edge of the tank rolled over like a combing to prevent water and elvers sloshing over the side. Inside it the water boiled like a jacuzzi with the force of compressed air from massive under-slung pumps. Churned endlessly in this enormous washing machine tank the elvers released their protective slime in the agitation and stress, giving off quantities of white foam, vump as we called it. It formed thick on the surface, trailed out of the back onto the yard like foam on a storm-lashed beach.

But the greatest surprise was the system of weighing; they didn't just weigh tight, they weighed till there was no water with the elvers at all. Two huge mesh bottomed bins stood by the scales to receive our elvers as we netted out the tanks, then left to stand. It was against all instincts of good husbandry. I could see our weight, and profit, shrinking, seeping out in a steady trickle at the bottom. At last when they were as dry as cattle cake and it seemed that they'd all be dead, they were put on the scales. I gasped at the end when we tallied up to find we were fifty or sixty kilos short of the half tonne I'd expected. It was my first introduction to Spanish weighing. Then it was all over; all the noise, the hammering of the compressors, the frantic activity, the leviathan was gone, leaving in its wake empty tanks and a great white trail of vump in Ernie's yard.

Up to then our elvers had gone to the restocking market or the eel farms. The elvers on the Basque lorry, however, were bound for the Spanish market, known as the dead trade, where they would be cleaned, cooked and packaged to be eaten in tapas bars, cafes and restaurants all over the Spanish-speaking world. A highly prized delicacy, particularly in north west Spain around the feast of San Sebastian in the third week of January, they were associated too with fertility: high in protein, the consumption of elvers or eels, it was thought, made you more fertile. (Certainly the image of human sperm under the microscope closely resembles elvers swimming upriver.) Not just in Spain, even on the banks of the Parrett, there were still fishermen who caught elvers not to sell, but for a feed and the after-effects. Anthony remembered an old boy on

118

the Parrett who used to cycle down to the river, net on his shoulder and bucket on the handlebars, and explain, 'My wife, she do love a feed of ilvers; they do make er proper frisky.' And he was over eighty.

Whatever the causes, the demand for elvers in Spain – and Portugal – was seemingly insatiable. The rivers of Portugal, Spain and France produced huge harvests of glass eels each year from October onwards. The main buyers were incongruously located in Aginaga, a small village in the mountains behind San Sebastian, close to the French border from where they controlled their gathering operations, buying elvers from all over the Iberian peninsular and south west France, right up to the Loire and the UK. Everywhere they had agents collecting for them, small elver stations manned seasonally where catches could be held until dispatched to the processing plant in Aginaga. The buyers were the grandees of the elver industry.

Years later in the nineties, one of them, Jose-Marie Manterola, took me to what had been his main holding site in the bumper years. It was vast, built like an amphitheatre into the side of the hill outside the village. Rows of concrete tanks were banked one on top of another. A mountain stream ran in at the top and the water cascaded down from one tier of tanks to another. There were one hundred tanks, each one capable of holding a tonne. In '79, he told me, they were all full, for weeks at a time. At 3,000 elvers to a kilo and three million to a tonne, all destined for the food market – and this had been going on already for 25 years - it was hardly surprising as the years went by that elvers would go into decline. Here surely was the largest single contributor to the decline of the elver and eel populations. No species, however prolific, could withstand that sort of decimation through the systematic removal of its brood stock.

★★★★★

In the first days of elvering on the Parrett, back in the Sixties, Anthony used to pay the fishermen on the last night of the tides in the Black Smock pub down on the river below Curry Rivel, the spot where I'd first caught elvers. Before decimalisation, it was two shillings a pound for elvers. It used to get very busy in the bar, much cider was drunk and not a lot of fishing happened. In the early years, we also paid at the end of the set of tides, fixing a day when the fishermen could come round to collect their money. I'd draw the cash from the bank and then we'd sit around the kitchen table in a ritual of counting and making up the separate pay packets with a list of the weights caught.

The phone would go. 'Just checkin' to see if me money's ready. Oh good, I'll be down later on.' Sometimes you'd hardly put the phone down and the speaker was there at the door, often with the wife. They were scrubbed up, wore shoes not wellies. It was often surprising to see them peeled out of their fishing garb, to see a face properly, a balding head or a mass of hair normally hidden at night under a woollen hat. The ritual was tea. They perched, shifting uncomfortable on the sofa, relaxing, 'Mind if I smoke, Mike?' talk about the tide, recall the high points, look at the pay packet, a quick look first, 'Yeah, looks bout right.' Nonchalant, but you knew it'd be pored over, minutely examined later, followed up with a phone call: 'Yere Mike, you know that night you said I had ten, well it should ave been twelve cos...'

In those early days we hadn't got into issuing tickets for each catch. Quite often the pay packet was passed straight to the wife. Elver money, depending on circumstances, could be about survival, paying the bills, but if a fisherman was in work, then it went on extras, which often involved furniture, carpets, white goods, 'That's for the missus,' they'd say,' 'er wants a new settee, keep 'er 'appy.' Sometimes messengers came. 'I've come to pick up Dad's money.' And there'd be a young face you'd recognise from the river bank helping Dad tray up. Often, they in turn became catchers, sometimes more successful than their parents.

On pay-out days they also came to the tanks at Bowdens. 'Come for me money Mike.' You'd be mid-hammer or saw, when a figure would appear. It had to be ready, it had to be there; it was not good to disappoint expectations. The Boys always came in a gang. Wads of cash would be handed over, theirs was always the biggest pay packet, and they'd divide it up then and there.

With the Bridgewater fishermen some fourteen miles away, I would deliver their pay to them and this time I was the visitor and the ritual was reversed: the front room, the sofa, tea and small talk and handing over the money. It was fascinating matching the household to the fishermen, often surprising. I saw inside houses comfortable and cosy, neat and ordered, then households so poor with barely a stick of furniture where the kids raced about, shouted at by exasperated young wives, dreams dead in their eyes. Often the poorer the house, the larger the television. Husbands went fishing to escape, to get away, not to the pub to spend, but to the river to earn.

And it was all cash, hardly ever a cheque. Cash was the oil that lubricated difficulties, slid unrecorded into their lives. Yet if you were unemployed on benefits, there was a genuine fear of being caught. There were always people who would dob you. Curtains twitched, neighbours disapproved. Nets and gear had to be hidden out the back, parked in a shed away from prying eyes. 'That ole bag next door...' might at any time inform the 'social' and when they came they didn't come for tea and a chat. And then there was the taxman. As more fishermen became involved from the late Seventies onwards and as prices rose, the local papers ran stories of how fortunes could be made by simply going down to the river to fish. They overlooked the fact that on many a night little or nothing was caught at all, that it required a deal of discipline, especially if you were working, to go out half the night. You might love it, it might reward you but it was never cosy, more like jumping into a tub of ice cold water. Many a new fishermen, keen as mustard, would melt away, back to the warm glow of the front room and the TV. Elvering was hard graft, yet it inspired a kind of collective envy from those who looked on.

And once it came to the notice of the taxman, goaded on by press and local television, he began to probe. He certainly wasn't going to come out on the river bank and ask the fishermen for their names; he'd have soon been learning to swim in the muddy waters of the Parrett. Instead he went for us, the buyers, the easy target. Word was that we were going to have to take out the tax due, dock it from the elver pay packet at the end of every tide, or, worse still, reveal the names of the fishermen. I felt sick, doomed. It was going to be very difficult; there was huge resistance from the fishermen; either way, to deduct tax or to reveal names, would be to lose every single catcher we had. The taxman waited, the fishermen watched us; whichever buyer found a way round the problem and ignored the deductions would have every elver off the river. They would all go to him. It was thanks to Peter Wood at Bristol Channel Fisheries that a solution was found just before the start of the season. His accountants challenged the proposed ruling, and successfully argued that elvers were essential direct costs of the business, that we were not employers and had no right to deduct tax; by issuing a ticket or receipt, with a number and the weight of catch, we had proof of purchase for the elvers, essential to our business, and the fishermen could remain anonymous. There was a collective sigh of relief and the taxman withdrew muttering. But he wasn't finished with us yet.

★★★★★

At the end of every season there was always one final drama. And it took place at the lock gates at Oath. All through the earlier tides the gates would have been lifted to allow clear passage to the tidal Parrett that swept on through, carrying the elvers upriver into the heart of the moors where they settled and grew to adult eels. Then, usually in late April, word would spread like wildfire, 'You 'eard, they gates is down.' In terms of managing the river, this was now the time of year when the rivers Parrett and the Tone were penned back to hold the levels of water needed on the moors for the cattle to graze all summer long in the rich meadows. For the fishermen it meant the tide would now bore upstream, sweeping before it any new shoals or older elvers hanging around from previous tides and deposit them at the lock gates. This was now the spot to grab, the chance to round off the season with some spectacular catches. Some teams specialised in fishing the gates and would forsake good fishing lower down in the early part of the tide just to stake out the long bend or the far bank below the lock. Boats were like gold dust; if you could get to the other side, competition was less fierce. Deals were struck over shared transport and shared profit. If the prospects were good, a lot of elvers still in the river, then some even camped for a whole week to guard their position.

'Yer Mike, you 'eard, they Abbotsbury boys, they'm camped out up there; that old chap, you know the one looks like a heron, 'ees sleeping out every night under 'is boat. Good luck to en, thass what I say.'

Each night you could track the progress of the elvers upriver; each night the catching moved a little higher and by the time they were expected at the gates, getting a spot if you hadn't bagged one previously was like trying to get a ticket to a big match. Every yard of the bank was marked out, claimed. Tempers flared,

'Now, just you shift back a bit there young man. I been yere since 4 o'clock; don't think you can just jump in in front of me, or I'll ave ee in the river.' Mostly though, these occasions had a good-natured, end of term feel to them. Generally it was the naïve who stumbled onto the seriously-held territory belonging to the big boys and they were quickly sent packing.

At high tide in the slack water the elvers were all over the surface. Then as the river turned and began to race back they'd hug the banks and drive for the gates, a swathe two feet wide, tight to the bend, straining against the current like athletes entering the final strait. For two or three nights there would be huge catches. But the biggest went to the lock keeper himself. His name was actually Fred Locke, and he was a tall, thin, old boy, always viewed as bad tempered, probably because we only ever saw him vigorously defending his patch. For this was his big moment, the only time of year that he entered the fray and caught elvers. No-one was allowed to get too close to the gates where the elvers massed, luxuriating in the sweet water that oozed and sprouted through the old doors. They were his absolute territorial possession. It was like a game of grand-mother's footsteps: the catchers would creep nearer and nearer to the gates until the old man would emerge and hissing like a rabid goose, drive them back.

'Back you buggers, you can't fish ere. Tidn allowed. I'll call the bailiffs. Now bugger off.' They would retreat, smouldering, muttering dark oaths, and have to watch Fred and his family dipping bucketfuls of elvers from where they congregated en masse below the fish pass on the far side. He filled deep white plastic containers that held eight to ten kilos and each time he crossed the gantry, you knew he was carrying another full one. We counted them, green with envy, seething with indignation. He was a Hancock fishermen; I never got a sniff of his catch. Hancock would park up nearby, on guard, to fend off nosey parkers. There'd be much rattling of chain on his pulley as he weighed and weighed the flow of buckets; fags glowed in the dark, low voices which we'd strain to catch. Word would get out, spread down the bank like a stain, 'th'old bugger had over ninety kilo, I 'eard.' But for Fred Locke it was his big night. And though they muttered and cursed, the fishermen knew that one day the old man would be too old to fish, and hang up his net. And then they would move in.

★★★★★

123

These were good times for the business. The season of '79 was a record, our best to date; we sold over five tonnes, put some money into savings, spent three months over winter visiting Utta's family and friends in Australia. The following year was back to three tonnes, just enough to supply the eel farms, but still creditable. Yet however good the prospects, we were always aware of the danger as a business of being wholly dependent on the elvers; the disasters of '76 had showed us that. We needed another string to our bow. Over the summers I was continuing to catch eels and take them down to the Dutch lorry but my catches were never consistent, the quantities very small and I still got the lowest price – as mine, the driver continued to remind me, were only good for 'cookink'. I'd already decided to have a go at smoking; now was the time to put the plan into practice.

One of the pleasures of having your own small business is the freedom to experiment: if you have an idea, want to try something new, you just do it. No meetings, no having to ask permission, going through proper channels. I'd always been interested in food and cooking. Growing up in Cornwall in the early Fifties, my father overseas, brother and sister away at school, I spent a lot of time with my mother in the kitchen. After married life in Burma with a cook and servants, her cooking skills were limited so she was quite happy to enrol me as 'help' and taster; we were big on bacon and eggs, toast, then rissoles on Tuesday followed by tripe in parsley sauce on Thursdays - the stench filled the house all day. Smoking, I figured, was just another form of cooking, there could be no great magic to it, you just needed to know what to do, a recipe. The trouble was, there didn't seem to be one.

I wrote off to MAFF – the Ministry of Agriculture Fisheries and Food and was sent a booklet from their Torry Research centre, their fisheries research unit in Aberdeen. Most of the information was on salmon but they did have a recipe for smoking eel and there were others I tracked down. They were all a bit vague, short on detail, and written by well-meaning folk who'd obviously never actually smoked a fish in their lives. But it was a start. One thing was certain: we first needed to build the smoker and the perfect materials were to hand. A tall wooden struc-ture, a water chute, overlooked the tanks. In the old days the water from the borehole had been cascaded down it to gather oxygen. It was now redundant, very rickety and ripe for recycling.

To help dismantle it, Bob, an amiable Welshman and work colleague of Utta's, joined me. He was a big shambly bear of a man, as strong as an ox, who came over on his days off to help. His standard of carpentry was slightly higher than mine but still in the rough bodge range. He was into massive nails. When he was pondering something, he had a disturbing habit, without knowing he was doing it, of moving his top front teeth - he'd lost the originals in an accident - jiggling them up and down so they moved independently of his face. When you first saw it, it was mesmerising; you couldn't take your eyes off it. It intrigued our children. Over the years, until his tragic early death from leukaemia, they were very fond of him. Not only did he do wiggly teeth, he shared his sandwiches which always seemed better than anything we ever gave them. They'd sit either side of him like dogs drooling as he ate his lunch and help him eat them.

From the planks of weathered pine, Bob and I built a rough wooden hut, with a door and hanging bars inside against the wall of the barn. For a chimney we cut a hatch in the roof that could be slid open or shut. When finished it looked more like an outdoor privy than a smoker. Ernie was intrigued. 'Wos this gonna be then, Mike? Oh, a smoker eh. You going to light a fire in there. You want to watch out ee don't ketch fire.'

From my holding tank, I chose a few of the larger eels, about two feet in length. They had dark brown backs with pale skinned bellies. While their heads were broad and rounded like the nose of a jumbo jet, the body quickly narrowed down to the tail. These were brown eels, immature fish, what my Dutch lorry driver described as no good for smokink. Well, I'd show him.

There was just one small problem. How did you kill an eel? I'd had plenty die on me, on still hot nights in the summer when the duck weed appeared and the oxygen levels plummeted. Whole netfuls of dead eel. Yet I'd never killed an eel with intent. With most fish, a trout or salmon, one good clock on the back of the head, and that was it. But with these eels, lying quietly in the bottom of the bucket, occasionally sliding over one another, rearranging themselves with the odd sucking sound, catching hold of one long enough to impart the fatal blow was nigh on impossible. They were incredibly strong and agile. I riffled through the Torry pamphlet. It wasn't much help either; killing the eel wasn't mentioned, something that happened somewhere else, off page.

I consulted Ernie. He had special experience in this department.

125

Each summer, when it was hot and sultry, his favourite pastime after work was to go clotting with the family. This was fishing for eels, not with rod and line, but with a pole, a length of wool, and a tub. The key was the bait. It had to be earthworms. I'd always know what he was up to as he prowled his veggie garden, very absorbed, muttering, looking under tiles or bits of wood. When he'd collected enough he threaded them onto a skein of wool until he had a big wormy, sticky ball that he then tied to the line of his pole and suspended it in the river. His favourite place was in the Isle below the farm, a spot he called 'the tumbling bay', where the river came over an old weir. Earthworm is caviar to the eel, and they'd home in on this delicious bait. As they bit into the wormy ball, their teeth would catch in the wool just long enough for Ernie to flick them out into his tub that floated on the edge of the river. The knack was to strike as soon as you felt a tug and whip the eel out of the water into the tub before it fell off. On a good night they'd collect fifty to a hundred eels, all small; the big ones always dropped off or tore the wool, even taking the whole ball of worm. It was a great outing, huge fun. Besides which, it was free food.

Ernie adored eel, cooked in parsley sauce. And to kill them he scattered wood ash over them overnight. This smothered them and at the same time absorbed their slime so that he could gut and skin them. The skinning was a brutal, yet awesome process. He'd impale the head onto a nail on the door of his shed, cut the skin around the neck just below the gills then with a pair of pliers gently ease it away from the flesh all round the neck, before pulling down with one strong swift movement and the whole thing would come away like a silk stocking removed.

Eels are smoked with the skin on so I only needed to gut them. I tried Ernie's ash method. It was crude and messy. Even though the poor eels had expired, I struggled to clean them. You don't always get the chance to test the accuracy of a phrase that has passed into the English language: 'as slippery as an eel' is a perfect description, obviously born of age-old experience, you can almost hear the exasperation in the phrase. As soon as I ran them under a tap to clean off the ash, it was as if they came alive in my grasp and it was like trying to hold a bar of soap. The only way I could grip them was by using wads of newspaper. Even then they slipped and I stabbed myself frequently with the knife. Even when I'd gutted them, I battled to get the slime off. From everything I'd read, this was apparently very important otherwise it affected the brining process, but no–one ventured to tell you how. I tried scraping it off with a spoon, then rubbing it off with more ash. In a short time the lean-to part of the barn I'd designated the 'gutting room clean area' looked as if some ghastly massacre had taken place, spattered with slime, ash, gut and bits of newspaper. It had taken me nearly an hour to gut and clean four eels, and badly at that. I shuddered at the thought of trying to do it on a commercial scale.

Then we had our first breakthrough. A Dutchman, an old friend of Pieter van der Schluwys who'd taught me to catch eels, dropped in with a fyke net I was buying from him. I described our struggles and he laughed, 'Oh, dat's easy. Wot you have to do is freeze em,' he said. 'Put em in a bag in the freezer to kill them, leave em for a couple of days, then when you thaw them out, all dat slime comes off.' He was right. Death by hypothermia, the deep cold sleep, seemed somehow kinder than the smothering in ash. And when thawed, you held the head and pulled the eel through the grip of your other hand, and the slime came away like snow off a roof. They were squeaky clean and ready for brining.

Curing or salting fish, I learned, was one of the oldest forms of preserving food. The Romans salted and dried the great tuna caught off southern Spain and the Dutch perfected the curing of herring, caught in vast quantities by salting and packing them in barrels. Smoking too was another form of prolonging the life of food but only worked if the product had already been cured or salted beforehand because the salt drew the water out of the fish or meat to allow the smoke phenols that did the preserving to penetrate its structure.

The Torry guide had little to say about the content or the length of time the eel was supposed to stay in the brine. So I made up a salt and water solution as I thought fit and left them in it for a couple of hours, before threading the eels onto skewers, and hung them in the smoker. At this point, as if in anticipation of eating the end product, Torry started to become highly informative, bristling with information about wedges to hold open the belly cavity so that the smoke could enter fully. I propped the belly flaps open with matchsticks; braced inside the hull of the fish they reminded me of seats in a rowing boat, but they were fiddly to attach. At last I lit the fire in the grate, damped it down with sawdust and shut the door. The handbook was very clear that the smoke divided into two parts: a gentle smoke of about an hour and a half, followed by a short blast at a much higher temperature to heat them through. Every so often I'd open the door and peek inside and admire the row of eels hanging in clouds of smoke. They looked wonderful. It was intensely exciting; the project was off the ground; I felt on the edge of something new. With a professional flourish I unloaded my first eel smoke.

Back home, in the cold light of analysis, euphoria quickly vanished. Out of the smoke, they looked miserable, they had turned a pale yellowy brown, the skin shrivelled, the belly distorted where the matches still braced open the flaps, worse still, they felt clammy and damp to the touch. We tried one in silence. It tasted sour and rubbery to chew. 'Not cooked enough,' Utta pronounced. 'More heat.'

It was back to the drawing board.

Chapter Seven

The growth in eel farming came as a boon for us, reducing our dependence on the continental market and providing a vital outlet for the elvers in those vintage years. Yet there was one significant improvement we needed to make and that was in the way we made our deliveries. Nearly all the elvers we sent out were packed individually, one kilo at a time, into polystyrene boxes, usually at night; and even though we were getting quicker at it, it was still a laborious business. I used to look with envy at the fish transporters of Peter Wood and Mike Hancock – Hancock's got more vast by the year, a measure of his growing prosperity. However tempting, they were hugely expensive, we couldn't afford one and even if we had been able to, outside the season there was no need for one. Many fish farmers simply hired the services of a specialist fish transport company – I knew several from the Two Lakes conference - but they too were expensive and had to be booked well in advance; with elvers you needed your own machine.

So it was that, at the beginning of 1980, I hired a flat-bed truck from the Abbey Hill Group in Yeovil. They were just getting into the truck hire business and offered an incredible deal for two months on a Fiat 7.5 tonne vehicle, the largest you could drive on an ordinary licence and with a carrying capacity of about 4 tonnes. Peter Wood's company, Bristol Channel Fisheries, generously lent me four fibreglass transport tanks that they had made themselves but no longer used. With the truck and the tanks on board I drove to Sparrows workshop in the nearby town of Martock.

Sparrows, in those days, was one of those old established companies with a depth of skills and craftsmen that would be hard to find now. They specialised in anything to do with water; originally they had been involved with mill machinery and resurfacing mill wheels of which there were several in the area, now they were into pumps and boreholes – they had sunk the one for Anthony at Bowdens and they had installed all the pipe work and pumps on the site.

Our contact there was Gordon Small, a soft-spoken, local man, tall and round like a bowling pin. Hugely knowledgeable in his field, he also had the gift of being able to divine water and could tell very accurately the depth and strength of the quantities involved; it was he who had located the springs that fed our borehole. Mostly I called him in times of crisis; he would arrive with Jim, his brother-in-law, and they would stand in the yard and listen before making their diagnosis, 'sounds like a bearing gone,' or 'needs a new volve' (Gordon's valves were always 'volves'). Or out would come an enormous set of stillsons, huge adjustable jaws on long handles capable of undoing the most stubborn, rustiest pipe and revealing its secret. 'See, ee's all choked up. That gotta come out. That's your problem.' He was our site doctor, providing a cure, restoring peace and order to the system. Gordon it was who suggested that I brought the truck to the Sparrows' workshops where they could properly get to work on it.

Their brief was to build us a fish transporter for carrying elvers that could be taken apart after each season and easily reassembled the following year without putting a single nail or bolt into the hire truck. It took them two days and as I watched, I could see they relished the challenge. The main problem was how to mount the diesel engine, weighing a good 200kg, which was to drive the compressor that produced the air. Physically there was no room for it; the row of tanks took up all the space on the flat bed. The answer lay underneath: the bed of the truck rested on two longitudinal box section girders with hollow ends. Into these they slid long metal arms and a frame – that they welded up there and then - onto which the engine and belt-driven compressor were mounted to form a sort of rear deck. The four red one metre cube tanks, set tight in a row on the back of the truck, were locked in place by the sides of the truck and linked by an airline to the compressor at the back, using standard irrigation black hose. Taps were added to control the airflow to each of the tanks.

My pride and joy was the diesel engine. It was an old Petter off a dumper truck and had been lying about at the farm until Anthony suggested we use it; it was more of a museum piece, the sort of thing that might have powered the generator in some remote farmhouse in the 1950's. It had real character. It started on a handle; you put it in neutral to get the flywheel spinning, taking care to keep your thumb forward in case it kicked back. When you flicked it into start mode it shuddered into life with a long, slow and rather reluctant, donk, donk, donk, donk that gradually gathered speed. Once going, it would run and run. As it did so, the compressor, belt-driven by the engine beside it, produced a plume of tiny bubbles from the H-shaped ceramic aerator bars, also borrowed from Peter Wood, fitted to the floor of each tank. The finer the air bubble, we were told, the more effective it was.

It was a major breakthrough. Loading directly from the tanks onto the truck was now so much quicker. At a 100 kgs per tank, two of us could start loading at 7 am and be away by 8.30, when previously packing them into boxes would have taken a team of six half the night. We queued up to be lorry drivers. It was smooth and easy to drive, had power steering, excellent mirrors and a radio, none of which existed in our ancient Transit van. And it was very quick. Sitting up high gave a commanding view and a sense of power as we hammered up the motorway to RHM at Drax or further north. From the back came the comforting thump of the Petter engine and compressor that beat like a heart through the whole body of the vehicle. The only drawback was that it came with a tachometer, a spy in the cab, that recorded every movement, every start and stop. There were all sorts of regulations about taking breaks, the overall time you were allowed to drive and record keeping. I kept forgetting to change the disc in the tacho so that they were totally indecipherable, like old barom-eter graphs. When I remembered, I used to hang them proudly on a nail in the barn in the event of official visits. Fortunately, as we came under livestock transport, there were several exemptions. Only once, on the way back from Drax was I stopped. But that was for speeding.

'Do you know what the speed limit is for this type of vehicle.'

'Er, 60'

'No, it's 50 on this road. Anyway, what's this you're carrying?'

They were young officers, immediately curious. Police talk fell away; they became ordinary people, fascinated and friendly. They hopped up on the back and peered intrigued into the tanks. 'From the Sargasso, wow, all that way. And with nets you say, they catch them on the tide.' The elvers entertained them for a good ten minutes but then as they clambered off and just as I thought they might wave me on, the tone of voice changed, like a switch thrown, from conversational to official jargon.

'And now if you have anything to say it'll be taken down in evidence...'

I got a speeding fine and points on my licence. To my huge relief they never asked to look at the tachograph disc. I don't think I'd even remembered to put one in.

Beside RHM and Marine Farm, we now had another major customer for our elvers. This was the cement giant Blue Circle that had diversified into fish farming. They had set up a salmon and trout unit in Sutherland in the far the north of Scotland and an eel farm in the county of Durham, just south of the Scottish border. Located on the banks of the river Wear in a deep valley amidst the wild high moorland of the northern Pennines, it used the waste heat from the cement works that stood beside it outside the small town of Eastgate to grow elvers into eels. A young Dutch scientist by the name of Peter Kastelein had carried out the first stages of development, but it was now run by Richard Berry, who had worked alongside Maurice Ingram as his right-hand man from the early days at Marine Farm. Richard ran a very tight ship, the place was spotless, the survival rates for the elvers very good and the water drawn from the river Wear was crystal clear: you could actually see what you were farming. Only the access was a little difficult, particularly for a novice lorry driver.

From Somerset, it was a long haul up to Blue Circle, but very straightforward, up the motorway, turn right at Penrith, over the top by way of Alston and down into the Weardale valley. With the radio or cassette blaring Abba songs and a stop to consume Utta's picnic, delicious home-made brown bread sandwiches, time whistled by. On my first delivery to the farm, I backed very slowly down the narrow approach to the unloading area where a flexible hose would drain the fish from each of our tanks into the weigh baskets. I had forgotten the extra length of the truck created by the added afterdeck of the diesel and compressor. It was odd, I thought, above the thump of the Petter, but had the reassuring voices directing me into position become suddenly more urgent, high pitched. A face appeared at the window of the cab, white with panic. 'Stop,' it yelled, 'you're going into the building.' The long spindle by which we cranked the Petter had just drilled a neat hole in the side of the new elver shed.

The truck could be useful in other ways, not just to make deliveries but as a mobile collecting station. Towards the end of the 1980 season, not a spectacular one, we still had orders to fulfil and took the truck to explore other rivers. I'd been given permission to fish for elvers at Beam Weir on the river Torridge; an elver trap had once existed below the weir and I'd heard accounts of fabled catches. It was a beautiful spot, a great bend in the river under deep wooded hills, where the otters whistled and fished at night – along with the salmon poachers. There were indeed elvers there, but not enough to catch on that particular visit. The problem, as we'd found on the Laxford, was that you had to have time to study a river, understand the tides and where to fish. At best you needed someone on the spot. In time we made contact with a local bailiff who resurrected the old trap, a wooden chute lined with damp straw, and supplied us for some years before we lost him to Hancock.

With orders still to fill that year and the season in Somerset nearly over, I drove the truck to another of the great elver rivers. Steering well clear of the Severn so as not to tread on Peter Wood's toes, and with Bob of the wobbly teeth for company, the truck carrying weigh scales and cash, we headed for the river Wye that loops through narrow wooded valleys to join the Severn near Chepstow on the northern shore of the Bristol Channel. Far bigger than the Parrett and over a hundred miles long, it was, then, still one of the great salmon rivers in the country. Each spring it also attracted a huge elver run. Just as Hancock dominated the Parrett, so too the Wye had become the personal fiefdom of an elver buyer by the name of Horace Cook. A farmer who'd started buying wild salmon, he had gradually drifted into selling elvers, first to the local Gloucester food market, for people to eat, and then to the Spanish market, the frozen trade. As soon as Bob and I trundled onto the river at Tintern and began approaching fishermen, we were met with a wall of suspicion and indifference. Horace's grip on the river was all too evident. Trying to persuade his fishermen to sell to us was like prising limpets off the rocks by hand. No, they were very happy with Mr Cook, thank you. Anyway they were on contract to him and that meant a special price exclusive to them. No amount of money waved at them seemed to make the slightest difference. The tide rose and fell, and there was little about anyway. We stopped trying to buy and chatted to the fishermen instead. One pair recalled their best catch the previous year when one night the elvers had run and run, a thick swathe around the long bend they were fishing; by dawn they had caught nearly three quarters of a tonne. Higher up river, in the village of Brockworth, we came on Horace Cook himself. He was weighing in elvers, then bit by bit, spreading them onto a sloping mesh table where they were washed and picked clean of rubbish to be frozen later. It was so simple; no tanks, no pumps, no worries about holding space. Just a table and a hose. I guessed that Horace's haul off the river in an average year might have been fifteen to twenty tonnes. Much more in a good year.

We returned to Somerset much sobered and still short of fish. Scotland that year helped some way to ease the shortfall but by the end of the season we had still not quite fulfilled all our orders from the farms. This was worrying. If we failed them again, if they couldn't rely on us, they would go elsewhere. It was ironic how the situation had altered. In the beginning we'd had elvers but few markets; now we had strong markets but, in an ordinary season such as '80, not enough elvers. Already we had enlarged our holding capacity by installing extra tanks to be able to buy in more, now we needed, in addition to our own fishermen, another source of supply, an insurance against a shortfall.

There were possibilities: from time to time I had already bought from the landlord of the Thatchers, Alan Gibb's pub on the banks of the Parrett, a mile or so above Bridgwater. It was an ideal spot, with good elver fishing above and below, easy for fishermen to drop off their catch, get paid and have a quick pint before heading home. His set-up was remarkable above all for the size of his weighing scales, ex British Rail, very accurate and so huge you could have weighed a battleship on them. He was a short, powerfully built, ex-Gloucester rugby player, plain speaking and very practised in the art of weighing; I noticed he weighed tight and bought no water. I always liked Alan, 'Gibsy' as he was called, but he sold mostly to Dr Grunseid in Gloucester, reverently referring to him as 'the good doctor' and when Grunseid faded from the scene, he supplied Hancock.

Then at the beginning of the '81 season, I heard that 'ee out Weston-zoyland way were thinking of packing it in.' 'Ee' was Terry Hamlyn, originally one of Hancock's best fishermen. Utta and I had met him one night in the pouring rain in our first year of elvering, when everyone else had gone home; he'd found a spot on the river jutting out into the current past which the elvers were still running and we had bought his whole catch that night to make up a load that was going out to Rosengarten.

Not long after, he got fed up selling to Hancock, having to wait for him to turn up and queue every night to weigh in. Along with a few others he had started running his catch up to Ted Clarke's elver station at Epney outside Gloucester where he was paid a better price, made to feel welcome and special. Over time, to make it worthwhile and cover the cost of fuel, he'd started buying in from other fishermen. He had become what was known on the continent as a 'ramasseur,' a small collecting station, whose strength lay in its links with the fishermen and buying from them, rather than finding markets. The ramasseur wanted shot of their elvers as soon as possible. They dealt with a single buyer. On the continent the big dealers would have several of these collectors, each on a different river, buying in from local fishermen. In Terry's case, the honeymoon period with Ted was over. The promises of better money hadn't materialised. Things were getting very scratchy by the sound of it. What's more, a 140-mile round trip each night was a long way and heavy on fuel.

Terry was a local man, friendly, easy-going, with a rusty laugh and never far from his roll-up fag, busy rolling the next one as he was speaking. After national service, he related, he'd worked for years in Bridgwater in the cellophane factory, the town's biggest employer in those days. He loathed it. 'One day,' he said, 'I just thought, I've had enough. So I picked up me gear and walked out.' He was much liked by the fishermen, they felt comfortable with him; he wasn't an outsider like Hancock or myself, he was one of them, trusted, and they were loyal to him. It helped too that he sold elver nets, beautifully made, and the trays to go with them, the complete kit. Moreover, his house on the edge of Westonzoyland, (close to the site of the Battle of Sedgemoor where the king's army defeated Monmouth in 1685), was just a mile from the river on the short cut back to Bridgwater; perfect for fishermen to drop off their catch, share a fag and a yak. His holding site was simplicity itself: an old plastic tank with a washing machine pump that re-circulated the water. Beside it stood his garden shed, a clutter of mugs and fag ends and a bench for his bedding, where he slept the season and could weigh in the fishermen who turned up all night. Terry, it was agreed, would supply us and we would pay him a straight fixed margin on top of the price he paid for his elvers. It was new territory for us, and one from which I was to learn some interesting lessons.

Throughout the first Terry season of 1981, things ran smoothly and he added a tonne and a half to our production, making it possible to supply the farms with over four tonnes of elvers and Rosengarten with nearly half a tonne. The decision to have taken him on seemed fully vindicated. In fact the season for once was perfectly balanced, with good, strong markets and the right amount of elvers. These were good times and we were blessed with another vintage crop of helpers. Roddy, who'd been with us briefly once before, tall, wiry and a tower of strength, was there for the whole season, helping at the start with a major enlargement of six new tanks that almost doubled our holding capacity. Jerome, who'd grown up in Drayton, had finished at Oxford and in-between writing, teaching and becoming world doubles champion at real tennis, was intrigued to see what elvering was all about. With the two of them and friends who came and went, our house seemed full of people.

And there was our growing family: Oliver had been born the previous November and during the elver season was held and cuddled by so many different men, he must have wondered which one was his Dad. Often when I got in late at night, I would steal him from his cot and, in an effort at parental bonding in case he was confused, sit with him in the chair under the clock with its peaceful pendulum tick, till we both fell asleep.

By day we would be out with the truck delivering to one or other of the farms; by night one of us slept in the barn at the tanks to weigh in the fishermen and be on hand in case of emergency. I loved those nights, when the fishermen had gone home and it was quiet again, a breeze with the scent of spring, an old moon in the sky, the cough of sheep from Ernie's ewes. And the drone of the pumps. I'd go round the tanks, checking, put it all to bed. I came to know the site so intimately, its every rickety wheeze and ailment, so attuned to its every sound that I could instantly sense, like the spider with its web, if a frequency had changed or something was wrong. And then to sleep, climbing the ladder to the wooden loft in the barn under the ribs of beams that held up the great weight of the tiled roof, like the keel and spars of a wooden ship. Sometimes if a gale blew up in the night, the whole building flexed and the floor moved beneath you. I loved the barn, we all did, as Roddy said, it was like rustic camping.

Normally I fell into instant sleep, broken only if a late fisherman called in or by an early phone call from the continent, already an hour ahead of us. Rosengarten had a habit of phoning early, so too did Serge Dodat in south west France. He was one of the most influential of the French buyers, originally an academic, fluent in several languages, now hooked on elvers. It was he who had originally sold to the Japanese market. You could sense he loved the adrenalin, the wheeler-dealing, brokering sales. He made it his business to be well informed. Never contacting us until the French season was over, usually in mid April, he always sounded vaguely bored, rarely expressed any emotion, yet I learnt this was just a guise: he was watching, waiting, sifting everything. In perfect English, he had a way of feeding you information, tempting you to match him. He would have made a fantastic interrogator. He could be very rude, very funny about various characters in the industry. Perhaps as a result he'd made many enemies: he loathed Grunseid and had for years been trying to wrest the Lake Balaton order off him; was equally dismissive of the Germans – who felt the same about him. To his approaches, I played the wide-eyed new boy and tried to glean as much as I gave.

On one occasion he came over to see Hancock and myself with the vague idea of buying elvers off us. In a temporary truce, Hancock and I met him at a nearby station and discussed this possibility. Nothing ever came of the meeting but it was a fascinating insight into the size and scale of elvering on the continent. Continental production, Dodat estimated, was then around 1,500 to 2,000 tonnes in a good year, perhaps 600 or 700 in a bad one. He recalled the season of '65 when there were such quantities of elvers, they'd had to stop fishing in March because the market was saturated. And all caught by hand-held dip nets; only in '67 did they start using boats to trawl. What surprised me was his view that, 'There aren't enough elvers, il n'y a pas assez de civelles,' he kept repeating.

A few nights later word of his visit got round the river bank, a mixture of wonder and suspicion fed back to me like Chinese whispers,

'Yer, Moik, you eard, some of Hancock's fishermen been saying, there's this yere Frenchman, chap called Dodo, ees so big, got so many markets, ee wants to buy everything he can. I don't like it meself. I'd just tell 'en to bugger off. Bliddy French, you can't trust 'en.' There was a chorus of agreement. Forever after and whenever Dodat phoned for his early morning chats, I could only think of him as 'Dodo'.

Once the phone calls were over, the lorry loaded for delivery, I would head home to breakfast, hungry as a hunter, to bacon and eggs, toast and marmalade, lashings of tea, the best meal of the day. It was a time for catching up with Utta and the children, an oasis of domesticity – I'd often not seen them since early the previous evening – filling in on the intimacies and minutiae of family life, on events at bath time, stories read, on phone calls, messages, 'your parents called, wanted to know how things were going, send their love, catch you later.' It was a precious time of restoring balance, putting things in perspective. Reminding you that there was a life outside the elvering, all too often so intense and all-consuming.

★★★★★

Things with Terry continued to run smoothly. He would usually appear at the tanks around mid morning in his little yellow van, the elvers on trays in the back. The quality was always good and what was useful was that he would often have fish when we'd had none, or very few, so that overall we were able to maintain a steady flow of production to meet our orders. I blessed the fact that I'd been to see him and secured his supply. Then one day, he came as usual but unloaded no fish. He was nervous, jittery, needed to talk. We stood in the barn and he sucked on his fag. His fishermen were asking for more money, they'd been approached by Hancock, he said, he wanted to hang on to them. Were we prepared to up our price to him so that he could pay them more? Of course, he understood if we couldn't, but there was a chance of losing them. I made fumbling mental calculations; we still had a good margin and it seemed a reasonable request. I agreed and the fish were unloaded. But now it was as if a stone had been thrown into a smooth lake, disturbing the surface. It made me wonder. Quickly Terry was back to his normal cheery self and the stream of fish kept coming. And then, after two or three tides, it happened again. The same ritual, the same story. But we were nearing the end of the season now, our margin with Terry still fair, and I felt we could manage the increase, so conceded once more. Coincidentally he was no longer delivering his fish to us. He had been unable to make the journey one day, so to help him out, we had collected from him instead and somehow it had stayed that way. After a phone call to check if he had fish to collect, Roddy or Jerome would set off, no more than a round trip of twenty miles. Not a problem when it was all going so well.

There was something else that was vaguely troubling. At the start of the season, the Boys had casually asked how elvers were caught in France and though I'd never seen it myself, I'd told them that the fishermen there used boats that trawled nets like great windsocks attached to a boom on either side of their vessel. They fished the estuaries of the rivers, holding the nets steady against the incoming tides, were capable of catching huge quantities, but the quality was poor as the glass eels were rammed into the back of the nets, damaged by the pressure. Of course quality did not matter because they would end up in Spain for the dead market anyway.

The Boys were intrigued. I thought nothing more of it, and was astonished a week or so later when they told me they had bought a boat, an outboard and made a huge flexible net like a giant windsock that they aimed to test in the lower reaches of the Parrett. This they did on the low tides and it worked. They caught quantities of elvers, but with them came piles of rubbish, shrimp and stickleback. Thankfully the Water Authority spotted them and forbade its use. Undeterred, they got rid of the boat and built another new net, this time, a huge box funnel that sat on the bed of the river with a mouth like a whale and swallowed whole shoals of elvers as they were born up river on the tide.

Not to be outdone, others copied them and soon there were three or four of these monsters up and down the river. They weren't always used, the conditions had to be right, but it represented, though I didn't know it at the time, a turning point in the life of the river and the elvering. Fishing with hand held dip nets was one thing, but this was industrialised fishing, a rape of the river; it stopped the shoals. Any fishermen trying to catch for at least half a mile behind such a net didn't stand a chance. I began noticing, too, imperceptibly, now and then, something different about our elvers; the quality was not uniformly the same. There seemed to be more damaged fish, they didn't swirl round the bucket quite as they used to and they didn't settle in the tanks in quite the same way, no longer lay peacefully under the shading. Stupidly, perhaps because the vast majority of fishermen were still catching in the traditional way, I never made the connection, never linked these changes to the use of the new nets; I put it down instead to the numbers being caught and to careless fishing. But it was the start of an entirely new problem.

★★★★★

139

Happy as we were living in Drayton, our dream was eventually to have a house of our own. Without regular incomes, however, we were seen as pariahs by the banks and building societies. When we approached the mortgage companies, their initial welcome would fade, congeal like fat in a roasting pan. 'And what are your earnings, yes, your annual salary? There isn't one. Oh, yes, I see, a seasonal business, eel fishing, (always a perceptible shudder here) and er, part-time nursing, ah yes..um, I think perhaps better come back again when things are.. er... a little more established.' Five minutes and we'd be out on the pavement like drunks chucked out of the pub.

The bank wasn't much better. Our branch was in the nearby town of Ilminster and the manager was one of the old sort, a benign, weary-looking figure, in his last post, dreaming of the sunlit uplands of retirement and golf. We met in his office across a desk the size of an aircraft carrier. He peered in some bewilderment at the figures in our accounts that I had proudly passed over to him.

'But you don't seem to be making any money,' he said puzzled. 'By the time you take out your drawings, there is effectively no profit. In fact,' he peered closer at another page, 'you're making a loss.'

'So, borrowing for a house...?' I ventured hopefully. He looked up aghast as if I'd asked to pee in his waste paper basket.

There was just one solution, we learned: build up a deposit that might just impress enough to get a toe on the ladder. The one great advantage of a seasonal business was that all our income, such as it was, came in one dollop. By the end of each season, before it melted away, we tried to stick as much as we could into savings, then live out the rest of the year on bits of nursing and teaching and any eel sales. The only trouble was, house prices were rising as fast as we could save. In '76, Skye Cottage, the first house we rented, had been sold for around eleven thousand. Now, five years later, it might have gone for double. Anything we liked dangled tantalisingly out of our reach.

Then suddenly we heard that some of the banks, though not ours evidently, had started to offer mortgages and were hot for customers. On the strength of this, we arranged to see a business manager at the Yeovil branch of Barclays. Garry Adams was a tall, crisp-suited young man with a handshake like a vice, whom we recognised as living just round the corner in the village. I'd been in the village panto with his wife. Very pretty. It was a good start. We told him about the business and like a couple of gardeners with prize tomatoes, showed him our savings account. He was impressed. He eyed us for a moment across the table, weighing the risk.

'OK, I'll take you on. I'll give you a mortgage. But I'll want your account. That'll have to be transferred here.' For him and the bank, this might have been one of the more regrettable decisions he made in his life, but on the pavement outside, we hugged and danced for joy. A door had opened.

★★★★★

Meanwhile, things had not been going well in my attempts to smoke eel. At every stage of the process new difficulties arose. For a start my smoke hut was too large; to make any adjustments to the fire or the fish, I actually had to get in there with them and would nearly choke to death from smoke inhalation. Worse was when I stoked the fire for the final cooking phase, as prescribed by the Torry method; it got so hot the eels would fall off the skewers and drop into the inferno below. Taking great lungfuls of air, I'd plunge inside, holding my breath, groping around in the stygian gloom, blinded by smoke, eyes streaming and try to hook them back up. Even wearing a mask and snorkel like a scuba diver didn't help. It would take several minutes, leaping in and out of the hut to take deep breaths like a demented jack-in-the-box, to restore order, by which time the fire was often out, all the heat lost. Over time the results grew marginally better but the eels still tended to be sour and rubbery, tasting as if they'd been scorched by smoke. Friends were encouraging, the feedback polite but never exactly enthusiastic. 'Oh, I adore smoked eel, we used to have it when we lived in Holland.' They'd try a piece, ruminating thoughtfully, 'mmm… certainly very smokey. A bit chewy perhaps, mmmm…' The look on their faces said it all: not there yet, not like the Dutch. Too many mmmm's.

The other problem that drove us nearly mad was trying to skin and fillet the eel after smoking. It seemed logical to work from the outside in, remove the skin then cut the fillets off the bone. These were the local brown eels I'd caught myself and when smoked they became very dry, their skin thin and papery; it kept tearing and was impossible to remove

141

cleanly. At the end the fillet looked terrible and bedraggled as if the creature had been suffering some awful skin disease. Just the occasional one was fatter, easier to process, but mostly it was like trying to fillet old leather belts. It would take hours to prepare even a few and the thought of doing it on a commercial scale filled us with dread. So much so in fact that we began to wonder whether the whole thing wasn't a waste of time and we should abandon the project.

And then, quite by chance, we mentioned our difficulties with the filleting to Herr Klinge who had come to collect elvers and was staying with us the night so that he could start loading early the next morning. 'What you need,' he said, 'is a spoon. I'll show you.' And with an eel I had just smoked, one of my better creations, he showed us how you removed the head, cut the two sides of the fish off the bone, then inserted the spoon between the skin and the tail and simply ran it up toward the head. If the eel was fat enough, then it peeled away easily. In a second he'd done what would have taken us hours. Eureka! Strange to get so excited about an eel and a spoon, but for us it was a major breakthrough.

We were still at this stage sampling to friends, or taking them as dubious gifts – on a par with home made wine - if invited out, when the owner of the deli in Langport, our local town, heard that we were smoking and put in an order for a dozen whole smoked eels for his friends in the wholesale trade. My first reaction was one of intense excitement. This was our first real order. Then panic. He wanted them by the end of the week. Working day and night, I could just do it. First I had to catch them. Then gut them, brine them, and smoke them.

When I proudly delivered my first batch of smoked eel, there was something of a stir in the shop, curious looks, the odd shifting away. I heard someone say, 'oh my god, just like snakes' but the deli owner was excited,

'Don't they look wonderful. And another twenty for next week, please Michael, they're going like hot cakes. All my trade contacts are really interested.' It was thrilling stuff but what was interesting when I thought about it, was that they were buying the name – smoked eel – on its reputation without having tasted what I was producing. It meant that there must be a market out there. A frantic few days followed. I set my nets but when I needed good catches, the eels were mostly small and I struggled to meet the order. It taught me a lesson, not to let the prototype run away with itself, not to run before we could walk. Significantly and not unexpectedly, the orders fizzled out, as his customers realized they hadn't quite got the quality they were expecting.

Further help was to come through Alex Behrendt who was always interested in my smoking efforts. On his recommendation I got hold of a German publication called *Das Raüchern von Fischen*, by two erudite gentlemen Edmund Rehbronn and Franz Rutkowski; it was an excellent handbook for people who wanted to smoke their own fish at home. As detailed as the Torry booklet had been vague, it was very teutonic, serious, thorough, with not a glint of humour, crammed with information on brines and smoke times, how to smoke all kinds of fish I never knew even existed. You half expected exercises and homework at the end of each chapter. Anyone hoping to rustle up a smoker out of an old barrel in the garden was definitely out of luck. For a start you needed an enormous German dictionary; mine hadn't heard of half the technical terms used, including one wonderful one for the wooden board used to clamp the eel while you gutted it, which it called a 'Schlachtbrett', literally a slaughter board. But all through the early years of smoking this was my Bible and I pored over it, translating it, faithfully trying to follow each and every step.

By now I was beginning, too, to understand the importance of having the right eel. The Dutchman who had weighed my eels the first time had been absolutely right. Brown eel, the ones I caught on the moors, were not ideal for smoking – only for kookink – they were too thin. What I needed were silver eel, the mature adult, full of fat-stored energy, fuelled up, ready to make their long journey back to the Sargasso Sea the other side of the Atlantic. These were perfect for smoking, plump and juicy, as were also the farmed eel I bought from Maurice Ingram's Marine Farm. Yet, despite some small progress, there was still an awful lot I did not know. I felt increasingly I was fumbling about in the dark. What I needed was to visit a smokehouse and actually to see how it was done. The problem was how and where. I'd already approached a smokehouse in Germany and had been frostily rebuffed over the phone.

Then, that autumn Alex invited me to provide smoked eel for the buffet lunch at the Two Lakes conference. The lunches were renowned, almost as highly as the conference itself, a delicious spread, beautifully prepared by Alex's wife Kathleen. It felt an honour to be asked, but it made me very nervous; this was going live, centre stage and there would be many delegates from the continent, real connoisseurs. I bought eels from Maurice – also present at the conference - and took huge care with the smoking. Utta filleted them beautifully. Laid on a wooden board, decorated with slices of lemon, the fillets looked wonderful and very appetising. After the morning lecture the delegates crowded into the marquee, serving themselves from long tables laden with all kinds of hams, meats, fish and salads. Fish farmers have good appetites. I hung around at the back of the queue, watching anxiously, self-conscious. By the time I reached the tables, it was as if a whirlwind of locusts had passed, there was hardly anything left and no sign of the eel; it had been cleared. I sidled up to a young man I knew, the owner of a small trout farm, standing munching from his plate piled high and asked him if he'd tried the eel,

'This is my second helping,' he said, 'The what… ?'

'The eel, someone said there was smoked eel.'

'Oh, was there? I don't know. I just went down the line and helped myself to everything. It's all delicious.' And he forked in another dollop. 'Lunch is always brilliant here. Best bit.'

I was greatly relieved, he must have eaten it, he was still alive. I was aware he was not perhaps quite the most discerning of food critics; you could probably have put fish pellets onto the pile on his plate and he would never have noticed. More discerning feedback came from a Danish delegate who approached me and said he'd heard that I had provided the eel. 'Yes,' I answered guardedly, 'how did you find it?'

'Good. But not quite cooked enough, not creamy enough, a little too chewy; it needs more cooking.'

Alex was very diplomatic. 'Why don't you have a chat with Dr Keller here, he may be able to put you in touch with someone over in Germany. And he smokes his own eels too.'

I had met Dr Keller already from previous conferences. This time he had given an excellent talk on the crayfish and its life cycle. Tall, fair, with very good English, he ran a successful family haulage business in Augsburg, south Germany but his real passion was breeding the European species of crayfish. And smoking eel. When I told him of my difficulties with the smoking, he generously invited me to Augsburg where he would show me how it was done. If I came the following spring, he said, then, at the same time, I could take part in the annual harvesting of the female crayfish.

So it was that at the end of April '81, as the Somerset elver season drew to a close, I flew to Germany, not to sell elvers this time but to learn how to smoke eels. It was to prove a turning point in our lives.

First of all, however, there were crayfish to harvest. The brood stock were grown in lakes, situated in remote wooded country a good hour's drive south of the city. The process of draining them down had already begun so that the morning after my arrival we were able to start at first light, gathering the gravid females, heavy with bundles of eggs under their tails.

These were the *Astacus astacus* variety of crayfish, known as Edelkreps - or Noble crayfish. Much prized, they grew to the size of small lobsters, some of them well over half a pound in weight, and eight inches long. Lying like submerged battle tanks under their hides, hunkered down, they quietly snoozed, their claws folded but as soon as you approached, the pincers reared up, slashing and snapping like scissors. They were very quick and could inflict a sharp nip or even cut if they weren't picked up with care from behind.

When gathered up, we placed them each in their own hatching box with a mesh floor in a long channel, a nursery area. When the young hatched out in early May they would spend some time around the mother before swimming free through the mesh; if they stayed too long, she would eat them. Either side the hatchery was lined with airbricks perforated with tiny holes in which the juveniles took up residence. Like all crustacea, they cast their shell in order to grow and would go through as many as seven moults in their first year. I was very interested in the hatchery as I felt I could do the same thing back home, making use of our tanks, which were empty outside the elver season, to breed crayfish and sell them for stocking like Keller.

For the sheer pleasure of it, I worked alongside a delightful Frenchman, Dr Laurent, a scientist whose special subject and passion was crayfish – 'astacologie'. He was a slight, bespectacled man with impeccable manners and exhaustive knowledge of plant and aquatic life. With boyish enthusiasm and wonder, he'd pick up a beetle or a bug or a plant from the lake and pore over it, marvelling, and exclaim 'oh, that's so and so,' the name given in Latin, followed by a quick resume of its features, ' so wonderful to see one here, just look at the colours on the back...' Or he'd hold up one of the berried female crayfish, her eggs like ripe black grapes under the bustle of her tail, 'oh, elle est belle, celle-là' and put her gently in his bucket.

The lake was a good acre and it took all day to empty and harvest the crayfish. In this, we were helped by Keller's family and friends, some having come all the way from Munich, as well as people from the village, all there to join in this annual ritual. We stopped for a picnic lunch, sitting on the banks in the warm spring sun; the dank, muddy smells of weed and lake mingling with the scent of pine and moss from the dark forest around us. I kept hearing the phrase, 'Das ist Arbeit,' - this is real work- and at first was faintly amused: if they thought this was hard work, they ought to try elvering all night. But then I realized that wasn't what they meant. Rather, the phrase expressed their huge pleasure in just being there, out of offices, out in the open, using their hands, puddling about in the lake, reconnecting them with the forest and the water, with things that were at the heart of the German soul, things so important to them and so often missing from their frantic lives in cities and towns.

That night, back in Augsburg with Keller's wife and family, we had a delicious Flusskrebssuppe – crayfish soup – made from the meat of the creature and stock from the shells that had been boiled and sieved. 'And tomorrow night,' he said, 'we will have smoked eel – that you will have smoked.'

Going on a course as a complete beginner is one way, perhaps the most obvious way, to learn a new skill. What was different and indeed so special about this trip to Germany was that I wasn't a beginner, starting from scratch. In a way I was already half way there, had done the ground-work through having made so many mistakes, I was eager, hungry to know where I was going wrong. I needed to be put on the right track and this is exactly what Keller did. In essence, I discovered that the method I had been following was completely back to front. I'd been starting with a gentle cold smoke with a hot snap at the end. And the resultant eel always looked wrinkled and unappetising. The German and continental method loaded the eels into intense heat and smoke, cooking them first, then let the temperature fall back as the smoke continued. They emerged bursting out of their skins, hot, fat and succulent. You wanted to grab one and rip into it – which was exactly what the Germans seemed to do if given half a chance, eating them with their fingers like sweet corn, juice dribbling down their chins, with a chilled beer or a schnapps to wash it down.

146

Keller was characteristically well-organised with his own preparation room in the basement of his house where he also kept his smoker. It was a home smoker, not a commercial one, but still capable of producing delicious results. About the size of a tall office filing cabinet with a removable lid for loading, it sat on top of a fire drawer section, with a draft control, that could be slid out to refuel. The eels were threaded through their gills onto smoke rods, six or eight to the bar, heads gazing upwards, tails hanging down. Using beech, which he recommended as the best for eel, he simply lit a fire in the drawer and when it had fully taken, slid it into place below the smoke chamber. This had an open slatted metal floor to protect the fish from direct flame and also helped to retain heat in the cooking process. Once the dial on the front told you it was hot enough, the eels were loaded in from the top, and with the lid replaced, smoked for half an hour at over 90 centigrade. You knew they were done when the belly flaps opened up. It was so simple, a revelation, and I was amazed: all that time I'd spent propping open the belly flaps with match sticks. Never again. Once cooked, the heat was allowed to drop and they stayed in the smoker for another hour or so, absorbing the smoke from the smouldering beech logs, turning a dark, roasted, coppery colour. It was so very different from my wizened attempts back home.

As soon as I got back to Somerset, I rushed off to the local blacksmith – who also happened to be German – and commissioned my first smoker based on Keller's design. We set it up in the garden at the Lodge, underneath our apple tree and began to practice. There was an immediate and dramatic improvement. For once as they emerged from the smoker the eels looked appetising, and tasted very good. When I showed Utta the result and we sampled them, I felt very excited. Now we were on track. This really was the start of a new venture, something to build on to the elver business, and give it stability. A good sign, too, was that Emily and Oliver liked the eel. As I filleted in the kitchen, little hands would appear from below the table or they'd run in from the garden, often with friends, requesting yet another morsel of smoked eel. It was like feeding small birds.

Keller had recommended beech as the best wood to use for smoking eel, and this we could find easily in the woods around us. But it would be good, we thought, to add another wood, readily available, that characterized Somerset and this, of course, was apple. There were six acres of old

147

orchard beyond our garden and many of the trees had sunk to their knees, covered in craggy bark and bristly lichen. Using old branches and twigs, mixed with the beech, gave off a thick sweet aroma of wood smoke to flavour the eel. Smoked over beech and apple sounded good, tasted good.

Much progress had been made but there were still disasters; I was still learning. In fact I discovered, with a live fire, not a machine, I would always be learning. Every smoke was different. That was the challenge, that was what made it so satisfying: to produce the perfect smoke. Like the perfect bread, or the perfect pot. It was one thing to smoke under the watchful eye of Dr Keller, very different on my own. Details of things that had seemed so obvious when we had done the smokes together at his house, now weren't so clear. I found great difficulty sustaining the right temperature, the fire would get too hot and there'd be an ominous, muffled thump from inside the smoke cabinet, often followed by another, as eels pulled off the hanging rod and dropped onto the slatted floor of the smoker. It was impossible to get at them without dismantling the whole thing. Apart from losing the fish, the smell of burnt eel pervaded the rest of what might have been a good smoke. It was demoralising, and expensive too: these were no longer my own 'free' home-caught eels but ones I'd bought in.

However, very slowly and surely, the consistency and quality improved. With a little more practice, it would soon be time to find a proper market.

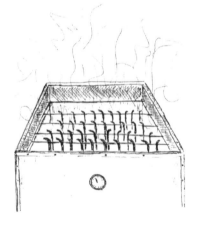

Our first proper eel smoker

Chapter Eight

Things seemed to be going well, almost too well. In Scotland, in the May of '81, after my trip to Germany, the elver run on the Laxford was a substantial one and we sold them without difficulty to the farms down south. We returned on a high, full of confidence and plans for the future. In the pile of mail awaiting our return was a brown envelope. It was from the Inland Revenue. And it made chilling reading. They wished to run a full investigation into our accounts. Even if there had been nothing to hide, the prospect would still have been bad enough, but I did have something to hide: I had stupidly not declared the income from my part time teaching. It had been so small to begin with, I had thought, not worth sharing with the revenue, but then as the earnings, still very modest, grew, the fault and the guilt compounded, it became harder, more complicated to confess; I was trapped by my own secret. Foolish, the accountant implied, because it was such a small amount there probably wouldn't have been any tax anyway. The worst part was the feeling that I had broken the trust of my accountant whom I liked.

In a strange way it was almost a sense of relief that the whole thing was out in the open; but beware, the accountant said, this is going to be tough, this could be nasty: deliberate evasion of tax was an offence inviting heavy penalties. Details of my illicit income were passed to the tax office. Nothing happened for a while and then like the distant rumble of thunder, things began to stir. They wanted everything, all primary records for the last three years. And that meant the cash books that recorded all the names and amounts paid to the fishermen. If they got hold of those, we were dead in the water – perhaps literally- we would lose all our fishermen instantly, none of them would touch us knowing their details had been passed to the Revenue. Once the initial shock was over, I began to take stock. There was only one thing to do: re-write the cashbooks and remove all identities. Fortunately this was long before the widespread use of computers and all my accounts were hand-written. So began a painstaking forgery. I bought three new identical ledgers and began the process; the payments were the same, but instead of the fishermen's names, I entered ticket numbers. These referred to cloakroom tickets I'd bought that correctly recorded the weight of each catch on the stubs but without names. Curiously, it became absorbing and if it had not been so deadly serious, I found I was actually enjoying the exercise, using different pens, applying coffee stains, rubbing out, dog-earing the pages, all to mimic the original ledgers. I'd obviously missed out on my career as a forger. Then came the final touches, the ageing process, I threw them around, stubbed the sharp new corners, rubbed them in a flowerbed outside. They would pass. Three old ledgers, without a fisherman's name in sight.

Then the questions began. All by letter, back and forth, through the accountant. They were relentless, exhaustive. 'The revenue would like to know how, why, when,' a continual drilling down into every detail. Each reply I wrote needed researching, careful weighing of information and each brought with it a fresh wave of questions, probing, pushing. What did we live on, what did we eat, drink, how did we spend our money. Provide details. Most of their focus, however, was on the elvering and the fishermen. Why didn't we have the names and addresses? Reply: it was dark, it all took place at night; I only knew them by their Christian names or nicknames, if even I knew those. Keeping up with it all was a job of work in itself. Each exchange, I hoped, would be the last, the end of it, but it was not to be.

In the early part of the following year, just before the start of the '82 season, I was summoned to the Tax Office in Bridgwater, an ugly stark building. It was a bitterly cold, grey day with snow on the ground. Outside in the car park, Bruce, the accountant, was sensibly dressed and wearing wellies and overcoat. The only warmth was his lovely broad Devon accent. We had a brief team huddle to discuss tactics, before being called in to a bleak office.

The investigator was quietly spoken, files and documents spread out before him. Quickly, as if an irrelevance, he dealt with the undeclared teaching: that was so much tax evaded, plus penalties, plus interest on late payment, making a sum payable forthwith. It was heavy but not disastrous. I dared to breathe a sigh of relief, glimpsing already the end of the meeting. Could it be over so quickly? But I was disappointed. 'And now coming onto the elver business.' What had gone before was evidently only starters. It was clear that this was the main course: all that money, cash being paid to the fishermen; and their identities, that's what he wanted to get his hands on. I could almost see him licking his lips, wondering which bit to go for first. It reminded me of facing a particularly nasty bowler in cricket. I tensed, waiting for his first delivery, watching the run up. The first question delivered straight, an easy one to answer. Another one, straightforward, and a good reply, right to the boundary. This isn't too bad, I thought, confidence, relief surging. Then suddenly a question probing from a different angle, awkward, straight through the defences. I scrabbled to answer. So it went on. The skilled tactics of the interrogator: a few easy ones to lull you into a false sense of security then, out of the blue, the question that came at you sideways, from an angle you'd never expected. And always impassive. No laugh, no smile, no response. Impossible to build a rapport. Just this ice wall.

Again and again he returned to the names. We skirmished. I stonewalled, repeating the explanations made in my letters. And then he drew out a list, 'Do you recognise any of these?' He read each name slowly, letting it settle in the air, watching me intently. Fortunately I'd never heard of any of them and couldn't help wondering just how many fishermen there seemed to be. There was a silence, then, 'If you don't let me have the names of your fishermen, Mr Brown, I will disallow all purchases of elvers, and you will not be allowed to charge these against tax.' In other words we were scuppered, wiped out. My insides turned to ice.

But sitting beside me, Bruce now sprang to the defence, wellies and all. He was bristling; I've never seen an accountant, before or since, quite so enraged.

'That would be totally unacceptable. And I have it from my client that this is a very vi-olent business as I am sure you know and if Mr Brown were to di-vulge,' he laid special emphasis on the words, 'the names and addresses of fishermen – even if he knew them – it would be high-ly (more emphasis) dangerous and might put my client at considerable risk.'

Actually this was probably an understatement. I thought of the visit I'd receive from the Boys; my mangled remains being sent in a jiffy bag to the Revenue with a note, 'Bugger off and mind yer own business.'

After what seemed like an age, we emerged from the soulless offices and Bruce said, 'Well, Mr Brown. I think that went rather well. I have seen much worse.' It was over, except for the bills, for the tax and the accountants' considerable fees. Fortunately it was to be a good enough year. But it had been a grim and salutary lesson; never again. Ironically a few weeks later, the whole matter of names was resolved in an instant. A new byelaw had been passed requiring the fishermen to obtain licences, for which they had to provide the Water Authority with names and addresses. This information, when requested by the Revenue, was handed over immediately and without question. And the tax man would now find, like a dog chasing rabbits in the hedge, that the task of recovering due payment individually from each and every fishermen was an exasperating and thankless one. That was his concern. For us, after all the years of worry, caught between Revenue and fisherman, the problem had evaporated overnight.

★★★★★

Talking to anyone involved in elvers who knew the good old days, they would probably cite 1979 and '82 as the two biggest years they ever witnessed. They were vintage harvests with record tonnages all over Europe as the elvers came in wave after wave of overwhelming numbers. For us the season of 1982 was all the greater because we were buying in from Terry; and certainly it remains more deeply etched in the memory for parts of it had a nightmare quality with its own set of dubious records: we bought in more elvers than ever before, over ten tonnes, but our losses were huge and our shrinkage – the gap between what we bought and what we sold – was nearly 20%; turnover more than doubled but the margin of profit was the worst in years. Certainly it was the year we came closest ever to coming unstuck.

To begin with, though, things started well. I felt confident: we had strong markets, with well over four tonnes required by the eel farms, and a secure back-up from Terry who was willing to supply us again. Normally the start of a season was the most difficult time to sell: the French still in full swing and dominating the market. Instead, happily independent, we were able to settle straight into supplying the eel farms. This year we had the dream team: Annabelle, Staff's cousin, was back with us, full of beans, and joined by Jacky, a fish farming student and friend of Alex Behrendt's.

They were probably the best team we were ever to have and certainly the most glamorous pair of truck drivers as they criss-crossed the country delivering to the eel farms and customers.

Up to then, the elver price paid to the fishermen had held steady, rising gradually with a moderate increase each year, but climbing in pence per kilo, never pounds. That year, all of a sudden things changed. Despite huge catches on the continent, fierce competition in the Spanish market was driving prices everywhere. Furthermore, back home, I think Hancock reckoned he'd had enough of us spoiling his patch; it was time for the knock out, time to get rid of Brown, the intruder. It was a classic manoeuvre. A short way into the tides, he put in rival offers to supply the farms at a much lower price - Blue Circle was the only one he didn't yet know about. At the same time he raised the riverbank price to the fishermen by a significant amount, well over a pound, thus clamping us between two barriers that potentially wiped out our margin. We were thrown right off balance. Fortunately the farms stayed loyal and I was able to renegotiate the price I sold to them. But the other immediate effect was a visit from Terry, not with elvers, but for a talk. Hancock had been to see him, had made him an offer for his elvers that promised a bigger margin. Could I match it?

'Course I'd much rather deal with you, Mike, I don't trust en, never liked en, he and I fell out long ago, but I got to look after meself, you know what I'm saying.'

I knew very well what he was saying. Without much hesitation, in order to retain him, I matched the price, desperate to have his extra fish to ensure we could supply the farms, so vital to us. It was my first big mistake: I should have said no. It would have been very different if he had been operating on a different river, a separate entity, but he wasn't, we were both buying from the same area, so he was both supplier and competitor. This meant that my hands were tied: if I raised the price on the riverbank to attract more fishermen, Terry would only have to match it, which meant that, with his margin on top, I would end up paying considerably more for his fish. Restricted in this way, I held back, hanging on to our regulars but not able to keep building our own team of fishermen.

I also became grimly aware as the season unfolded that while we were so busy servicing his needs, I was not only neglecting my fishermen, but Terry, like the parasite feeding on its host, was growing bigger and stronger as we remained static or even shrank. With his elvers collected each day – a job that was beginning to consume more and more of our time when we were already at full stretch – he was free to devote his time to his fishermen, developing a whole network of catchers, disaffected Hancock men, on the Brue north of Bridgwater. Furthermore by getting rid of his fish each day, he suffered none of the weight loss we experienced when elvers were held for days, even weeks. Imperceptibly I noticed changes in his site; he was expanding, putting in more tanks, better pumps and equipment. The whole place had smartened up. And what was so galling, if I allowed myself to think about it, was that, with low overheads, few money worries, he seemed as happy as a lark.

★★★★★

Before the season, and prompted by Anthony, I'd been wrestling with the problem of emergency back-up. Holding a crop as valuable as elvers in a system that depended entirely on electric pumps made me quake when I thought of a power cut. And they did occur, sometimes for an hour or two. Certainly long enough to wipe us out. The problem was finding a generator big enough to meet the power requirement of what was now a sizable site. Then Ernie suggested 'one of they generators they use for they there floats'. Every autumn, towns and villages around took part in the annual carnival processions, where lorries were decked out in spectacular tableaux with thousands of lights and moving parts. I got in touch with a carnival committee who were happy to loan their spare generator out of season for a small sum. It took a long time coming and when it finally arrived, towed by tractor all the way from Bridgwater, I could see why. It was enormous and had been used to power searchlights during the war. We parked it in the old hay barn and gathered round for a demonstration. It was so big that it had its own starting platform, which was like mounting an executioner's scaffold – as the victim. A starting handle the size of a tree trunk fitted onto the flywheel that had to achieve considerable velocity and momentum before it would awaken the sleeping giant.

'Make sure you keep your hand to the front,' said the driver who'd brought it and who in working life was, I learned with interest, a tax inspector.

As I prepared to wind, Ernie said helpfully, 'Remember to let go when 'ee starts , old son, or you could be the first man on the moon from round yere.' After what seemed like minutes of stirring the great flywheel faster and faster, the monster broke into a roar that nearly brought the barn down. Ernie's chickens exploded in all directions like star shells as I leaped from the platform. It was so loud no-one could hear themselves speak. But it worked. In fact it provided enough power for the whole village. Fortunately it was never needed.

In the midst of a busy season, it was often easy to overlook what extraordinary creatures the elvers were, to forget that we were holding not farmed, but wild fish taken from a vital stage in their migration and life cycle. Whenever you drained a tank and tried to wash them out, they would persistently swim against the flow of water, as it was their instinct to swim against the current, up stream. As nocturnal fish they would lie up by day in a dense mat under the shading we kept over the tanks, then at dusk, as the sun went down and they sensed the shift in the angle of light, they rose to the surface and streamed against the flow of the pumps, rippling the water. They were migrating within the tank itself in tune with the migration in the river a few miles away. It would only last a few minutes but it was very poignant and always made me feel ashamed that we held them captive.

★★★★★

By April we had already brought in a record tonnage. Each tide seemed bigger than the one before, and some nights were huge, with massive catches. All the way down from Stathe and Burrowbridge, past Moorland to Bridgwater, the river was thick with elvers as the shoals kept coming. Normally, skill, local knowledge and perseverance rewarded the best fishermen, but now they were so prolific even a beginner could throw in a dip net and catch a bucketful. Down on the river it was bonanza time. Over the Easter holidays that April, whole families came with picnics, children and dogs, sitting out the afternoons in the warm spring sun on the buttercup grass, the blossom of orchards behind, lining the banks like spectators at a festival, waiting for dusk, and the moon and the tide that would swell the river and serve up the elvers. I remember driving past them one evening, on the way back from Terry's, seeing them all, envying their care-free spirit, the sense of festival, and the adventure, wishing I could join them. Young and old, they would remember those times forever.

We did too, but for rather different reasons. Night after night the flow of elvers onto site seemed never-ending. I thanked our lucky stars that we had enlarged our holding capacity the previous year, and had put in more tanks. Yet, as fast as we could get the fish away to the farms, making space, they would instantly fill again. It was back to shovelling sand. Once we'd stowed the fish at night, bedded them down, we had then to find space for Terry's fish the following day. I used to hope his catchers had missed out to give us brief respite but it never happened.

One night stood out above all others. The river had been full of elvers, shoal upon shoal. There were vast catches weighed in, and to cap it all the Boys with their monster nets had weighed in over three hundred kilos. In all we took over a tonne and with what was already in stock, we were now holding well over two tonnes. With the help of Jacky and Annabelle I managed to stow them. Every tank held more than it had ever done before. Any more and I felt the site would burst like an over-ripe seed. I didn't dare think what Terry might have for us. Reports suggested that his fishermen hadn't done too well. That would be such a help to ease the strain. Before climbing to bed in the barn, I took a last look round. The moon was low in the sky. Surveying the scene, I was very aware that more than our entire worth and savings were now swimming around in the tanks. And losing weight by the minute.

I was woken at five by the sound of a vehicle in the yard. Outside a large, red van had parked by the tanks. I recognised the driver, one of Terry's fishermen.

'Hi Mike, good night was it? Got something for you. Yere, round the back.' I followed him and he opened the rear doors of the van. Inside a bleary-eyed Terry crouched in one corner and behind him, stacked from floor to ceiling, were trays and trays of elvers. He looked terrible, grey through lack of sleep.

'I was just holding the trays,' he explained, 'to stop 'em tipping over. There's about three hundred kilo there. All me tanks is full. These been on trays all night so I wanted to bring em up quick. 'Course there's bout another four hundred in the tanks for you to collect later on.'

It was one of those moments when I just wanted to run away, crawl under a stone and hide. We were already full up; there was nowhere to put them. I hadn't got a market for them. I felt sick inside. It took two hours to weigh off, and we worked in silence. I stopped worrying about our ability to hold them; simply focussed on dividing them equally between the tanks and piled them in. There was nothing else to do. As Terry unloaded, he became visibly happier and lighter of mood as the weight of ownership shifted from him to me; they were my responsibility now. And there was more to collect later.

'Hope you got a market for these, Mike, ave ee?' Ernie said, joining me, worried. 'They idn looking' too clever. Best get they away so fast as you kin.'

The trouble was, I didn't know how or where. Over the days that followed, I hardly left the tanks. Things were pretty desperate, like one of those simulators for training pilots when everything goes wrong at once. We had run out of space, we were full up. We were running out of markets, the farms had had enough; Rosengarten, and our continental contacts weren't interested. The price of elvers was climbing, forced up by Spanish buyers who were now approaching the fishermen direct. The overdraft was at its limit; Garry was getting very twitchy and beginning to phone nearly every day. I was becoming very weary, finding it hard to think with any clarity, just enough to trudge on. Most worrying of all was the quality of the elvers themselves. Not long before, we had prided ourselves on quality, it had been our hallmark, how we'd got into Germany. Now every day there were losses in the tanks; you always expected some initially and normally they settled down, yet now they persisted. The fish seemed weaker, never settled properly and when we shipped them to market, the stress of delivery would cause further unexplained losses.

What we did not yet realize was that they were being damaged by the force of current that rammed them into the back of the big nets that the Boys and others were using. And though many fishermen still caught good fish by the old dip net method, it only took a small percentage of badly caught elvers to spoil a whole batch. Doubts began to creep in; my confidence shaken. It was like walking on rotten planks, never knowing when the next would give way. I tensed each time the phone rang, dreading bad news. Peter Wood at Bristol Channel Fisheries in Gloucester was a lifeline at this time. He and his business partner, Glynn, had just

157

built a trailer capable of carrying two tonnes of elvers, an extraordinary piece of engineering with its own re-circulation and chiller systems to transport elvers to the continent and far into eastern Europe, even to Russia. They would often have space, a tank or two spare. But our unreliable quality was in danger of upsetting this arrangement - and the client. I worried they'd wash their hands of us.

Yet somehow we moved enough fish to keep our heads above water, chipping away at the sales, eating into the pile of elvers that never seemed to shrink. At last, the peak of the tide passed and the catching eased, earning us some small respite. What we needed desperately was a single big lift to clear us out. To this end, I had been badgering Herr Klinge from Hamburg, knowing that he was back and forth to Hancock with his truck. I urged him to come: we had enough for him now, we could fill an entire load – and the rest if he wanted. He promised he would and we waited. And waited. Then the phone rang one morning early: the truck was on its way, he'd be there at the end of the week. Instantly my spirits soared as if a cell door had opened. The worry had closed me down, locked me in to myself; suddenly I felt alive again. After the phone call, I cycled slowly the couple of miles back home, aware and seeing everything as if for the first time in days, breathing in the smells of spring and grass, past lambs that bounced and raced in Anthony's fields, to the rooks that cawed and squabbled in the trees above the village church; I was hungry for home and the family.

Running any small business is full of highs and lows, but elvering pushed you to the limits physically and mentally, and the dark tangle of worry blocked out all else. It could become very lonely; there was only so much you could off-load onto the family. Then again the pressure would release and bring, by contrast, that sheer joy of being alive. It had an intensity too, an adrenalin which gripped us all. Life was never quite the same again.

In the end, Klinge's truck came twice, loading and delivering into Poland before returning to collect again. There was something hugely reassuring in the knowledge that he was on his way, that we just had to hang on till he came, and when he did, the great beast with its multiple tanks filled the yard with its noise and the thump of its compressors, and cleaned us out, departing with a trail of vump like a huge snail. It was while we were in the process of loading the second time that the phone rang in the barn. It was Garry from the bank. Increasingly he had begun to call as he watched our mounting overdraft. Buying in so many fish, we were perilously close to our limit, perhaps even over it. We were very fortunate that the eel farms paid us almost immediately. But the last few weeks had put a huge strain on our resources. Garry was courteous, but there was a steeliness in the voice.

'So when can we expect this figure to come down?' For once I was able to sound genuinely reassuring. I knew Klinge would be paying for both loads, leaving a cheque for over thirty thousand Deutsch marks, enough to bring temporary relief to the account. Garry was reassured, impressed even, as I put down the phone.

What he did not know was that we still owed an awful lot of money for elvers yet to be paid for. Terry had been very understanding of the pressure on the overdraft, was happy with just enough to pay his catchers and leave the rest till the end of the season. So too with the Boys. It was part of their bargaining strategy. Gaining the best price for their fish, but taking payment at the end. 'We'll leave it in to the end, Mike, that way we can't spend it.' It was indeed a great help in easing the strain, yet their trust and confidence in us almost increased the pressure: what if we went bust, were unable to pay them? In their eyes, we were rock solid, utterly dependable. Each time they came to the tanks and saw the fish had gone, the tanks emptied, they knew that the wheels were turning, were reassured in their view that we were dependable. But as the end of the season approached, there was a massive amount to find. In early May I went to the bank and drew the cash that was owed. Though due to be split several ways, it was enough to buy a small house in those days, filling two blue bank bags, stuffed to the brim. Nearby where one of them lived, they were waiting, breathless, like pirates for their treasure. As they opened the bags, eyes gleaming, they became engrossed in the counting and division of spoils. I was invisible to them and quietly slipped away.

Eventually the market for live elvers, for farming or restocking in Europe became saturated; everywhere was full up. This might well have led to a sharp drop in the price yet the Spanish were still buying hard, driven by fierce internal competition, turf wars and macho rivalries, outbidding each other to supply the dead market, the food and tapas trade. A Spanish agent working out of Plymouth even turned up on the river, causing great excitement, buying cash on the nail, direct from the fishermen, loading what he bought straight into sacks to take back for processing. Terry sold to him and the Boys too. I was actually much relieved as I'd no idea what I'd have done with their fish.

'I've frozen the elvers you brought up the other day,' Peter said on the phone at the end of the season; 'they're worth more dead than alive and they're a lot less trouble.' Cleaned and frozen in three kilo tubs, we now had over a tonne, along with Peter's three, sitting in cold store waiting to be shipped to Spain. Or that was the plan. Overnight in July the whole thing ground to a halt. A foreign market, in Mexico it was said, had collapsed. You couldn't sell a single kilo of frozen elvers. At least, they were safe in the freezer, though it was nearly two years before they sold and for a fraction of what they'd cost.

★★★★★

Throughout that April, following the invasion of the Falklands by Argentina, news of the British Task Force and its progress south was a constant backdrop to the daily dramas of the elver season. It seemed so incongruous in the warm spring sun in Somerset to think that this conflict was about to unfold. Most of the fishermen, to my surprise, were against intervention, 'Let the bliddy Argies ave it, tis so far away. Nothing to do with us.' To them, engrossed in the elvering, it was an irrelevance, something happening way beyond their horizon. Maybe also it was a measure of their dislike of Mrs Thatcher, stirring memories of strident, hectoring mothers. But for Somerset as a whole there was a direct interest and emotional involvement. Many served at the Royal Naval Air Station at Yeovilton, or at the Royal Marine base near Taunton. Others worked at the Westlands factory in nearby Yeovil making helicopters, desperately needed. Everyone seemed to know someone, a son, a husband, neighbour or friend, on the task force heading south.

As the fleet approached, the Exocets began and the tension rose. Each night we listened to the measured, sepulchral voice of the government official who intoned the grim news. I remember, early in May, the shock of hearing that the Sheffield had been hit, causing terrible fires and loss of life. It made me aware of what it must have been like for the generation before us – my parents had been in the Far East – listening night after night to such news that rocked the world.

160

As the great season drew to a close, none of us knew that we would never see anything quite like its magnitude again, nor that this marked a turning point, the very top of the wave, the beginning of the downward slide. In fact, long before the end of the season, many fishermen had had their fill and drifted back to work and normal lives. For us it was time for Scotland, a working holiday but a time to repair and recuperate; the annual reward.

These were boom years for Kinlochbervie, now fourth in order of tonnage landed in Scotland. The north west fishing grounds were yielding consistent catches, the harbour crammed with boats. Development money was pouring in to support the infrastructure. The road, still single track, had been resurfaced all the way from Lairg, the bridge over the Laxford strengthened to take the pounding of the fish lorries that headed south throughout the night. Lives had changed too; you could sense the prosperity in the local economy and a tiny supermarket had appeared by the harbour. Since our first visit seven years before, the rusty pickups that carried fish had been replaced with gleaming forty tonne trucks. The pier had been transformed and a huge warehouse built the length of it to house the daily landings. Each night it was full of fish, row on row, as the auctioneer, like a priest performing last rites, moved slowly up and down the lines of boxes, the fish glistening fresh, rattling away in a language so foreign that only the buyers seemed to understand; with an imperceptible nod, flicker of an eye, they bought, and a buyer's label was slapped on the box.

Across the road from the fish house and pier was the Seaman's Mission, steamy with trawler men and porters in oilies, mugs of tea and plates of 'hadie 'n chips 'n mushy peas', local papers and a telly going full belt over it all. In some ways it was like a trucker's café except that it was for seaman and it had better facilities, excellent showers and loos, and rooms upstairs to sleep, and the food, the fish especially, was simple but delicious.

At first we thought it was a no-go area, for seamen only, and were surprised to find the public were welcome. We loved reading the notice boards, a peep into the life of a small community so different from ours: a hand wanted on a trawler with an Ullapool number given; porters needed at the pier, apply to the harbourmaster's office; for sale, marine diesel engine; and news of local events in Kinlochbervie and Durness further north. Striking was the number of families with similar names: on a list of two local football teams due to meet, almost all were either Morrison or Mackay; hell for anyone trying to report on the game.

Our favourite stop in Kinlochbervie was next door to the Mission, the chandler's shop, a sort of DIY for anyone with a trawler. Here you could get anything from Y-fronts to engine parts, even the complete engine; from a humble tin mug to a hawser that would tie up a liner. It smelled of oil and plastic, things new; it held that fascination that you get from any stores serving an industry, supplying all sorts of weird and wonderful objects from another world of work. It was always bulging with stock and reflected the thriving growth of the fishing industry itself in those days. Over the years a return to the chandlers became an obligatory part of any visit to Kinlochbervie. You just felt you had to buy something in there; you'd look at an ice shovel, or the coils of rope or the carabiner clips and wonder what you could use them for. We'd end up buying Useful Things for the tanks back home: tough, open mesh fish baskets, or nylon cord, or penknives, sharp as razors, for filleting - or gardening.

The elvers on the Laxford were as prolific as they had been down south. They came in three great shoals, almost one a week, during the time we were there, entering the estuary and massing at the falls beneath the bridge. I caught over three hundred kilos, mostly on my own as Utta had to stay back with the children. I never saw such numbers again. Fortunately the farms were a ready market, using the elvers to top up on earlier losses they had incurred. With friends or family staying, it was hard to tear myself away from good company and conversation round the table and to go down to the river. On my first night I was greeted by the small whiskery face of an otter, eating the elvers out of a hollow bowl in the rock where they collected at the side of the rapids. It looked up at me like a diner in a restaurant with a mouth full of spaghetti, indignant at being disturbed.

Once I was there, sitting with my net, out on the spine of rock in the middle of the river, like a raft in the darkness, the magic of the place took hold. I loved the rush of the river, the smell of water, the soft scent of spring in leaf, sudden splash of fish jumping. Fishing alone in the dark was good thinking time, mulling over the season, the highs and lows, the lessons learned. It had been a roller coaster few months and we had been lucky to survive intact. Our turnover was impressive, but our costs and losses were also huge. More than ever I recognized the need to reduce the dependence on the elvers; to start selling the smoked eel.

Past midnight the Kinlochbervie fish lorries would pass, often coming in pairs, lights probing the dark, slowing to cross the bridge, lit up like carnival floats, twenty tonnes of fresh fish, iced in boxes, heading down to Aberdeen or further south. Despite the disparity in size and operation, there was a parallel, a common link between the truck and the man beneath the bridge: both were taking fish as if there were no tomorrow, as if stocks would last for ever; neither gave any real thought to how long the boom might last; it just seemed so infinite, this boundless supply from nature.

★★★★★

Back in Somerset we started looking for houses in earnest; the trouble was that anything we liked was well beyond our reach. Having lived in two lovely cottages with gardens, we had great expectations. We had been spoiled. Then one afternoon I came home to find a note from Utta directing me to a property she'd seen about two miles away; I was to go and look at it immediately, this bit underlined. I could tell she was very excited. However I wasn't quite sure of her directions. Next-door to a crumbling building with a demolition order attached to it, I found a low white washed bungalow beside the river and bridge. I looked inside; this must be it, I thought, it was certainly very pleasant with its lawn and garden but I couldn't quite see what had caught Utta's imagination and told her so when we met that evening. 'No,' she said, exasperated, 'No, not that one, it's the one next-door. The ruin. It's wonderful. It's got such potential. And', she said triumphantly, as if this cleared all further need for discussion, 'it's south facing.'

She was right. It did have great potential. But it came with a demolition order for it was literally falling apart, the beams rotting, riddled with woodworm, the stonework slipping. Unlived in for years, part of it served as a wood store for the owners who lived across the road and was inhabited by a fierce squadron of geese. The roof, once thatch, had been destroyed by fire during the war when Italian prisoners, billeted there to help on the land, had cooked on open fires and it had been replaced by ugly asbestos sheeting. There were lavatories and urinals everywhere: it had belonged to a local firm processing the willow – the withies for baskets - off the moor and the men's needs had been amply provided for, especially with an old pub just down the road. Utta had a vision of what it could be like, she had a gift for that; all I could see were the bills and the cost of rebuilding it. But it was beautiful and it would make the most wonderful family home with space for four good bedrooms. The river Parrett flowed round the end of the large garden, bounded by a raised levee. Kingfishers nested in the opposite bank. Across the road was West Moor, one of the most southerly of the wetland areas that make up the Levels, enclosed and secret, covered in withies and poplar, a wilderness of water and rhines, sedge and birds. You could walk for miles on droves and tracks and never touch tarmac.

We did our sums. By a piece of sheer luck it just happened that the government was giving grants to improve buildings and housing stock. From preliminary enquiries it looked as if we could well qualify – and for the maximum amount – of £6,000, a fortune in those days. Garry from the Bank came to look at the ruin and agreed to lend us the balance of the money, to be converted to a mortgage when the house was finished. Thinking back, it was remarkable that he took the gamble and was prepared to back us.

It was an agonising time. The property was being sold privately and would be taken off the market at whim, only to be put back on again a few weeks later. Frustrated by lack of progress, we asked an estate agent friend to act on our behalf. Meanwhile the council grants were beginning to dry up, if we didn't clinch the sale soon we might lose out altogether. A builder, we noticed, was also interested, stopping to inspect the ruin. Several times we'd seen his vehicle outside as presumably he weighed up the prospect of buying to renovate and sell. After months of waiting however word at last came through: our offer had been accepted. Equally the grant was allocated, payable on completion of renovation at which point the demolition order could be removed. Twenty thousand for a ruin; my parents and other elders in my family thought we were mad. We tipped our entire savings into the purchase and the bank lent us the rest. It was the last time we were in credit; from now on it was overdraft all the way. In honour of its past we called it Willow Cottage.

The ruin was in two sections. The main part built of the local blue lias stone, compressed clay, while the smaller, older attached cottage was of warm-coloured brick, hauled up-river on the barges from Bridgwater. With limited resources, we decided to concentrate on restoring the larger stone part first and leave the other till later. We couldn't afford an architect so we used a quantity surveyor and drew plans ourselves. By December '82 the builder had removed all but the end walls and raised the floor level by nearly a foot. There was good reason for this. Every year in the winter, as it had done for centuries, the river flooded the whole area, turning it into an inland sea. Many villages on marginally higher ground bore the suffix '–ney', meaning 'island' in Anglo-Saxon, as in Muchelney, Midelney and Thorney.

Till well into the 1950s many communities were cut off from each other for weeks at a time and transport was by boat along the roads or over the hedges. Some years before, the bank that bounded our garden and protected Thorney had been raised to hold back the river and allowing it instead it to flood the fields and moor the other side. We'd been told our house never flooded now. Keen to see for ourselves we drove over to inspect what happened when the first floods came. The road was just accessible, the garden soggy, the height of the river swirling by, held back behind its raised bank, in line with a point about half way up the kitchen window. But the house, or what was left of it, was dry on its new raised floor. 'This is going to be your new home,' we burbled with excitement at the children. Surrounded by flood water in the stub of a ruined building

Willow cottage restored

they were understandably puzzled, not hugely impressed. Oliver meanwhile was having trouble with his one of his wellies that wouldn't fit on properly. Exasperated, I tried to help, jamming it onto his foot without success, until on closer inspection I discovered that a squash ball had taken up residence in the toe.

Meanwhile the renovation of a building that had stood empty for so long drew much local curiosity and interest. People knew people who'd lived there, or worked there when it was a withy yard. An old boy on a bike would cycle past and stop to tell us repeatedly that he used to drink there, when it was a pub. No, we said, not here, that was the Old Rising Sun next door. It must have been very easy to lose your bearings after several helpings of local cider. Rebuilding a ruin, it was inevitable I suppose that we should go over budget. The plan had been to retain the end wall of the house that ran along the road but when all else had been removed the bend in it was so pronounced that it had to come down. The builder went to his van and made a quick calculation. A photo captures the moment as I face the camera looking distinctly bilious, as if I'd just swallowed something very unpleasant: the fact, no doubt, that rebuilding the wall was going to add another twelve hundred pounds.

For the rest of '82 as building work continued, we stayed on in Drayton, keeping ourselves afloat financially as best we could. Utta was nursing, I was teaching English part time to foreign businessmen at a nearby language school in-between selling a few wild eel - for kookink - to the Dutchman and making my first attempts to sell the smoked eel. With the quality so much improved, I thought it would be easy, that the orders would flow in.

But I was mistaken. Perhaps it should have come as no surprise: in those days it was still difficult to find fresh garlic in Somerset and ginger was still a mystery ingredient that only came in bottles. Prawn cocktail and chef's pate were still the most popular starters when you ate out. Good, safe food. No wonder smoked eel didn't appeal. Local chefs would be very enthusiastic as I left them with samples but no further orders ever came. The difficulty was underlined when I was visiting yet another restaurant to drop in yet another whole eel for the chef to try. Entering by the kitchen door, I was greeted by the owner's wife, whose eye chanced to fall on the board I was holding with the smoked eel. She sprang back, her face a mask of fear, hands to her mouth, and let out a scream loud enough to be heard in the dining room, 'Aaaah, SNAKE.' I beat a hasty retreat.

I was almost indignant, I couldn't believe it: after all the time I'd spent learning how to smoke the eel, now no-one wanted to buy it. It never occurred to me that I might have usefully surveyed the market beforehand. It was just at this moment, however, that a friend of a friend, an entrepreneur who had once had his own salmon smokehouse, threw us a lifeline.

'Why don't you look at mail order?' he suggested. 'There are lots of people out there, scattered about, who would love to get hold of smoked eel, people who've eaten it abroad but can't buy it locally. Try putting an ad in the papers at Christmas.' To emphasise his point, and having stayed with us a few days, he sent, as a thank you, a slim wooden box, like the kind used for cigars or liqueur chocolates. Inside, between layers of waxed paper, lay thin slices of the most delicious smoked salmon we had ever tasted; it was the most wonderful surprise and it decided us: we would follow his advice and try the mail order route.

At about this time we also heard that the Royal Mail was offering a special deal to encourage small businesses: you could send up to a thousand items free of charge as long as they were all the same. Perfect for a mail shot. I had a single sheet printed, brown on cream, in slightly rustic lettering - the local printer was very proud of the effect. It offered Brown and Forrest's Somerset Smoked Eel, smoked over beech and apple, in fillet packs or they could buy it whole eel if they wanted. For the fillets we bought shallow polystyrene trays lashed down tight with cling film, popped inside Jiffy padded bags. With a half slice of lemon as decoration and the black on gold Brown and Forrest label with storage instructions ending with the flourish 'Bon Appetit', it actually looked quite professional. Rustic and professional. The storage instructions I made up, borrowing the language from perishable products I found in the chill counter of the local shop. You had to start somewhere.

Annabelle Archer was back with us after a summer working at the Ridgway's School of Adventure. Together she, Utta and I drew up a thousand names, starting with friends and family, then friends of friends of friends, then delving into Good Food and Restaurant Guides, ending up randomly selecting names from the phone book - Colonels and ex-servicemen seemed likely targets. We wrote the addresses by hand on the envelopes and posted them off, free; we also placed one ad – all we could afford – in a Sunday national paper. And stood back to await the result.

There was intense anticipation each morning when the post came. We hovered about like children waiting for Christmas; a small wad of letters would thump onto the mat, envelopes with cheques, postal orders, even cash. They ordered mainly fillets but whole eels too. Often there was a letter attached saying they were so glad to have found us, they used to buy eels in Germany or Holland when they'd lived there, but hadn't been able to get them in this country. What was so amazing to us was that the whole thing worked at all, that they'd actually bothered to reply. There is nothing so exciting when you have a small business as the moment when the idea becomes reality and you make the first sale; it's like the child's model aeroplane, painstakingly built, that actually flies. It took us right back to the first elver shipment to Rosengarten.

The advertisement also produced results. It appeared at great cost in early December, a tiny half inch of text on one of the Sundays' Food pages, surrounded by much larger ads for smoked salmon by post. I was annoyed that they had misspelled the 'beech', printing 'beach' instead, but no-one seemed to notice. And no-one else was offering smoked eel. The next day there was a phone call from a man in Norwich, he'd like three whole eels please, as soon as possible. He ordered with the confidence and authority that suggested he was used to smoked eel and knew a lot about them, wasn't in the slightest bit concerned about the cost. It was our largest order to date. I was so excited I could hardly take down his address. As with all the orders there was a moment of euphoria that would then quickly fade as the grim realization set in that I had to get out there and produce it. The whole eels in particular had caused me much headache beforehand: how to price them when every eel was different in size and weight. In a shop you'd simply put them on a scales and charge accordingly, but you couldn't do that with mail order: customers had to know how much money to send. In the end I worked out an average price that bracketed all sizes, large and small. Consigned to the post, wrapped in greaseproof, rolled up in long cardboard tubes, they looked like architects plans – or walking sticks.

While the renovations continued on our new house, we were still in the cottage at Drayton, with every part of it used in production. I did the gutting in the kitchen, the brining outside, then smoked them under the apple tree at the end of the garden against the woodshed. It snowed heavily in December and grew very cold. I was forever trudging back and forth, dressed like Scott of the Antarctic, muffled and hatted, with armfuls of eels and though a little awning over the smoker helped keep the weather off, it was hard work getting the fire up to the required cooking temperature. When they were smoked, we filleted them inside on the freezer top in the hall, and packed them on the kitchen table. David White, still our neighbour from across the road, dropped in from work one night to see how we were getting on, and surveying the scene with his usual good humour said, 'I think this is what might be rightly described as a true cottage industry.'

Fifty yards down the road was the village post office run by the highly efficient Roseen. It was tiny, the converted front room of her house, not much bigger than a walk-in cupboard, but an important meeting place and the hub of local news. The bundles of parcels I took to her were individually weighed and stamped as a queue formed behind me, and I listened to news swapping back and forth; anything of note, any juicy morsel of information could be round the village in five minutes flat if let slip at Roseen's.

In the accounts book for 1982, beside the total sales for the season's elvers – over eighty thousand – stands the figure in the column marked 'Income from Mail Order': £840, a tiny amount, yet somehow one that had given us greater satisfaction. As well as holding greater promise.

Our veg garden at Willow Cottage

Chapter Nine

The late 1970s and the early 1980s were the vintage years of the great elver migrations as we knew them. Of course, long before any commercial exploitation, elvers had been coming for thousands, even millions, of years. But what none of us guessed at the time was that from now on, as a result of our activities, especially the removal, year on year, all over Europe of the brood stock of the species to feed the Spanish appetite for elvers – 'angulas' – we had passed the peak; things were never going to be quite the same again. There would be more good years, times when we thought – we hoped – that nothing had changed, that the good years were back, but inexorably in the decade that followed the movement was downwards. The decline had begun.

Looking back with hindsight, this should have been the time to have taken measures in the UK and on the continent to preserve the species, by setting closed seasons at the appropriate time of the year, ensuring free passage of elver migrations upriver and adult eels downriver; restocking waters to create sustainable eel fishing – as on Loch Neagh in Northern Ireland and restoring habitats. There were many things that could have been done, that are now being done, though it is almost too late. I always used to think that as we were all involved, we ought all to contribute, buyers and fishermen alike, to the preservation of the creature. Many of the fishermen I bought from were equally concerned and would have been happy to have contributed to a scheme, like a levy linked to the licence - there were over two hundred licences on the Parrett and nearer a thousand in Gloucester - say one kilo a season per fishermen which we buyers could have passed on to the river authority for restocking. I used to phone up the relevant department in Bridgwater and put this to them but they were never very interested. They were too busy. And the evidence seemed to show that there were elvers aplenty. What was the problem? What they were concerned about was the illegal netting and to give them their due, they were devoting considerable energy to stop it. But I always felt that, as much as anything, it was an image problem, almost a social thing: no-one really cared about the humble eel. If it had been salmon, the public school of the fish world, they would have reacted immediately. Wild salmon were always up there in lights, getting special treatment while old eel, once poor man's food, came and went by the back door.

What made the decline so difficult to detect was that it happened so gradually, and imperceptibly. And it didn't help that the reality was hidden by the shadowy, secretive nature of the industry: no-one ever knew what the total European catch was, or could ever collate accurate figures and shout a warning; so much of the trade here and on the continent was done in cash, off the books, invisible to officialdom. Equally as catches dropped, fishermen worked harder to make up the shortfall driven by the rising prices. In the old days they fished just the set of high tides, then went home for a week, now they fished the low tides as well, so they were out every night of the season once it started. And were just discovering that if the tide rose in the dark, they could fish the morning tide too. So catch effort was increasing, helping to maintain the levels and mask the truth. It was only when you looked back and compared past and present catches, like seeing the drop in level in a reservoir, that the decline became evident.

There were also other big changes afoot. In the early Eighties the economic downturn was having a direct effect on the eel farms. Most of them had been set up in prosperous times when there was money around for the creation of new business ventures, now as things got tougher they were vulnerable to cut-back and closure. An even greater vulnerability was their reliance on waste heat, the warm water to grow the eel, supplied by a primary source they did not control, like a power station, whisky distillery, cement works. If these were to cut back, they were doomed; you couldn't farm eel on cold water. By the end of '82 Richard Berry at Blue Circle in the Weardale valley had been ordered to close down the highly successful elver-growing unit he had built up. With the slowdown in the economy, the cement works was working part time. For a week that autumn he employed me with our DIY truck, hastily reassembled, to run fingerlings – small eels – they had reared from Weardale down to the RHM site at Drax in Yorkshire which was still going strong and where they could be grown on to adult eels in the warm water lagoons. What

171

was striking to us as a small business was the way in which large companies could so ruthlessly switch projects on and off, invest millions in fish farming ventures, then abandon them when things didn't go right. To us, it seemed such a terrible waste.

★★★★★

Meanwhile by early summer of '83 we moved into Willow Cottage, our first very own house. We had no money for a painter so while the children were in bed and I stayed to look after them, Utta, who, with good reason, took a dim view of my decorating skills, worked night after night with roller and brush. Ernie arrived with tractor and trailer and helped us move the couple of miles from Drayton to Thorney. Conditions were somewhat spartan; we lived on concrete floors and bare boards upstairs for we couldn't afford carpets, but by knocking the whole place down we'd been able to redesign the old interior, creating rooms that were spacious, light and airy and a huge kitchen. South facing, the sunlight poured in. It had a warm and friendly feel. Moreover, renovation had given us four bedrooms, enough space for us never to have to move again. In front lay a large garden, though still covered with builder's rubble, and an orchard bounded by the river where kingfishers flashed. The heron flapping slowly home to roost, the urgent rasping flight of swans overhead, the sound of the mill weir upstream, all reminded us that we lived on the edge of a watery land.

What made it even more special was the area of West Moor that lay just across the road, surrounded by hamlets and farms, one of the most

Hay cut on West Moor

172

private and secret places. Like so much of the Somerset Levels, it wasn't grand or majestic, in fact to the casual passer-by it was probably flat and uninteresting. But as you got to know it, a whole world opened up; it had a stillness, an intimacy, a sense of peace. It was a soothing place of willow-lined ditches and wide open skies, and light reflected on water; it teemed with birds, mute swan and waders, snipe and curlew and lapwing. Warblers arrived in the spring and skylarks soared in the air like bubbles of song, lifting the spirits. In summer the cattle grazed knee-deep in grass, in winter it flooded for weeks at a time, returning to its ancient state. Green lanes, tracks bordered by ditch and rhine gave access to the every part of it. A large part of it in those days was still planted with withy beds – the willow for basket-making – jungles of wands through which you might catch the flicker of roe deer or fox. And on a clear day, from one spot on the raised river bank, you could make out the square towers of up to nine churches set around.

The moor was our sanity, our space and place of retreat. And in the house we had found the perfect home to bring up a family. As long as we could hold onto it.

The excitement and pride of ownership was tempered only by the change in our financial situation. Things had altered dramatically. We no longer had the reassuring lump of savings, they had been consumed by the purchase of the house. Instead we had a mortgage. For years it never seemed to shrink, indeed it even grew as mysterious chunks of interest attached themselves to it like barnacles. And along with the mortgage we were now the proud possessors of an overdraft. Of course we had had one every year to see us through the elver purchases, but then it had only been temporary, easily wiped out at the end of each season. This was permanent. It was like a great fat tick, a parasitic creature, fastened on to our lifeblood. It hung around, like the unwanted lodger. It had an insatiable appetite. Whatever we shovelled at it never seemed to make the slightest difference. At times it shrank but it never went away; we were shackled to it and it became part of our lives for years. Friends and family would casually ask after it, as if enquiring after a lingering illness or some crotchety relative. To begin with I thought it was a terrible stigma like leprosy but was much relieved to discover that most of our friends with small businesses, and certainly farming friends, enjoyed one too. The only difference was that they usually had assets to set against it. Our only asset was Willow Cottage, and the bank cheerily assured us whenever it sent a statement that it could be repossessed at any time if we failed to meet our repayments.

Considering our business evidently as a fragile plant that needed careful tending - or perhaps more accurately a sick patient on life-support - Garry, our bank manager, insisted on a Review, at six monthly intervals. This entailed a rigorous inspection of plans, profit and loss, budgets and cash flows; these projections of income and expenditure were particularly nasty. I used to stare gloomily at the income column, and wonder what I could possibly conjure up that might add a little gloss to the doom-laden picture, the only item of revenue of any certainty being Utta's nursing. In the end I came to realize what a useful medicine it was. Garry taught me the financial disciplines of running a small business, the need to know how much things cost, what the margins were and the need to carry them in your head; taught me not to confuse turnover with profit: not to think that just because sales were up and business booming, we were making money. And as time went on, I began to relax and he became an ally and mentor, one with whom I could be quite open about the business and its problems, asking him for his help and advice and involving him in decisions. It was the very best of old-fashioned banking.

When he was promoted, which happened regularly, he would phone up and ask if we'd like to follow him, move our account to the branch of the town or city where he'd been posted. Each time we accepted with alacrity. So we trailed along in his wake, trundling the overdraft behind us, like camp followers hitched to his rising star. In fact he was crucial to our survival and it was one of those pieces of rare good fortune that we had met him. Not that he came free: an old account book from the time reminds me that at four percent over base for our overdraft, we paid, relative to the size of the business, vast sums in interest for the privilege – which of course only swelled the overdraft further.

★★★★★

As soon as we moved to Willow Cottage, we set up the smoker outside against the wall at the back. This part of the house in old red brick, where geese had been kept, was almost a separate entity, a tiny attached cottage, a one-up and one-down, that we had not yet had the funds to renovate.

Instead we used it as a wood store for the voracious wood burner installed in the kitchen next-door. This piece of equipment had been sold to us as the last word in wood-fired cooking and heating. Made in Italy, and badly, it had razor-sharp edges, a large appetite and needed constant cleaning. To boil an egg or raise the temperature in the house to just above freezing it required armfuls of logs. The only time it ever warmed us was when we were shovelling fuel into it. Otherwise it sulked, dreaming of la dolce vita and puffed soot morosely around the kitchen. Fortunately we had a surfeit of timber, old boards and beams from the renovation work to feed it. Next-door to the room that stored the logs was an outhouse that ran down one side of the cottage. Though in a decrepit state, it had a sink and water and a worktop and with a good clean served as my gutting room and processing area. I tacked hardboard on to the walls, covered the surfaces with self-adhesive material for easy cleaning and very soon we were back in production.

I had almost stopped catching my own local eels now as so few were suitable for smoking. Most of our eels at this time were from Chard reservoir about ten miles away, netted by a young man, Andy Carpenter, who had married into the family that owned the fishing rights to the water. It was about fifty acres in all and had been dug in the nineteenth century and linked by subsidiary channel to the main Taunton-Bridgwater canal. The reservoir was shallow, full of nutrients and warmed like a rich soup through the summer months. Fish thrived in it. Ernie could remember the time when they'd drained the lake before the war to remove the silt. The size and spectacle of the eels that lived in it had passed into local legend and oral history.

'I knew chap wot lived up Chard who were there at the time,' Ern recalled, 'Ee said they eels were massive, six foot long, and they barked like dogs.' Apparently they had been taken away by the cartload, free food for all.

Andy brought me fabulous eels, all around a kilo; they weren't silvers in the sense that they weren't caught in their migration, rather by the fykes he set in long strings down the lake, but they were of silver quality, had a bronzy sheen to them, with firm, even bodies and sharp noses, all of a size as if they'd been graded. Perfect for smoking. They made an impressive sight in the holding tank at Bowdens. I used to keep them under shading where they'd lie longways, side by side, gently swaying like weed in a river against the flow of water. Now and then a tail would come up, exploring the lip of the tank like a thief at the window. If they could get their tails over the edge, find purchase like a grappling hook, they'd flick themselves out and over. They were the Houdinis of the fish world. Ernie warned me to be careful, to keep the water level low or they'd break out en masse.

I learned that if I was holding eels in the tanks for any length of time, they were much happier if there was shading, better still if they had places to hide, like sections of pipe placed on the floor of their tank; in minutes they vanished inside them. It was a characteristic amply born out by a description in *The Tin Drum* by Gunther Grass that I happened to be reading at the time and which graphically describes this predilection for going inside things: an eel fishermen on the Baltic shores casts a horse's head as a lure into the waters. When later next day it is hauled in, the horse's eye sockets and mouth are crammed full of eel. It is such a grisly yet accurate account, I felt sure Grass could never have dreamt it up; he must have witnessed it, or heard about it.

From time to time I would be asked by schools or parties to give a talk at the tanks on elvers and eels. It could produce widely-differing reactions. On one occasion Garry brought the local Lions club and as I showed them the Chard eels, draining the tank down so they could see them better, I asked, 'Would anyone like to try and pick one up?' There was a gasp of horror and they took several steps back. This was followed soon after by a visit from one of our local primary schools. When it came to draining down the tank and inviting them to hold an eel, a forest of little arms went up with a chorus of voices, 'Sir, sir, please, sir. Can I, sir? My Dad caught an eel once.' They had to be prevented from diving in a heap into the tank to do battle. Eventually one small boy was awarded the honour and with the help of a cloth to grip the slippery skin held it up to much applause until the creature slid effortlessly out of his grasp; he was the hero of the hour.

Once we had started smoking in earnest, I was always on the look-out for good eels we could use. The Chard ones were perfect for selling as whole smoked eel but it seemed such a waste to have to fillet them down for the smaller packs that we offered. Smaller eels were better suited for filleting and these we bought from Maurice at Marine Farm, as well as from RHM at Drax, who were beginning to sell a considerable tonnage to the continent. What was interesting was that suppliers of eel would often get in touch because they'd seen our advertisement for smoked eel at Christmas, or received one of our early primitive mailings. One such contact came from the secretary of the fishing club of the huge reservoir that fed the Port Talbot Steelworks in south Wales. He was a retired director of the works, a bundle of energy, and became a regular customer. With the Welsh hills behind and the great industrial sprawl of the works with its mile of steel rolling mills, it was a strange place from which to collect eels.

The actual management of the water fell to three delightful ex-miners who had improved the fishing by re-stocking with trout from the hatchery they'd built. It was they too who actually caught the eels using fyke nets. Aubrey was their chief spokesman and it was he who took charge of weighing. For this, we carried a large black bin with holes in the bottom like a colander to allow water to drain out before it was hoisted to the clock scales slung from a tripod. On one occasion, just as Aubrey was bending over the full bin to peer at the dial, a great tail rose up out of the writhing bodies beneath him and, encouraged by the lip of his chest waders that seemed to offer a nice dark place to explore, began to slide down inside his front to his nether regions. With a startled yell he jumped back, and to the extreme merriment of his fellow men, ejected from his waders like a man possessed – which in a way he was.

When first buying eel, I could never get over how quickly we seemed to go through them, and how much weight was lost, especially if they were being filleted. After smoking, the head, skin and backbone all removed, there wasn't an awful lot left. If I did a smoke that had weighed thirty pounds at the start before any of the gutting and cleaning, we were lucky to recover twelve pounds of actual fillet, a yield of barely forty percent, or put another way, a loss of sixty percent. This meant that smoked eels were very expensive. Not only was there a huge weight-loss, there seemed to be considerable waste from filleting: succulent pieces still left on the backbone, sections of fillet put to one side that were too long for the size of the pack. Very early on we realized we had to make something out of these leftovers that were just as delicious as the fillets we sold. Quite by chance at this time I heard an interview on the radio with Sir Charles Forte, the then-head of the food and hotel group, who was asked what had been the secret of his success and he'd replied, 'Good housekeeping, not allowing waste'. It had struck an immediate chord. We

177

should try making a pâté to make something out of all the little bits. A friend who was a cook suggested a very light pate, more a pate mousse. With lemon juice, horseradish, black pepper and single cream, we mixed the eel bits in the blender, not making it too smooth, but still with some texture, then folded in a measure of double cream that had been whipped separately. The result was delicious, enhancing the creaminess of the eel and the subtlety of its flavour. Emily and Oliver, our tasters, ate it by the spoonful and came back for more.

It was extraordinary how word got around that we were smoking eel. Through bush telegraph, word of mouth, people would drop by at Willow Cottage, curious, wanting to buy some. It was actually very exciting, for it showed that for all those who were squeamish about eel, there were also those who were passionate about it, and thrilled to have found it again. One elegant couple – she was Swiss - had already discovered us at the Lodge in Drayton when I'd been experimenting with juniper berries thrown onto the fire to give additional flavour to the apple and beech smoke; they'd been intrigued and captivated by the idea as much as by the rusticity. The juniper idea hadn't lasted long as the berries were expensive and difficult to find. When the couple found us again at Willow Cottage they brought friends and the Swiss lady acted as a sort of tour guide in front of them as I worked away, 'You can see how he's using the beech and the apple wood and also the juniper berries. Ahh'...She breathed in deeply and they all dutifully filled their lungs with imagined juniper-laden aromas, 'Such a lovely scent and such a wonderful flavour.' I didn't have the heart to disillusion them that there was not a juniper berry within miles. But the most memorable visit came from a more unexpected source. One morning in the autumn I was busy with the smoker when a large police car turned into the drive. Utta came rushing through to the back, 'Michael, it's the police, the police.' I must have been harbouring some deep-hidden sense of guilt, because I remember saying, 'Oh, my God, they've come to arrest us.' At which point two very large police officers appeared round the back by the smoker. But there were no handcuffs, just smiles.

'Sorry to bother you, wondered if we might buy some eel,' the one said. I was so relieved I almost hugged him. I can't remember how he'd heard of us, perhaps a friend had passed on our mailing, but he was to remain a good customer for years after.

We did not seek or encourage customers to the door; they just found us, and we were happy to supply those that did. It seems odd in retrospect that we didn't build on this obvious demand and open a shop but we never even thought of it then. Besides, while that might yet come, our main focus was very much still on the elvering. Although we had begun with the mail order method of selling, in order to reach out to potential customers far and wide, we found as time went on that mail order actually suited us very well; we could fit it in around our often chaotic lives, the elvering and the nursing with their different demands on time and place. It gave us a certain freedom, not being anchored to one spot, or having to run a shop with fixed opening times. We could take orders, smoke and fillet and pack them at any hour of the day or night - which we often did - as long as they reached the customer by the date required.

In the winter of '82 we had done our first ever mailing, sent 'blind' and at random to a thousand addresses. When it came to repeat the performance the following year it was sobering to find that only fifty people had actually ordered from us, not exactly an outstanding success. Yet in the next four or five years, the number of customers steadily grew. And it was thrilling to see how, once we'd reached a critical mass, a few hundred names, the momentum gathered. Mail order seemed to have a life of its own. It increased exponentially. Especially if what you sent was good, then each customer was your best recruiting sergeant, extolling its virtues, capable of gaining more custom: smoked eel served and enjoyed at a meal with friends could often lead to several people ordering. Equally someone who'd received it as a present would order of their own accord, both for themselves and for others. It was the ultimate network, a spider's web of connections, best illustrated when customers would explain how they'd found us, 'I met someone on holiday who'd had your smoked eel at a meal with friends and remembered your name....' It was like the message in a ship's bottle washing up long after the event. But most fortuitous of all, mail order was payment with order, providing vital income; it kept us going.

Very soon, probably as early as our second mailing, our customers began asking, 'And what else do you do, besides smoked eel in all its forms?' Did we do salmon for instance? We didn't, but we had kept in touch with Jacky who had helped us in the '82 elver season who was now working for a small salmon smokery outside Bath, under an hour

179

away. The company was helpful, friendly, still small and what they were producing, using mainly farmed salmon, tasted very good indeed and came well presented. Borrowing heavily from other brochures, we offered a choice of small packs as well as complete sides of salmon that came sliced or whole. Suddenly with one accord our list of products on offer had doubled, here was a range of eel and a range of salmon. Whereas before, potential customers might have been put off by the untried eel, they were now reassured by the smoked salmon with which they were more familiar and over time they might end up trying the eel. Quite unintentionally, the inclusion of the salmon suddenly opened us up to a wider public and helped to bring more people through the mail order door.

It also enabled us to approach the corporate market where businesses sent gifts to their clients at Christmas. In the autumn of '85, armed with the salmon, I got in touch with a marketing company and bought a mailing list of five thousand named executives – the marketing or sales directors – of small to medium companies in the UK. My local printer in Langport created an impressive logo, an oval shape, into which he scanned a photo I had of the fishing boats in Kinlochbervie harbour with the mountains behind. It had just the right feel. Together with our list of salmon and eel, I attached a covering letter that I spent weeks composing, ending with the hopeful phrase, 'Surprise and delight those on your list this Christmas,' which I borrowed from a promotional letter from a company selling cakes by post. With this collage of efforts thus assembled, I posted the five thousand letters causing a temporary crisis and shortage of stamps in the Langport Post Office and awaited the result with anticipation. As the label on fireworks used to say, 'Light blue touch paper and retire.'

The results were astonishing, not I think because of the logo and the persuasive text but because smoked salmon was still new and exciting; what better than a side of salmon at Christmas, something different to the diary or the whisky. Of the five thousand, only about half a percent, twenty five to thirty replied with an order, but this was ordering on an entirely new scale: seventy sides for a shoe manufacturer in Leicestershire, forty of the largest sides to a milk products company in Sussex, another thirty to a paper company. And the variety of businesses was bewildering, paper companies, chemicals, car parts, oilrig services. Some of them even sent their cheque with the order, causing an unusual seasonal blip to our finances and a shrinking, only fleeting, of the overdraft that had

Garry from the Bank almost as excited as we were. Receiving quality and service, many of these companies were to stay with us as loyal customers for years to come and formed the bedrock of our Christmas mailing.

However getting an order is just half the battle, the other is expediting it, making sure the right product is packed, with the right message, on the right day. There is an old saying that 'retail is detail'; mail order is absolutely about detail. You had to be methodical, work a system, one order at a time, constantly cross-checking. And the responsibility for despatching the business orders really struck home that first year when the Christmas packing still took place at Willow Cottage; especially when directors or bosses would ring up for reassurance, to see how their orders were coming along, or to give me some change of address. In their imagination they no doubt saw some huge smooth factory operation with lines of packers – certainly not a kitchen table, boxes all over the floor and the children just home from school. With the posting deadline fast approaching, I sought help from Bob of the wobbly teeth; yes, he'd come in early the next day and get ahead with things, he knew what to do. I did the school run and various errands and returned to find Bob still outside the house, looking rather sheepish.

'Sorry Mike, I just can't get in. There's a dog in there and it just won't let me past the kitchen door. It's already had a go at my leg.' The animal in question was Scuffles, my sister's ancient, arthritic but much beloved wire haired Jack Russell that we were looking after. From the other side of the door came a low bubbling growl of fury from this small canine. With Scuffles removed, we made rapid progress and caught the post in the nick of time. In those days, major disruption was caused when I turned up at the post office with sackfuls of parcels that all needed stamping individually while long-suffering queues formed behind me. Word must have got back to headquarters because I was soon invited to enrol in a contract that charged on the average weight of the parcels and needed no stamps, just a posting book. The post office and much of Langport must have breathed a deep, collective sigh of relief.

★★★★★

In October 1984 at the Two Lakes fish farming conference, I met up with the young man who was the farm manager at the RHM eel farm at Drax.

This was usually the time of year when he would give me a rough idea of their elver requirement for the coming season. It was always a good solid order, somewhere in the region of two tonnes, and far and away our largest. It gave a comfortable feeling, something bankable, something I could wave like a flag at the bank manager at the next Review.

'How's it all going?' I asked him casually.

'It's not,' he replied, 'because of the miner's strike, the power station's been shut down; we've had no waste heat, no warm water for months. In fact they've just made the decision to close the farm. I was going to give you a call but I thought I'd see you here. So I'm looking for another job. We all are.'

I didn't hear much of the next lecture. I was desperately thinking. What would we do? Blue Circle had gone, RHM had gone, only Maurice Ingram remained and he was only taking three to four hundred kilos. Of course there was the continent and Rosengarten whom we still supplied with one or two shipments a year. But we could not rely on them; a good year in France and they weren't that interested. Besides, the price of elvers was rising inexorably, around ten pounds a kilo by now, putting ever more strain on the overdraft, already looking very corpulent. The future looked pretty bleak. I was not looking forward to the next Review meeting with Garry at the bank.

Peter Wood of Bristol Channel Fisheries and his business partner Glynn Wright were also at the conference and must have heard about the demise of RHM for not long after I received a call from Peter casually introducing the idea of some form of collaboration on the elvers. It seemed an excellent idea, a possible solution to our situation. I liked and trusted them. We had already worked together on many occasions and they had saved our bacon in both '79 and '82 by taking our elvers when we had run out of markets. Outside of elvering they were both vets, very intelligent with analytical minds, both very focussed, extremely hard working, bordering on the workaholic; any liaison could be an interesting experience.

We met at the elver tanks at Bowdens on a freezing cold day in the following February. One of the options mooted was that they bought us out. Peter surveyed our set-up, the tanks and the barn that I'd swept and cleaned till they squeaked. As it was all rented, there was nothing to buy, he pronounced imperially. And his accountant nodded in agreement. At that we decamped to a hotel in Taunton where Garry from the bank had kindly agreed to join us and support me in the hard bargaining session I'd assumed would take place. It was not a relaxed meal, the conversation nervy and forced. Peter's accountant, whom I got to know and like later on, suffered from a serious squint, while Garry had a nervous tic and a sniff. These two squinted and sniffed at each other as they sparred across the table like boxers circling, looking for an opening. The only meaningful conversation took place when I went to the loo followed by the accountant, who said as we stood, 'I'm sure we can work something out. Don't worry about Peter. He's a good man. You can trust him. Come up to Gloucester and have another chat.'

I did, meeting with Peter and Glynn. It was agreed that I would be their man in Somerset for the duration of each elver season, buying elvers on their behalf off the river Parrett and delivering them to BCF at Gloucester. I was to be paid a management fee and they would cover all the elver-related overheads. I would also fish and supply them with the elvers from Scotland and negotiate on their behalf any sales to Rosengarten, so retaining my connection with him. Part of me was of course aware that this tie-up meant losing our independence as an elver supplier, but it only extended to the elvers and the elver season, it had nothing to do with the smokery or any other business ventures we might have. Knowing that elver prices were rising on the river bank, I was very aware that, on our own, we were pretty soon going to be out of our depth financially; very deep pockets were now needed to survive in the industry. What the arrangement gave us was a degree of financial stability, something else beside Utta's nursing that I could mark on the cash flow. It meant too that I no longer had the worry of finding markets for the elvers, or how to get them there. This was now the concern of Peter and Glynn, and a huge weight off my mind. Much more important, it freed me mentally and physically to develop the smokery. It was an arrangement that worked very well and was to last for the next fourteen years.

The new arrangement, which only Anthony and Ernie knew about, brought interesting changes to our elver season and to our pattern of working, though partly these things were happening anyway as a result of the imperceptible but steady decline in the elver catch. Previously our fishermen had always come back to Bowdens for the nightly ritual of the weighing in. Now increasingly we were weighing on the riverbank. It was all to do with quantities. If in the old days you had ten trays full you didn't mind bringing them all the way up to our site – a good half hour's drive from the lower end of the river - but if you'd only caught a kilo or two you thought twice about it and took them somewhere closer, to Thatchers or Terry, or Hancock who'd always weighed in on the river; in short, catchers were becoming our customers and if we didn't adapt to circumstances, give them a good service, then we would lose them.

The fishermen were changing too. The 1980s saw the passing of an era. The old guard from the farm, Shep, Ernie and his family, and men from farms around who'd been the backbone of our catchers when we'd first started and when it had been possible to catch elvers all the way upriver to Langport and beyond, had all hung up their nets; they didn't like 'this yere newfangled fishing', this weighing in on the riverbank, this fighting for a spot. More to the point they saw the elvers weren't there in the same quantities; Ernie couldn't fish his favourite spot in the old orchard because only rarely were the elvers making it that far up river; they were all being caught down low by 'that Bridgwater lot'. He'd 'rather stay 'ome and watch darts.' I still had the Boys and Mick, Merv and Bruce and their network of friends, but in the place of the old guard, lured by the rising price, came younger fishermen from the Bridgwater housing estates, perhaps at most just a mile from the river, perfectly positioned to tumble out of bed and fish the night tides. Increasingly, therefore, the focus of the elvering was shifting down river, becoming more urban.

To enable me to go to the river, rather than wait for the river to come to us, I was kitted out by BCF with a flat bed vehicle carrying two tanks on the back, a smaller version of the truck we'd hired in earlier days. To be supplied by someone else rather than trying to cobble it all together myself was an entirely new and wondrous experience. Glynn was the master of the re-fit, like Q in the James Bond films, revelling in adaptations and gadgetry: an overhead light on an extendable pole lit up the back of the truck like the deck of a trawler; a metal weighing arm that slid out of the bodywork to save carrying a tripod for the scales; all kinds of important-looking dials and gauges in the cab. At the back was a small compressor producing a mass of fine bubbles in the tanks to keep the elvers alive and happy. The water in them looked like a jacuzzi; if it had been warmer, I'd have been tempted to get in. I once shared these thoughts with a fisherman one evening as he was weighing in his catch.

184

He was a big, bovine smallholder-farmer with a sly tendency to include with his elvers as much mud and stones as he could get away with to bulk up his catch.

'Wouldn't you just love to get in there with your missus and wallow in there,' I said to him, proudly showing him the bubbles in the still clear tanks. He sucked on his pipe thoughtfully and took so long to answer, I wondered if he hadn't heard, and then at length replied, with an enormous grin, 'Yah, but it'd be a lot more fun with someone else's missus!'

★★★★★

The Eighties brought other changes too to our working lives and the elver seasons. Utta and I were now in our late thirties, and our supply of friends, or friends of friends, many from overseas and down under, who had been such a rich ingredient of the early years, had eventually dried up, as they themselves began to fashion their lives, got serious jobs or married and started families. Through Alex Behrendt and his Two Lakes conference, I turned to Sparsholt College near Winchester for our supply of helpers and made contact with Chris Seagrave, one of the senior lecturers on the fish farming course. It was one of his jobs to find placements for students to give them practical experience during their academic year. Chris would phone up like a salesman from a new car showroom, 'I've got a very nice lad here, Michael, very reliable, hard working, driving licence, I know you'll like him, he's just the right sort of person. I'll send him down.'

They came usually in March or April for three weeks at the height of the season. They lived with us, worked with us, fed with us and were forcibly part of the family. Hardly had they stepped out of their ancient and battered jalopies than they were ensnared in the logistics of our family life, often coming with me straight down to the riverbank to meet the fishermen and learn the ropes. There was a hidden agenda for this rapid introduction: little did they know it, but, besides learning about elvers, they were about to become child minders. The most complicated time for us as a family was the start of the new set of tides. The early tides would be around seven or eight in the evening, inconveniently just around the children's bedtime, and just when Utta would be leaving for work if she was on nights. I'd send the student ahead with the truck to set up ready for any early fishermen, swapping over with them later. This gave me time

185

to put the children to bed and read them their stories. Often sitting on the bed beside Emily or Oliver, relaxed after a meal, a delicious darkness would engulf me like a black wave and I'd fall fast asleep mid-sentence in the middle of Jemima Puddleduck or Postman Pat, to be woken to sharp nudges and cries of 'Dad, Dad, wake up, you've gone all funny, you're saying it all wrong!' Sometimes, when there was no student and we couldn't find a sitter, they had to come with me to the river. Emily would help with the weighing, writing the fishermen's tickets and winning votes, while Oliver, blessed with the gift of being able to sleep anywhere, curled up like a small dog and slept in the foot well of the van.

Over the years through Chris at Sparsholt we received a regular stream of students, nearly all of them turned out to be useful, some delightful and some outstanding. Whatever the experience they got out of working for us, we certainly gained from them: news, information, glimpses of life from all over the world of fish farming. With at least three placements a year, they came with all sorts of experience, from working at fisheries, trout farms, helping river keepers on the chalk streams, to labouring on isolated salmon farms in the outer isles of Scotland. When they came to us, they'd work mostly with the elvers, servicing them by day and often driving them up to Gloucester to the BCF holding station, but as the smokery grew, they were able to help me there. One student, Willy Dawson, a delightful fellow, had worked in a well known smoke-house in Scotland and not only taught me the basics of cold smoking to produce smoked salmon and trout but helped me with the design of my first cold smoker. He made it sound very easy, 'Ya just hang the fish in this sort of wooden cupboard, set light to a load of sawdust underneath that smoulders away for a while and there ya go.'

But I was to find it wasn't quite that straightforward.

★★★★★

It was not long after I had teamed up with Gloucester that the wisdom of buying elvers from Terry Hamlyn was called into question. With his margin on top, his fish were expensive; while I had been supplying the farms, I had needed him for security of supply, indeed become over-reliant on him. Now things had changed, it was far better, Peter said, to buy direct from his fishermen. When I went to see Terry at the start of

186

'86 to tell him I could no longer afford his elvers, it might have come as a surprise to him but he understood and he was a survivor; he knew he could find another buyer. Very soon he was supplying first Mike Hancock then Horace Cook on the Wye. This meant that my hands were now free, and I was able to approach Terry's fishermen armed with Peter's cash. What was revealing was the size of the network he had built up, particularly on the adjacent rivers of the Brue, the Axe and the Yeo, and how loyal they were to him, the local man. He was one of them, they liked him and they took some prising away.

Persuading them to sell to the new man, the outsider they'd only vaguely heard of, was a delicate, gradual process of building trust, taking several weeks. It was like unblocking a pipe: once I'd coaxed one team of fishermen to sell to me, and they saw they were paid the promised rate, then others who'd been hovering, waiting and watching, were soon to follow. The key was the collection point; I needed somewhere close to the river where I could be easily found. After some searching I hit on the ideal spot and word soon got around that 'that there Brown chap from over Langport way were paying more and you'd find 'en parked out on the Bristol road, edge of Bridgwater, on the way out to the motorway.' Yet once that had been established, I had to be there; it was a commitment, part of proving my reliability.

It may have been the perfect spot, as convenient for my own fishermen as for any new ones I was trying to attract, but it was also a soulless godforsaken place on the edge of town opposite a sprawling industrial estate, deserted and artificially lit. Over the years I came to know it all too well: if I strung together all the night hours spent there waiting for the fishermen to weigh in, it would have added up to months. But, in the midst of this urban desert, my diary recorded that at just after four, most mornings in April, a blackbird would start to sing in the blackthorn hedge beside me, a pure sound, just as the first lorries began to thunder out of town. Close by, hidden behind a banked-up levee, the river Parrett wound its way between oily banks of mud down to the estuary and the Bristol Channel. It was treacherous fishing; as the river fell lower and lower, the fishermen built trackways of old crates, bits of wood, tyres, anything they could find on the shoreline, to make safer the access to the water. They'd wear waders, and weigh in, plastered in mud.

The low tides, or 'droppers' as they were called, lasted about a week.

All this time the fishermen caught 'down low' on the muddy river, or on remote clappers scattered about the estuary and on lock gates set against the sea. Each night low tide was later by three quarters of an hour; the first around eleven at night, the last, a week later, at around six in the morning. It was hard on the body, yet the week of lows had a ritual all of its own. On a typical night I'd grab a few hours sleep before I left, going to bed just after the children. Utta would wake me on her way to sleep – our bed was like a helicopter landing pad with frequent comings and goings though the night - and I'd take my picnic and a large thermos of tea and my basket that contained my office, and set off before midnight, aiming to be on my spot in good time to catch any fishermen wanting to weigh in early.

At that hour the world was your own, the roads deserted. In the early part of the year often a clear sky, full of stars, the cab of the truck freezing, it'd take a mile or two to clear the frost off the screen. A barn owl would waft across the road; with the emergence of spring came the badgers, busy, trundling about, very purposeful and I'd pass orchards blowsy with blossom. For several years in late April I used to stop on the way and listen to a nightingale in the village of Aller on the edge of the moor just beyond Langport. It had taken up residence in some dense bushes. I'd stand in the dark and listen to the liquid, rising notes that led up to the magical, ravishing song, fluid as silk. It set me up for the night.

Often, when I got to my pitch on the road out of Bridgwater, there'd be a lone fishermen off the sea gates on the Brue or the Axe, waiting to weigh in, then it might be an hour or more before others began to drift in. In the waiting, I found that it was not a question of having to pass the time, rather I valued this oasis of peace to catch up on office work, or compose the seasonal letter to our mail order customers; most of all it was a time to think and take stock and plan long term – a rare opportunity for a small business, with the need to juggle so many roles and immediate demands.

While I worked, I had for company the radio, tuned to BBC Radio 4, with the late night news, followed by Sailing By, (a signal to break out the picnic) and then the Shipping Forecast. I loved the measured rhythm of the names, 'Viking, North Utsire, South Utsire, Fortes, Cromarty, Forth, Tyne, Dogger'... and so on, round the coast. It was like the rhythm of a prayer, and it reminded me that we were an island nation, and as I listened, especially when it spoke of 'gale, force eight, rising storm force ten' I thought of the trawler-men out of Kinlochbervie tossed about in the dark seas off Cape Wrath. There was a kind of intimacy about the night time forecast as if it was being delivered personally to the few who listened. One evening as it reached the end of its long litany of weather stations and lightships, there was a short pause, then the voice calmly announced that what we had just received was actually the forecast for the previous twenty four hours and that it would now read the new one, so I was treated to an unusual encore.

After the forecast came the World Service, which I'd never listened to before but on which I now became hooked, returning home to greet, and bore, the family at breakfast with extraordinary interviews, news items I'd picked up in the night. It caught things as they happened. I remember listening in disbelief to the news of Chernobyl in April '86 as it broke in the middle of the night, an event so chilling I could almost feel the shudder of the reactors. Or sometimes there'd be live commentary on a Test match, a winter tour of New Zealand or Sri Lanka. The fishermen were never very interested in cricket, their main sports were football. And boxing. On occasion, I could pick up extra fishermen because word got round that I was tuned into some big fight: Tyson v. Bruno or the middle-weight battle between rivals Marvin Hagler and challenger Tommy 'the Hitman' Hearns, live from the USA.

There'd be whole week of nights in Bridgwater and then, as the tide pushed upriver, the fishing moved up with it. For us all, it was a relief to get out of town into the country, to smell the grass and feel the breeze, see the tide swell the river; hear the bark of a fox. At one spot where I used to park at dawn, jackdaws visited an old dung heap in a field beside the road, fossicking for grubs and picking out the straw for a nest they were building somewhere. And every night, we'd bend our heads to wonder at the moon in all its stages from the first thin sickle in the early evenings, through to the old one, worn and pale, slipping quietly into the night sky through banks of shingle cloud. There were intense stars, too, like Hale-Bopp, or a fleeting comet, its stream of stars trailing behind it for millions of miles. Our necks craned, we marvelled in awe, 'Tis bliddy luvly.' Elvering was stargazing.

Sometimes if the fishing was good, there'd be a long wait and they'd all turn up together; then, as I worked feverishly to weigh each one in, they'd hang around to see how others had done. On one particularly busy occasion with cars and old vans parked at all angles, blocking the limited access to the space we used, I appealed to them in my best public address voice, calling out, 'When you've finished weighing, would you mind moving on to make room for others.'

They took not a blind bit of notice. The fisherman I was weighing in, a man I knew well, took note and said, 'Yere, Mike, let me handle this. You gotta be a bit more direct round here.' And with that he strode into the middle of the melee and yelled,

'Yere, you lot, just fuck off 'ome.'

At which, still talking but without the slightest resentment, they all departed. And brought to close yet another night.

Poplars on West Moor

Chapter Ten

Smoking the eels at Willow Cottage did not last long. We soon realised that space was limited and that, while there was room for an office at home, it would be far better to move the smoking operation over to Bowdens, across the moor from Thorney, where the rambling old barn gave plenty of scope for expansion. Now that Gloucester handled all the elver shipments, the lean-to tacked on to the front of the building (scene of so many all-night airfreight packs) was no longer required and readily converted into our production area with the smoker at one end behind a partition wall and open to the outside world. The swallows were very pleased with this arrangement as it meant they could still access this part of the barn and for some years, until the area was enclosed completely, continued to build their nest in a corner of the rafters to one side of the smoker. I loved their arrival each year, the first breathless visit to see their nests were still there, then later the little heads peering over the lip of their mud-walled home, the whoosh and swoop of a returning adult and the gaping mouths and excited twittering that greeted the arrival of food. What was amazing was that they seemed not to mind the smoke or the noise as I loaded eels or split logs to feed the fire.

Inside, which had once been the workshop and store and where the elvers had been boxed, the barn was perfect for mail order dispatch. The loft upstairs where we'd slept during the elver seasons became a packaging store. Downstairs, set against the wall, were long sturdy tables with broad worktops and storage shelves, ideal for mail order packing, which I bought for a song from Blue Circle when the eel farm closed down; I knew the man who'd made them and they always reminded me of elver deliveries in the truck. Friends and family happily offloaded old fridges and freezers; some of them, already ancient, lasted for years. A second-hand cling film machine with a heat sealer to wrap the eel fillets was our only piece of hi tech equipment.

During this time we had obviously appeared on the radar of Environmental Health for they phoned to arrange a visit. I was dreading it and pleasantly surprised when the lady who came was positive and helpful. On her recommendation – and we learned that when an Environmental Health Officer recommended something, it meant, 'Do it'- we built a small separate, clean room, like a box within the barn, with tiled floor and wipe-clean walls, to serve as a filleting area. We were lucky: this was before the stream of edicts that later flowed from Brussels. When I happened to mention her visit to the builder who was at the time renovating the remaining dilapidated part of Willow Cottage, he said,

'Oh, yea, I know 'er, she does building inspections for us too. Yea, she's all right, she is.' Then he added, 'Er's got nice pair of legs. Best when 'er goes up a ladder.'

Ernie, as ever, was on hand to advise. He showed me how to put up partition walls. He'd call in to the barn on his way to his lunch or from checking the sheep. He was always intrigued by any new project: he'd turn it over in his mind, and come up with a much better idea, 'So, youm puttin' the smoker yere, are you Mike?' He'd consider the idea, his boot tapping the wall, 'Wot about turning ee round and putting in this way, then you got more room to work, see.' However, by the mid-1980s Ernie had not been well for a while. Ever since I'd known him, he'd dropped by during lambing to complain, 'Cor, Mike, I feel so weak's a kitten.' Which was hardly surprising when he'd been up half the night, though his resemblance to a kitten was hard to detect. This was more serious though. He always seemed to be on a 'new setta tablets' but they weren't working and he began to complain of pains in the stomach. He was diagnosed with cancer and began to go downhill very quickly. He died in the winter of '86. It all happened so fast I never had time to visit him in hospital and tell him how much he'd meant to me and valued his friendship and support over the years. I wished, too, I'd been able to tell him what a privilege it had been to know him, this kind, gentle man of the moors.

★★★★★

As well as moving the smokery to Bowdens, one of the most important developments in these early days was the creation of a fresh identity for the mail order. A recent mailing had produced only a muted response. The initial spurt of growth seemed to have faltered. In despondent mood,

I dropped in to see John Leach, the potter, who lived just down the road from us and showed him the leaflet I'd sent out in the mailing. Very diplomatically he suggested that it might be an idea to improve our design and image. He put us in touch with his PR lady, Marian Edwards, who came to meet us at the house. Wearing a smart white suit and dark glasses, very chic for Thorney, she was business-like, not one to pull punches. It was a chastening exercise; she didn't flatter, but challenged our ideas, made us stand back and look with new eyes at our fledgling smokery business: the price list we'd just shown her was fine for a village fete or a wholesale butcher but not for the market we were trying to reach. It needed to convey something much more professional, to lend weight to our identity and to the name 'Brown and Forrest'. It was invaluable feedback, and we took heed, but her justified criticism stung just the same.

Marian put us in touch with a young graphic designer, Neil Lumby, whom we met and briefed. What he came up with a few weeks later was a completely fresh look, a reinvention. The 'Brown and Forrest' had become a brand, quietly confident, the typeface suggesting old-fashioned values of the well-established purveyor, supplying quality and service. In the weight and feel of the paper there was friendly reassurance. Below the Brown and Forrest name and between the sections of the mailing list were woodcuts, images of rural scenes by the eighteenth century wood engraver Thomas Bewick: a boat drawn-up on a beach, an old mill and waterwheel, all suggesting links with fish and eel, with water and river. For us, for the business, it was like being given a new set of clothes; it gave a huge boost to our morale and confidence. In autumn '86, when we sent the redesigned mailing in its new format, there was a marked response, a buzz and

The Mill at Thorney

stirring, lots of approving phone calls and letters, one customer saying, 'the print work all looks so good, you almost want to eat it.' The orders flowed in; the mail order sails filled again.

In the very beginning, before the arrival of a computer, we kept the names of all our customers on index cards stored alphabetically in shoeboxes and wrote the addresses by hand onto the envelopes, working round the kitchen table, a very companionable activity. In this we were often helped by a small group of friends, Sally, Biddy, Vivienne and Pat, whom we had got to know since moving to Willow Cottage. Encountering such lovely people was the start of a long association, one of those pieces of rare good fortune. They came from round about, mostly from Muchelney, busy wives with busy lives, but with husbands away or children growing up, beginning to have more time to welcome some work, part time. They were to become the core of a new breed of helpers at the smokery, vital to its growth and on whom we relied entirely, from the taking and processing of orders right through to filleting and packing. None of us was skilled; it was new to us all and we all learned together. Without them, I don't know what we would have done and the fact that they knew and liked each other created a tight-knit family feel, a team that worked well together. What made them so special though was that they cared; it mattered to them that things were done well, and they gave one hundred percent. Anthony Lang, always a shrewd judge of a workforce, used to say, 'Michael, you're very lucky, you've got a wonderful team up there at the smokery.' What he didn't add, being too polite, was that they all happened to be stunning women.

In those early days there was something very special, very personal, about the mail order customer, especially before the computer and on-line ordering. The relationship was simple and old-fashioned, developing either over the phone or by written word. The girls were all naturals at it. In those days, we hardly ever met our customers but they became a large family, a friendly tribe that loyally supported us. We got to know them, their interests, families, gardens, dogs, had glimpses into their personal lives, bereavements, holidays, grumpy husbands. Some were lonely and loved to talk; some polite, quick and efficient, some scatty, in a tearing hurry, never with details to hand. There was a delightful, elderly lady who loved cricket and listened knowledgeably to every ball of a Test match commentary, her father and brother having been fine players; there

194

was another whose dog not infrequently ate the parcel she'd ordered from us as it dropped through the letterbox; then there was the very elderly Colonel in Norfolk with exquisite manners who always wrote a thank-you letter when he'd received his order, telling us how his dinner party had gone and how much the smoked eel had been enjoyed. There were moments, too, when, despite the formality of address, you just clicked with someone on the phone about something – trivial or sad or funny - and for a few brief moments talked as intimately as if you'd known that person for ever; that I enjoyed most of all.

Obviously sensing we were beginners, they gave invaluable positive feedback: don't use ink on the address as it can smudge or wash off in the rain; please put a fresh form in with the eel so that I can order again; why not use a system of codes to save writing out the full name of each item. All these things helped strengthen the relationship between us as if they too were involved in the growth of the business. Other things helped smooth our way as well; being able to accept credit cards over the phone was a huge step forward and immediately increased our sales.

To avoid set office hours and keen to pick up any phone order whatever the time of day or night, our order form invited customers 'to use our 24 hour telephone answering service.' I always thought this sounded very grand, reminiscent of a large organisation and ladies wearing headsets sitting at phone exchanges. What customers did not know was that this was our home phone number and before the answer machine was switched on at night, if we remembered at all, they would often be surprised to hear a real voice on the line. We took orders during meals, at the weekends, in the garden, in the bath, in bed. We took to positioning pens and paper strategically around the house. It was interesting to hear in their voices how relieved and grateful people were to be able to speak to an actual person and know that their order had been received. When they did leave messages though, it was a reassuring measure of their confidence in us to hear messages as brief as 'Hello, Mr Brown, could you send two packs of my usual and charge my card,' often forgetting, or not even bothering to leave their name, which they knew we would recognize.

Of course the list of names didn't just grow of its own accord. It needed encouragement; like a log fire needed fuelling. Customers dropped off the list, drifted away, found some other passion; you couldn't expect them all to be excited and ordering forever. The knack was trying to hold them, feeding them reminders, special offers, new things we were smoking. This was where the seasonal mailing, and the Customer Letter came in.

In this I was much helped by another Michael Browne – this one with an -e on the name. Michael had been director of the Blue Circle fish farming ventures and I'd met him when we were supplying them with elvers. In order to market the salmon the company were intending to produce, he had built an impressive mailing list. When the recession closed the farms, he bought it for a song, and set up on his own a very successful mail order business, with just a secretary and a small array of packers to help at Christmas. It was an extraordinarily neat, lean operation with a low overhead. He never got involved with smoking; he bought all his salmon from a smokehouse in Scotland and just packed and delivered it. It was very good quality, and he gave an excellent service. I don't think his customers ever visited him or knew where he really was; they imagined him somewhere up in the Highlands, gazing onto the mountains as the aroma of oak smoke drifted from the smoke kilns over the valley below, which is just how he devised it. Michael's expertise was in marketing.

Besides giving us help with use-by dates, packaging, costing, all the nuts and bolts of mail order, it was he who advised us how many times a year to mail customers: 'They all go to sleep if you only mail once,' he said. Equally if you mailed too often they got fed up with you, so he'd settled on three a year, spring, summer and autumn. In his case, the customers received a newsletter that was brief and to the point, never personal, and written under the fictitious Scottish name he'd created. When, in the mid-1980s, I came to write our first newsletter, I found it excruciatingly difficult. We were such a small player I felt overawed by the giants around us and terribly self-conscious, like someone up on stage for the first time, not knowing quite what to say or how to say it, whether to use the language of the marketing man or just to be natural. I tore up draft after draft. In the end, I wrote the letter and sent it for a second opinion to Marian who'd advised on the brochure. She was a helpful and reassuring editor, always aiming to be succinct. Gradually, I grew more confident and able to go it alone, writing about our small family business, smoking eel and other things. People seemed to welcome a more personal approach, a peep behind the scenes. But it never grew easier, keeping it fresh, finding something new to say. The Easter one was often composed at night in the cab of the truck as I waited for the elver fishermen to appear. Seasonal mailings came round with startling rapidity, while Utta and Emily, as she grew up, became my new editors.

As the number of customers grew, the laborious assembly and dispatch of each seasonal mailing became a major operation: gummed label with Freepost address, inside order form, inside price list, inside letter, inside envelope. Address label on envelope, stamp on, ready to go. There were companies that specialised in bulk mailing dispatch. Instead, in our case, I planned the mailings for holiday or half-term and unashamedly used child labour: our children, Emily and Oliver and their great friends Laura and Harriet White. They were between seven and ten years old when they first started. For years they were 'chief lickers, stickers and stuffers'; a highly organised labour gang, run with frightening efficiency under the gimlet eye of Laura and Emily who vied for supremacy and to whom I could happily hand over complete responsibility for the whole operation. They did a fantastic job, far more accurate, far quicker than we adults. With a language all of their own, 'What are you on?'

'I'm on thinnies into thickies. Oliver's on stickies into thinnies, Harry's on stuffing and licking.' Occasionally Oliver, the youngest of the team, would rebel or collapse from fatigue only to be hen-pecked back into an upright position and lashed to his post. Harriet once licked so many stamps that her mouth nearly gummed up and had to be unglued with helpings of tea. At two hourly intervals they'd have a break, rush outside and whack a ball around for ten minutes before returning to the production line. Not knowing quite how much to pay them, I consulted the Agricultural Wages guide for casual workers, which only started at thirteen, and paid them accordingly. I remember counting into each of their hands the vast sum of three pounds fifty, representing several days' hard labour and seeing such a look of absolute wonder and thrill they might just have won the lottery.

★★★★★

Our working year was taking on a distinctive seasonal shape. The elver season started in January and went on till May; the mail order ran all year, building up to its busiest time from September to Christmas. In the summer there were sales of crayfish and ornamentals. All the time Utta nursed. The hinge in the middle of the year, marking the end of the elver season, was the pilgrimage to Scotland, to the Laxford and Sutherland. Perhaps pilgrimage is the wrong word, for it denotes obligation, duty; for us Scotland was more a migration, a journey we longed for, could not do without. In the old days it had been for six weeks, now it was for only one, two at the most. Yet it was as important to the children as it was to us: seeing good friends, Sandee and Sinclair Mackintosh with their daughter, Mary B., Emily's age, and having time to reconnect with wild places, having time to stop and stare. It was our spiritual recharge.

In Scotland, the elvers still arrived at the end of May, coinciding in the south with the flowering of the lilac and the children's half term. Ever since Utta, driving down from Scotland on her own with Emily as a baby – I had gone ahead in the van on a delivery – had had to kidnap a startled hitchhiker and press him into childminding, we had long since decided that the best way to drive the seven hundred miles without too many, 'Are we there yet?' was to go overnight. Over the years, as with any pilgrimage, this journey had shaped into a kind of ritual. A platform was built in the back of the little van, our kit stowed underneath and the children, dog and bedding loaded on top - without a seat belt in sight. Utta made up goodie bags for the children that included a picnic, sweets, and a puzzle book. Usually by eight o'clock we were on the road, down river past elver fishing spots, battlegrounds of recent drama now forgotten, sinking gently in the darkening night, onto the motorway and heading north. By Bridgwater Oliver had eaten his picnic and sweets, and fallen asleep.

For Utta and I, after a hectic elver season, a house full of students, helpers, friends, that drive through the night was often the first proper chance to catch up, like meeting up after a long break, a special coming together to talk uninterrupted, mull over the season, make plans for the months ahead. In the back, just behind us, the children slept, crammed to one side while Lilly, our lurcher, sprawled sideways, taking up all the room.

Somewhere south of Manchester we'd begin to tire and one of us would climb into the back, swapping with Emily who would come forward into the passenger seat to help keep the driver awake, keeping up a steady stream of conversation while passing pretzels, crisps or sweets to munch. We did hourly shifts through the night, rolling on, leapfrogging north, past the Lakes, past Glasgow and Perth, the dawn breaking through the Highlands on the A9 to Inverness, stopping for breakfast near Tomatin, at a Little Chef that never served porridge though we asked every time. But who cared, we were nearly there. Past Lairg, by Loch Shin, we'd make the ritual stop and listen to the lap of water, the silence, breathe in the pure air. Then over the hill and down to the long dark water of Lochmore, the road running alongside its pebbly shore, in the shadow of Stack, and Arkle, down the Laxford to our rented cottage.

On the first night, we walked the path by the river down to the estuary, peering under stones for the any signs of elvers. Sometimes they were waiting for us, sometimes we'd wait a day or two. They always came, but now there were the first signs of change. Unlike Kinlochbervie where the trawlers were still landing four to five thousand boxes of fish a night as if there was no end to the boom, our elver catch was dropping. In the old days we'd caught some two hundred kilos a season in Scotland, more in good times, but as the 1980s drew to a close it was down to a hundred, then seventy, then forty, as the shoals became thinner, lighter. As we were the only fishermen, we were all too aware that the elver run to this remote river at the outer edge of the migration pattern was slowly drying up.

Now, with less catch to store and to save the nightly trek to the hatchery at Achfary that could add a good hour to the night's work, I had mesh-sided wooden boxes made that could be sunk like coffins in the stream beside our cottage. Each one could hold about twenty kilos of elvers. One evening I went down to check them and saw an extraordinary sight: a large eel nearly three feet long had appeared and was peering through the mesh, like a thief at a jeweller's window, working its way round the box looking for a way to enter and feast on the elvers inside. I was just about to scare it away when, out of nowhere, another monster eel appeared and the two, enraged by each other's presence, had a vicious fight outside the keep box, their bodies coiling and writhing, each seeking to grab the other in its jaws to apply the bolt-cutter bite. The water boiled around them and I could see the scars and marks from their encounter scored on their skin. Then, as I yelled at the family to come and see, the eels were gone, vanished as if they'd never been.

★★★★★

However much we loved Scotland, however important to us, home was Somerset. We returned refreshed - always inspecting the veggie patch first to see what had come up - and ready to pick up our working lives. By the end of the decade, we'd enlarged our mortgage to complete the remaining part of Willow Cottage, finally removing the demolition order that had hung over that part of it. With the overdraft ballooning, Utta, already doing regular part-time psychiatric nursing, now went full time, starting a pattern of night duty, seven on, seven off, that was to last for years. Relentless though it was, night duty served us well. During the 'off' she was a normal Mum at home; when she was working, the impact of her absence on the children was minimal: she left as they were going to bed and was home by breakfast.

When she slept by day I looked after the children when they weren't at school. In the early days I'd used the empty elver tanks; well shielded from the wind and filled with toys, they were perfect play areas. When Oliver was very small, I used to carry him in a backpack as I worked at the smokery, having to remember to bend from the knees and keep upright when I stoked the fire in the smoker so that he didn't slide out like a parcel. As they grew older it was easier. In the summer holidays, I'd take the children, the dog and any of their friends to Bowdens and while I worked, they played in the old hay barn. It was the ideal child minder and nanny, a wonderful place to play. Stacked high with bales, the little ones like Weetabix used as bedding for the sheep in winter, it was ideal for making houses, hides and tunnels. Every so often I'd be visited by a creature covered in straw, 'Dad, Dad, we're going to hide, can you give us ten minutes then come and find us.' Somehow I always forgot, a phone call or a crisis with the smoker and an hour later another figure would appear, very indignant, 'Dad! Dad! We're still waiting. You were supposed to come and find us!' It was not difficult; whispering from within the bales and the real give-away was Lilly guarding the entrance to the hide, tail wagging. The Langs were very long suffering over their barn and the dishevelled state of the stack.

It was one of the greatest benefits of having our own business and working close to home that I'd always been able to take a full part, hands on, and share in the children's lives as they grew up. Yet I was never very good at shutting work out: often I'd be playing with them, but preoccupied, not quite fully engaged, gnawing on problems, thinking of jobs I had to do. And I'm sure there were times when they could sense this. I used to envy the nine to five dads who seemed so carefree with their children. I found it was never quite possible to close the door on the business; it was always there like someone waiting to come in.

★★★★★

Not long after the move to Bowdens, my first smoker, which I'd had made on my return from Germany in '81, was beginning to show signs of wear and tear. It had been just the right machine on which to learn, but I always found the top loading awkward, and it didn't allow you to see the gradual opening of the belly cavity – such an important indicator of how the eel smoke was doing. And besides we were beginning to need something bigger. The Mark 2 model was based on a design I found in my German guide to home smoking, Das Raüchern von Fischen. Made from metal by a young blacksmith in Langport, it was much bigger than its predecessor and double walled for better insulation, with the same fire drawer in the bottom. The principle difference was that you loaded it from the front, not the top, swinging back a single large door to load the racks of eel, reaching in as if to hang clothes in a wardrobe. It even had a chimney, the smoke piped out through the roof, a refinement of which the swallows must have approved. But the *pièce de résistance* was a little window, a regard, set at the right height to peer and check on the fire, watch the belly of the eel slowly open as it cooked. Now I felt like the real pro. As with all new ovens I had to learn its ways: it took longer to reach the correct temperature but it held it better and for longer than the old one. Production improved, became more consistent.

Our mail order range was growing. Besides the choice of eel and salmon, sliced or whole in various packs, we had begun by popular demand to sell fillets of trout. I started by producing them myself but by the time I'd bought the fish, smoked, filleted and packed them, it was far more expensive than buying them ready smoked. It was a lesson we learned: specialists in other products could often do them better and for less, and if they did, it was no shame buying from them. Over the years we regularly bought from other smokehouses and they from us. The fillets, recommended by one of our customers, came from a trout farm in Devon, which also smoked their own trout. They were delicious. I was almost as proud of them as if we'd smoked them ourselves. And that, I found, was the key to building the range: you had to be passionate about what you sold, whether it was yours or purchased from outside.

But this wasn't the only addition. Hot smoking had become our speciality and the eel our flagship product. What I was keen to experiment on now was cold smoking. Already Willie Dawson, our student helper from Sparsholt college, had taught me the rudiments of the process based on his experiences in Scotland. Cold smoking, probably one of the oldest forms of preserving food, is everything that hot smoking isn't: where hot smoking is short and sharp, with high temperatures for the initial cooking and all over in an hour or two; cold smoking is a long, slow, gentle smoke with an optimum temperature of between 20° and 25°C. It can take a day to cold smoke a salmon, several for a ham.

But before anything else I had to build my smoker. We had a large wooden storage chest the size of a freezer that was no longer used. Setting it on end, on blocks, beside our old wood burner I ran a flexible pipe low down into the side of the wooden chest. When the sawdust was lit in the wood burner, the smoke was supposed to meander slowly up through the pipe, cooling as it went, and produce a thick smoke in the chamber alongside. The only trouble was I couldn't get the sawdust to stay alight. I tried a blow torch; it would flare for a while, then go out. I tried firelighters with the same result. I went through so many bottles of methylated spirits that the chemist in Langport must have thought I was harbouring a secret drink problem. Eventually I found if I made a separate fire and embedded the embers in the sawdust, they provided just enough steady glow to get a smoulder going.

Whichever method of smoking used, hot or cold, it was still necessary to salt or brine beforehand. Salt draws water from the flesh, allowing the smoke to enter and preserve. As I'd found already from experience, if I forgot to brine, the taste was awful, smoke on its own was sour, very unpleasant. I made up a brine of water and salt, a good measure of brown sugar and then, having read somewhere that the Queen Mother's salmon supplier added whisky, I gave the mixture several generous gurgles from the bottle. Since we were already buying in trout fillets, which were hot smoked, I wanted now to have a go at cold smoking larger sides of trout, four to five pounders, the size of small salmon. I split the fish into sides and gave them two hours in the brine before hanging them to dry in the chiller. I'd been partly inspired in the choice of trout from a one-day course I'd attended, run by Peter Black, manager of Alex Behrendt's Two Lakes Fishery. He offered an excellent service to the fishermen who came there, a captive audience, smoking the trout they caught each day in the lakes; something I noted and thought we might offer to anglers in the future when I'd perfected the technique.

I was very excited, full of anticipation, as I opened the door of the cupboard to look at my first-ever cold smoke. Picturing neat rows of sides, smoke still drifting upwards, I was somewhat puzzled to see a set of hooks but no fish; they appeared to have vanished. Then I saw to my horror they were lying scattered, crumpled on the floor of the chamber; they'd torn from the hooks; the chamber was like a sauna, far too warm for cold smoking. Despondently, I gathered them up to throw away but just by chance pulled off a piece to try. To my surprise it actually tasted very good, rich in flavour with a hint of peat. Perhaps that was the whisky.

Over the next few weeks, things improved; I managed to drop the temperature by adjusting the rate of the sawdust burn and by adding a chimney to the chamber. Very soon we were ready to sample our customers, highlighting the cold smoked trout in the next newsletter. Sliced into packs, sealed in gold bags by our newly-acquired vacuum packer, it looked wonderful and tasted delicious. It became an instant success. It was one of the best bits about the smokery, this freedom and versatility: you could try something new, perfect it and within weeks it could be on the mailing list and selling to customers.

★★★★★

In those early days, before we renovated the barn, the business was physically split in two with the office at home and production in the barn at

Bowdens, five miles away. At the house Biddy or Pat processed the orders that came by post or over the phone; the first contact with a company, a smile in the voice that greets you can be so important; they both had just the right friendly manner and I would hear them chatting away to customers as if they were old friends. The office was at the back of our house, freezing cold and not much larger than a cupboard. With just room for two desks and chairs, the best way to reach my desk, if either of them was already at work, was to crawl along the floor beside the wall. Once installed, I got in a sleeping bag, which excluded all drafts but meant a kind of sack race hop if someone came to the door. When a seasonal mailing was sent out to our customers, it would be followed by a surge in orders and the tempo would rise; at Easter and in summer this might last only a few weeks, a short burn, before returning to normal, but at Christmas it would build and build. And with the orders came the money, cash up front, a vital flow of income to feed the ravenous appetite of the overdraft, swollen by the multitude of seasonal costs.

Our biggest expenditure, and indeed my greatest worry, was the autumn buying of the eels. It was a measure of our growth that we were beginning to need significantly more. Not just for our mail order customers but for wholesale orders, restaurants, distributors and other smokehouses we had begun to supply. By far the largest of these was Pinney's of Scotland. With their royal warrant, they then ran one of the largest and most prestigious mail order lists in the country. Their speciality was smoked salmon but they offered other things to their customers, which, like us, they bought in from specialist suppliers. In '87 I'd been beside myself with excitement and overawed when asked by Jean McPhail, who for years had run their mail order department, to send a sample of our eel fillet. For months we heard nothing, then out of the blue she placed a Christmas order so huge, for so many packs of eel, that it totally dwarfed our own annual production.

It was thrilling, yet daunting. Knowing the wastage involved from fresh eel to fillet, from river to plate, it was evident we were going to need at least double the amount of eel we already required for our own mail order customers. With the closure of all the UK eel farms, I had to buy wild, but what made this the more complicated was that wild eel hibernated over winter, and weren't much available till the following June, a long blank stretch, which meant I had to buy enough for Christmas and to last through the first part of the year. Not good for the cash flow. I'd spend hours trying to estimate the number of fillet packs and whole eels we were going to sell up to Christmas, and beyond in the New Year, then convert it all into the weight of eel required. Basically, it was lots. Squillions as my niece used to say.

Some of the eels we bought were from fishermen using fyke nets; most, however, were from the eel racks. These were permanent structures, often centuries old, a catching method perfected by the monks, consisting of a grid of vertical bars, like the teeth of a fine comb, set across part of the river to filter the adult eel out of the water as they migrated downstream to the sea heading back to the Sargasso. These barriers known as 'risers' were set at a gentle angle so that the eel swimming at speed and with the current of a swollen river behind it wasn't slammed against the grid but instead lifted gently upwards by the sloped bars out of the water onto a horizontal platform formed by another set of similar bars, aptly known as 'the stage'. There the river keeper would brush them into a holding tank or underwater cage, some of these beautifully built, smooth-floored with stone, capable of holding over a tonne of eel at a time.

But to work the trap, you had to be able to control the level of water; no good trying to catch eel if the river was over the top of the rack or way below the risers. It had to be just right so there had to be a weir or hatches close by to adjust and fine-tune the water level. For this reason many old racks were positioned close to a mill, sometimes even occupying a separate raceway to the wheel itself. The miller had been after all the arch controller of the river, able to raise or lower levels, directing the flow as and when he wished down through his leat to power the wheel. Or to run the eel rack. It must have been a profitable sideline, certainly a source of free food: bread from your own milled wheat with your own eel – and delivered to the door.

At this time I was buying from wherever I could: from Bristol Waterworks which owned Chew and Blagdon reservoirs where the eels were massive, big as cudgels, but caught infrequently and at odd times of year; from the Severn at Gloucester, and its tributary the Avon at Evesham, though a large proportion, at least a third of the fish were small, male eels, barely a foot long – very time-consuming to gut.

Occasionally I bought lovely eels from Loch Neagh in northern Ireland, a shining example of a sustainable eel fishery, stocked with elvers every year, and run by Father Kennedy, a catholic priest, whom I never met but enjoyed speaking to every year if only just to hear the measured rhythm of his voice.

Then there was Iford Mill, a beautiful house near Bath, whose owners were mail order customers and had restored the eel rack on the Little Frome which annually produced several hundred kilos of eel, large and silvery. To store their catch, they had rigged up an enormous holding tank but with no way of draining it, so I always arrived armed with waders and a net and would get into the tank with the eels to fish them out into the weighing bins.

I collected, too, for many years from Brendan Sellick and his nets in Bridgwater Bay, but some of the best eels at this time came from another professional fisherman, Richard Fleming, a likable man from Hereford, jack of all trades, charcoal producer, and cider maker, who had the licence to trap Llangors lake in the Brecons, a large, shallow body of water lying in the shadow of the Black Mountains. Over the centuries the elvers had probably entered it from a stream that connected it to the river Wye to the north. Certainly in the records and chronicles of itinerant monks and passing travellers it was widely noted as a source of fine fish, tench and eel. Hancock, when he worked with Anthony back in the 1960s, knew the area and had bought eels from the lake. It hadn't been trapped for years then and Ernie used to say they were huge, always escaping from the tanks at Bowdens; he could remember them, slithering down the drive to meet him, 'so long as my arm and so thick's me wrist.' It was a good measure: Ernie's wrist was very impressive. To keep the population going, Hancock had even stocked the lake with Somerset elvers. When smoked, the Llangors eels had a succulent sweetness that was hard to match.

All these were valuable, if irregular, sources of eel supply but not enough to meet our growing demand. Partly the problem was that we weren't yet big enough, nor had the freezer holding capacity to buy tonnes at a time from the big estates who liked to deal with one main buyer. I could have managed part of their output but not all of it: we simply didn't have the space – and I probably couldn't have afforded it anyway. With the estates, it was the keepers who took care of the racks and the sale of the eel. A different breed to the elver fishermen, they had secure jobs, they were busy on the river, they didn't have time to shop around; if they had a fair price and were given good service they were loyal, happy for one buyer to take the whole lot year after year. But they did like cash. It was one of their perks: so much to them, so much to the boss, each estate had its own arrangement. Strange for a trade that was always considered a little dodgy, a little slippery, or perhaps because of that, the rule was always cash on the nail: you weighed the eels, and paid then and there, counting out often two, three thousand pounds. It put huge, additional strain on the overdraft, a re-run of the old elver days: I desperately needed the eel – the whole business depended on them – but at the same time I used to lie awake at night wondering how the hell I was going to pay for them.

It was intensely frustrating. I'd hear on the grapevine of massive catches, but they went elsewhere. Many of the rivers had been selling for years to either Hancock, or the Dutch, or the London jellied eel market and would not shift allegiance. A good example was the chalk streams like the Test, and the Itchen, famous for their salmon and trout - and their eel. When I approached the river keepers I was politely but firmly told that, thank you but no, they were well looked after. Nearly all of them sold to a flamboyant gentleman by the name of Fred Cook, an East Ender, trading in the jellied eel market and with eel pie shops of his own. It was said that he used to turn up on the river wearing red braces, carrying wads of cash and driving a truck with the number plate – EEL. Years later I met him in a Radio 4 studio when Derek Cooper was making a special edition of the Food Programme devoted to eel, one of his favourite foods. Fred was very complimentary of our smoked eel - and still wearing the red braces.

Though unable to supply us, one of the estates on the Test put me in touch with a keeper higher up river who did not produce the quantities to interest London and who often had to wait weeks for a pick-up. Offer a better service, it was suggested, and he might be interested. Very quickly I was in touch with a Fred Kemp, a very likeable man, who looked after a mile or two of river at Whitchurch. It was my first introduction to the Test. Though at this point still not far from its source, it had a grace of its own, the water like glass with a luminous light, tinged green from the long tresses of weed that rippled and swayed on the bed of the river. Trout hung in the current waiting for fly. Fed by underground aquifers, its chalk spring waters encouraged a rich diet of snail, fresh water shrimp, crustacea and fly that once supported not just trout and salmon but grayling, pike and all kinds of coarse fish long since removed. For this was now one of the most exclusive rivers in the country, groomed for brown and rainbow trout.

From talking to Fred, I saw that though it gave the illusion of peace and serenity, of wilderness tamed, it was in fact a highly managed river, requiring constant upkeep, with successive summer weed cuts, mowing of miles of grass along the banks, maintaining the right level of fish in the river; ironically, most were not wild but introduced from hatcheries run discreetly out of sight by the riparian estates.

Fred's eel rack, sited in an old mill, regularly produced about two hundred kilos over the season. He was to supply me for years and through him I got to know other useful suppliers like Rupert Dawney lower down at Hurstbourne Priors who had painstakingly restored his own mill and eel rack; lower down again was Mike Crate, keeper of a stretch of the Anton, a tributary of the Test; all of them yielding regular quantities that kept us going over the summer months. The Test eels were beautiful fish, always around a pound in weight, a perfect size for fillets. When freshly smoked, as the skin was peeled away, their flesh had a pinkish hue, the result, I learned from the Germans, of a fine diet of crustacea, snail, and shrimp. At the top end of the river the eels started to migrate in early summer and ran like clockwork month in, month out, during the dark phases of the moon until October. The trouble was that by the autumn, with orders for Christmas pouring in, we had nearly always got through them and our stocks were melting away at an alarming rate. Once I remember being down to the last fifty kilos – and with Christmas to come. I desperately needed some big hitters, suppliers who came on stream in the autumn and could meet our growing requirement.

An eel rack on the Test

Then, out of the blue, I had a phone call from the Avon. Unlike the Test, the river never yielded much in the summer. It was a classic autumn river for eel. The keeper's name was Mike Trowbridge, and he looked after the fishing on the Radnor estate just south of Salisbury. He had eels; was I interested? He had, he thought, about seven hundred kilos. I couldn't believe our luck; it was in the nick of time. I arranged to meet him the following morning, which gave me time to draw the necessary cash from the bank. We were so close to our overdraft limit, I had to draw cash on my credit card as well to top up the shortfall.

Mike was an ex-Marine, tall, wiry, ramrod straight, and softly spoken; we could hardly hear ourselves speak for the boom of the river. After the long dry spell, several days of heavy rain had swollen the Avon, colouring the water, lifted the river; ideal conditions to trigger the eel migration. He had caught a few early ones, sensed their restlessness, their longing to set off; he'd guessed they'd come. He'd gone down early and set the rack and they'd run all night. 'Probably a few more to come,' he said as I set up my weighing tripod and scales on the narrow bank. Alongside the rack was the old fish house where great cages had been sunk in the riverbed to hold the eels. In the gloom I could just make out the great dark mass of eel gently swaying in the current, before Mike put on his waders and climbed in to net them out into bins. We worked flat out for nearly two hours. As the weighing bin was hoisted to the scales, great tails would lick up the side, explore the lip, seeking purchase to flip over and out. Some of them were huge, up to five pounds, nearly three feet long, perhaps from some lake upstream, warmer than the river, where they had lain and flourished. When each weight was recorded, Mike would lift the bin off the hook of the clock scales and tip them into the baskets lined with strong black bin liners that I held open, directing him, 'Keep coming, more, more, enough, stop!' as he poured the eels that emerged like spaghetti. There was a knack to sealing the bags. You had to twist and tie them as fast as possible or a tail would block the neck. Occasionally there'd be the odd escapee that Mike would deftly gather up in the net or I'd grab with a dry cloth carried for the purpose. Steadily the van filled, creaking as it settled under the weight. I took over half that day and returned two days later for another load by which time he'd caught some more. They were big, the Avon eels, always bigger than the ones on the Test, averaging about a pound and a half but just as good for smoking and

209

ideal for whole eels where customers wanted bigger ones. As I counted out the cash, I thought bugger the overdraft, at least we had our stock for Christmas. I drove home very slowly, the van creaking under the weight, bonnet of the vehicle pointing skywards, the inside steamy and pungent with the smell of river eel, a smell that mixed mud, dark waters, weed – and wet dog.

Meeting Mike was the lucky break, for through him I got to know two other good men who were to become, with him, our main suppliers each autumn. Rob Flett looked after a stretch lower down the Avon at Bickton below Fordingbridge. Rob was also an ex-Marine, proud of his service, having joined as a bugler in the band at the age of fifteen from his native Orkneys and ended up attached to the Special Boat Service. Rob was less organised than Mike, his net with as many holes as a colander and patched with electrical ties. Precariously, he'd balance on his keep box set in a side stream, swaying as he fished out his eels. He never quite knew how many he had, always erring on the side of caution and frequently – to his delight, and ours – we'd end up taking nearly double his estimate. Below Rob, with nets on the Avon and a rack on the Stour was another supplier, Roger Castle, a former maths teacher, gym instructor, mentor of young offenders, and professional fishermen, a delightful man with an exhaustive knowledge of eeling. Roger sold to the Dutchman but was happy to sell to us too. In a good year he could be worth a tonne. For the next decade, and more, the eels from these three men went a long way towards supplying what we needed for Christmas and the months that followed.

But it wasn't quite the end of our worries. However dependable the suppliers, there was always an inherent uncertainty about wild eel; they ran when they felt like it, or when the conditions were right. Often the early autumn brought a long, dry spell of settled weather, weeks of golden October days, cold and frosty at night, when the rivers were gin clear, full of the reflection of autumn leaves. In such conditions nothing moved, not an eel caught. What it took to trigger the migration was a change in weather, a westerly gale with heavy rain to fill the ditches, to swell the carriers, the side streams, to lift the river, colouring it brown, sending it booming and swirling down the valley and carrying with it fallen leaves and branches - and thousands of eels, a scene Thomas Hardy describes so vividly in his poem, Night-Time in Mid-Fall:

The streams are muddy and swollen; eels migrate
To a new abode;
Even cross, 'tis said, the turnpike road;
(Men's feet have felt their crawl, home-coming late)

If stocks were low, waiting for them to come was one of the most stressful times – worse even than wondering how I was going to pay for them. I'd phone round, just to make sure, but nothing had been caught. My parents would phone, just as concerned. Anthony would come by the barn, knowing how I felt, 'Don't worry, Michael, they'll come, we just need that old rain, you'll see.' And still the orders kept coming. The worst time was at night around three or four, when worries magnified and loomed grotesque. I'd toss and turn, envying Utta's peaceful breathing beside me. I kept coming back to what I would say to our customers if we couldn't supply; and to the dread of the house being repossessed.

Then, at last, the weather would break, rain streaming in from the west. And from the Avon and Stour, all of a sudden, so many eels I didn't know where to put them. Feast or famine; but at least we had them.

The smokery was growing fast, turnover rising; after Christmas '89, the overdraft shrank to its lowest level for nearly a decade. We cheered and Garry at the bank nearly fainted. It didn't last long, about three weeks before it was again looking glossy, well-fed and smirking, but it was a promising sign. Yet, as the big bills came home to roost in January, and as I prepared the figures for the bi-annual review, we never seemed to be making any progress with the smokery, little more than breaking even. Where did it all go? we asked ourselves. Undoubtedly it was the endless costs: the raw materials, the wages, equipment, overheads and the eternal stock of eel. All these things devoured any margin of profit. On bad days I'd moan to Anthony, who'd always encourage me with, 'Just stick at it, Michael, it'll come right, you'll see, just stick at it.' In odd moments of clarity I could glimpse the promised land, 'growing the business, controlling the costs' as Garry put it, but it was a long old haul, a case of onwards and upwards or, in Churchill's famous phrase, 'K.B.O'. Keep Buggering On.

211

Chapter Eleven

Every winter the land around us flooded, the river swirling past the end of the garden on a level with the kitchen windows, but the bank held and the house stayed dry. Flooding was part of the Levels; it had happened for thousands of years. But like snowfalls, or elver migrations, we remembered the big ones. And 1990 was a big one, a massive flood. It came in the January and it lasted for weeks. Villages, like Muchelney became islands once more, silent in isolation. Folk began to reach for their boats and waders. When I phoned the elderly canon to tell him that the village was cut off and therefore, I assumed, choir practice cancelled, (Emily being much relieved,) he was in defiant mood and I was told triumphantly that, no, he'd got hold of a boat and was expecting us all to be there, in true Dunkirk spirit.

With my brother who was staying, we rowed Emily and Oliver and their small cousins down the road to the church. On the way home in the wind and the waves, it grew difficult to steer between the hedges, so we elders jumped out and pushed. But this was nothing to the round trip undertaken each day by Alan, husband of Vivienne who worked for us, who with his tractor and trailer took over the school run; the children, ours included, sitting on bales as he navigated between posts and hedges, where the road had once been, an experience they would never forget. Health and Safety, had they known, would have had a fit.

Drawn to the floods, all sorts of water birds would fly in, great flocks of widgeon, duck and teal, squadrons of geese and swan. Out in the middle, afloat on this sea, with canoe or boat, drifting on the water, it was magical as the sun set and the moon came up, the darkness full of the sound of their watery calls, the burble of voices like a great congregation come from afar to the new feeding grounds.

Perhaps because of the flood, the scent of the sweet water miles out in the ocean, that year produced a huge run of elvers. Though not on the scale of '79 or '82, it was still a big season and all over Europe collecting points, closed for years, were hastily reopened to cope with the volume of catch. Hancock took ten tonnes, it was said, off the Parrett while we took over four, ferrying them almost daily up to Gloucester. But it was a strange season; things did not go well. The quality was poor, fish damaged by the use of illegal flow nets and we were buying badly, a lot of mud for a start, and there were big discrepancies between what we bought on the riverbank and what was weighed off in Gloucester. The fault was really mine. The smokery was very busy with the spring mailing. It was also peak season for sales of ornamental fish. My attention was diverted from the elvers and I delegated too much to a particular character.

I'd met L the previous season on the river. Older and more mature than the Sparsholt students, he'd already worked on fish farms and seemed the ideal helper. What's more he was living locally and could be on hand at any time. He was a keen fisherman and soon became fascinated by the elvers and the money that could be made. On his nights off he would fish, along with the elver men, very close friends with some of them. Too close. He was both buyer and seller, poacher and gamekeeper.

Then I began to notice odd things. If he had been fishing, queuing up to weigh in, his elvers were always very clean, no mud, no weed, as if they'd been caught in a different environment. When I mentioned it, he said it was because he was fishing another river. And I noticed too on these occasions he avoided eye contact. There was something shifty about him, but I never thought anything of it. There was no reason to doubt him. Then, one morning early, a customer came to buy a few kilos direct from our tanks. The site had been emptied the previous day but I had deliberately left enough fish for his order. When I removed the covers however, I couldn't believe my eyes: the elvers had gone. Worse was to follow. Towards the end of the season three full tanks, this time about one hundred and fifty kilos, vanished overnight.

We never found out who'd taken them. They would have been quickly slipped into the system, sold on to other fishermen to sell to other buyers. I might even have bought them back myself. All along I never suspected L for I trusted him completely. And there was no evidence to suggest that he'd done anything wrong. It was only the following year I began to wonder, when the fishermen would hint darkly, 'there were a lot going on, Mike; you don't know the half of it.' I didn't, and I couldn't ask because by now he had taken a job in New Zealand on the other side of the world. But I did discover one thing. A year or two later, I came across someone who'd employed him at his trout fishery before he came to us: he'd been caught taking fish and selling them to the locals.

Good things often come out of bad; this unfortunate episode was to prompt direct but positive consequences. After Ernie died, Richard Lang, Jane and Anthony's son, had moved into the house at Bowdens. While he was happy for us to continue to use the old barn for the smokery, the tanks formed part of his own backyard and understandably he gave us notice to find a different site for the elvers. At this news, Peter was unperturbed. He and Glynn were becoming increasingly aware that over-handling of elvers caused them stress and damage. Buying from Somerset involved at least three separate operations, transfers from one tank to another. Much better, particularly now that security was an issue, not to unload each night as we had been doing, but to leave them in the tank on the vehicle which could hold up to 100kgs – perfectly adequate now that there were fewer elvers. There they could rest in the gentle stream of oxygen carried on board. It meant too that when I drove home at the end of the night, I needed no longer to unload at the tanks, but could park directly under our window at home. What it did mean though was that, for security's sake, the vehicle could never be left; off duty we'd arrive at friends or family with the truck and its tank full of elvers, like prisoners shackled to ball and chain. The vehicle had become our mobile elver station; from now on, it was eels on wheels.

In the past few years there had been huge changes in the elver world. Empires were crumbling, new ones building, figures once powerful – Grunseid, Ted Clarke – were long since gone to fishing grounds in the sky. At Gloucester this left the two main players, Peter Wood on the Severn and Horace Cook on the Wye, locked in battle over the elvers. Yet through changing market forces, the unthinkable was to happen and by the early 1990s, these mortal foes had teamed up to work together, forming a new company, UK Glass Eel. In Somerset, meanwhile, Mike Hancock had died of a sudden heart attack the previous year, the business carried on by his two sons. Terry Hamlin, too, had retired suffering from cancer. The Boys, who'd been our main fishermen for a decade, had found a new elver river and disappeared from the local scene. Maurice Ingram's Marine Farm at Hinkley Point, the last surviving eel farm in the UK, had finally been forced to close in '88 unable to pay the increased rents demanded by its landlord, the ECGB. Around this time new competition had arrived on the Parrett: Peter Neusinger, once employed by Peter and Glynn, had set up on his own; initially buying elvers to grow on, but now selling in direct competition with Gloucester.

Changes were also taking place in the way the elvers were fished. In the old days, we waited till the tide turned, then fished 'on the crawl' as the shoals came into the side of the river as the line of least resistance against the current, the elvers swimming into the back of the net. Now, as the shoals became thinner, the fishermen didn't wait for the turn. Instead they fished the 'push', or the 'up' as the incoming tide was called, using huge nets on long, extending poles. The elvers, born on the tide, were rammed into the back of the net where they were held by the force of current; little wonder that the quality of catch was dropping.

Underlying, indeed causing, all these shifts and changes was an inexorable decline in stocks, so slight at times and offset by good years like '90, that it only became clear over the long view, over a period of time. As a result, competition grew fiercer and the elver price began to rocket. They were becoming too expensive now for the Spanish dead trade for angulas and tapas, (where an artificial substitute, an exact look-alike, was now being sold.) There was still some restocking, but the main market was to the European eel farms, and increasingly to the Chinese, farming eel cheaply on a huge scale in lagoons warmed by the sun. Production was already around one hundred thousand tonnes. With insufficient quantities of Asian elvers – anguilla japonica - they were dependent on elvers from Europe. Every producer wanted a slice of this lucrative but high-risk trade. When I first started, the cost of elvers rose a few pence at a time, now it jumped by pounds, often five at a time, and to customers it rose at an even greater rate.

Against this background, it became ever more vital to buy elvers accurately; buying waste, mud, sticks and vump – the elver slime – so much part of the old days when elvers were cheap and plentiful, was no longer possible. Following the disasters of the previous season, it was decided in '91, we'd hire no helpers. Instead, Glynn Wright, Peter's fellow director, would give me a hand and in particular introduce a new system of weighing. With his dark, swarthy looks Glynn could have been a Lebanese trader. In fact he was from Derbyshire. He'd arrive in the early evening, have a meal with us then we'd head down to the river where we'd work all night, before he drove the elvers back up to Gloucester. He was good company, very professional, investing everything he did, however menial, with a sense of its worth. He had a direct manner with a wonderful turn of phrase. Once, looking to carry out some delicate repair to the van, he quizzed my motley tool kit, 'No, I don't think you have what I want; I can see you're more of a hammer and string man.' And when the large easy-to-see calculator I'd acquired for the van stopped working, he advised, 'Just because it's got big tits, it doesn't mean it's more reliable.' It was under his guidance that the new set of scales was introduced. In the old days the elvers were weighed on old clock scales to the nearest half kilo. Now we used electronic ones that measured to the nearest few grams and the fishermen transferred their catch to our clean mesh container. What came up on the digital screen was the exact weight of the elvers, a statement, not an estimate. There could be no argument. How I could have done with them during those long nights of haggling with George years ago!

It was one thing to introduce the perfect system, quite another to put it into practice. Several fishermen drifted away to find a more lenient buyer. Neusinger, 'that there new bloke,' was still using old scales. And what's more, they didn't like having their catch cleaned, they'd always sold a few sticks and a bit of mud, that was what elvering was all about. The scales too were viewed with deep suspicion. How did they know they were accurate, hadn't been doctored for our benefit. Sometimes, like a conjuror, a fisherman would whip out a kilo bag of sugar from his coat to test them. A tense silence, all eyes on the read-out. I'd breathe a deep sigh of relief as it came up, bang on. But the new scales were highly strung, prone to nervous breakdown and blacking out just as a queue was waiting to weigh in. Moments of utter panic, if on my own, as I feverishly fumbled to resuscitate them. If you couldn't weigh, you lost your men and they might never return; very soon I was carrying the old clock set just in case. For all that, what we bought in Somerset now matched what we weighed off in Gloucester.

When they dropped by the truck for a chat at the start of each season, the police would quote the interesting statistic that during the elver season the Bridgwater crime rate dropped by some forty percent. This was a whole new world of elvering, utterly different to the rural

216

scene I'd met when I first arrived in Somerset. While a few still came from outlying villages, the majority of fishermen were from the council estates in town, the rougher ones like tribal areas, warrens of big families, where, if you called to see a fisherman, you checked your vehicle when you emerged; where many were officially unemployed, skilled at working the system, dabbling in whatever made money under the radar, out of the way of the Taxman or 'Social'. Often, talented and skilled, they'd have flourished if only they'd been given the opportunity. I often used to think they would have made brilliant soldiers – resistance fighters. They were resourceful, lived on their wits, comfortable with new technology; when mobile phones first appeared, there was one who built listening devices to pick up the conversations of the elver buyers – and the police.

Many, though, did have jobs, working in factories, in construction, for the council, and there were always surprises: one fisherman, always covered in mud at the end of the night, owned a string of houses and could never fish on a Thursday because that was rent collection night. At the end of the season he'd come for his money in a sleek sports car, a totally different figure out of his fishing overalls. Then some, like suppliers of picks and shovels in the Gold Rush eras, made more from selling nets and gear than they ever did from catching elvers. Yet despite the decline in stocks, a good fishermen could still catch fifty to sixty kilos over the season, earning himself four to five thousand pounds; to do that however, he would have fished a hundred nights on the trot, and quite possibly held down a job as well. But it wasn't just the money, one and all they loved the elvering: it was the excitement, companionship, and escape from drudgery and humdrum lives.

And as they gathered to weigh in their catch, smoking skinny roll-ups from breast pocket tins, their chat floated round me as I worked,

'Well, ee was fishing my spot so I turned round an' I said to 'en...'

'When I said to 'en all about it, 'ee turned round to oi......' There was a lot of 'turning round,' it could make you dizzy. The accent was not as deep or burred as Ernie's had been yet the language was rich in expression, black humour never far away. The most commonly-used word, acting as adjective, verb or simply filler, was 'fuck'; it peppered their sentences, though not aggressively, it was just the easiest word to use. You could overhear a good-natured exchange any night between two catchers that might run, 'Yere, you fucker, give us a fucking fag.'

'No, I fuckin' won't cos you fuckin 'ad the last one.'

Surprisingly, like flicking into a different gear, they didn't swear much when they were chatting to me, only when tensions rose over price. And they were always highly amused if I was to swear,

'Cor, 'ark at 'ee, d'ee hear, Mike just said fuck.' Then, often, intrigued by my accent, I was asked, 'Where you from then, Mike? You sound different like.' And when I told them, from Devon, 'Ah, that's it then, I knew you weren't from round yere.' When things got heated, the fuck rate rose like a temperature gauge on the side of a greenhouse, up to forty fucks a minute.

Over the years, I got to know about their families, money worries, interests: coarse fishing, racing pigeons, allotments, the floats they were building for the carnival each autumn; it was an insight into the lives of people I'd never have otherwise met. Best of all, perhaps because it signalled the prospect of bed and sleep, I remembered the farewells as they signed off for the night, the 'What time's tide tomorrow?' and 'Cheers en', as they stabbed out fags, or 'Well, time to fuck off 'ome now', or, as one with an unfortunate stammer, used to manage, 'Well, I'm gonna f- f- f- fuck off home and sh- sh- sh- sh- shag the missus.'

As the decade ticked by, the battle to supply the Chinese eel farms intensified. From around 1995 onwards, Chinese buyers appeared, equipping and funding a group of fishermen to buy for them directly off the Parrett. The price seemed to change almost weekly, daily. After a brief settled spell would come the familiar signs that things were on the move: phone calls at home to check the price; a face round the corner of the van, watching from the side, one you'd never seen before, who'd ask, 'What yer paying, mate?' before slipping away. Even though it was Gloucester's money, not mine, I still felt the same sense of dread when one of my regulars dropped the warning, 'Matey up the road's paying a bit more.' And when a regular catcher failed to turn up, you always wondered; had he gone elsewhere, or just not caught? It was galling to see the man you'd chatted to for nights on end, weighing in to the opposition, a sense of deep betrayal. Yet money talked. And the fishermen were past masters at manipulating the buyers, doing the rounds and winding up the price.

One ploy was to hawk a good catch from one buyer to the other. There was one gang that fished the sea gates on the Huntspill Relief Drain that specialised in this auction approach. Each year they hacksawed their way through massive locks that were supposed to secure the remote site operated by the Water Authority and prised open the hinged clappers to allow the fresh water from the man-made canal to flow into the estuary, attracting the shoals of elvers as they passed. Huge catches had been recorded there over the years. 'Yer, Mike, we got over thirty kilos in the back of the truck. They'm lovely fish. What's the very best price you can give us?' It was tempting, very tempting but the danger was that if you bought them at a higher price, news would spread like wildfire and everyone would demand the same. I was hopeless at bargaining and I never managed to get the Huntspill elvers.

At the suggestion of Gloucester, and in an effort to steady the situation, I introduced a system that offered a basic riverbank price, a sort of bank base rate, common denominator, payable to all. Added on, as an option, was a bonus - an extra pound or two per kilo - payable at the end of the season if the fisherman stayed loyal. The bonus was the variable part negotiated privately between buyer and fisherman. Designed to take the heat out of the market and to encourage loyalty, it worked well - for a time - until inevitably pressure moved from the bank price to the size of the bonus. It became so complicated that I could never remember who was on what, when, or how much, forever tripping over the coils of my labyrinthine arrangements. In the end I kept a list to remind me. On one awful occasion, the classic leaked document, this master list, lying on the front seat of the van, was read through the window by a group of catchers who, armed with the information, gleefully roared off to the opposition down the road to secure a better price and never weighed in with me again.

To attract new fishermen, the biggest lure, though, was the offer of cash. Cash on the nail, on the night. It drew them like moths to a lamp. In the early 1990s the country was in recession, a lot of unemployment in town. The price of elvers was now such that I carried a float of several thousand pounds on the vehicle each night. It didn't buy much, and I'd be down at the bank in Langport almost daily to top up. I used to thank my lucky stars that it was Gloucester's money, not ours; we could never have stood the sums involved: just to buy the elvers over the season was well over a quarter of a million and rising. Beyond taking obvious precautions, I never felt overly concerned about carrying so much cash because I felt protected by the fishermen themselves: it was as much in their interest that I wasn't robbed.

This was perhaps naïve. Certainly someone had other plans for at about five one morning, at the beginning of April 1992, just as I was about to set off for the early morning tide, police and detectives turned up at the house in a rush of cars and banged on the door. Not to buy smoked eel this time. There'd just been a tip-off: I was going to be rammed by two cars on the straight road into Langport and mugged. I was being given Police protection. Though grateful for their concern, it all seemed quite surreal, as if I was taking part in some badly-made cop movie. A large policeman was bundled into the back and hid behind the tank while we set off down to the river with a police car following. There was no sign of ambush. Needless to say, chaperoned by such distinguished company, I hardly saw a fisherman and was avoided like the plague. This went on for two weeks. Each night a local constable came with me, placing himself discreetly out of the way behind the tank where he sat like a large bird on its nest. The catchers would come to the door of the van and in the middle of chatting would suddenly spot him. 'Got company then, Mike; wondered why the Hancocks were doing so well.' And they'd hurry away, not even waiting to weigh in. Police protection was turning out to be the kiss of death.

There were other dramas too, like the night one of our students was on his way back from Gloucester where he'd been delivering elvers in the new van, Glynn's pride and joy, fitted out with all the latest kit. Coming home on the narrow road that ran beside the river, he pulled over to avoid another vehicle and slid like a pudding off a plate into a ditch some five feet deep. The van lay tilted on its side like a great beached whale. The riverbank seethed and buzzed with excitement; a crowd of fishermen gathered; advice on where and how to haul it out flying in all directions. A tractor appeared, ropes were fixed, its wheels spun, but the van, sunk deep, never budged. Only in the morning with proper lifting gear was it uncorked, emerging unscathed, with soft sucking noises as if reluctant to leave its soft bed of peat.

And then there was P. Just before his sad death in '92, Terry handed me a piece of paper, 'Yer, no good to me now, Mike, I'd rather you 'ave these than they go elsewhere.' It was a list of the names of his top catchers, the ones who really mattered, the core of his team. 'And ee,' he pointed to one name, 'above all hang on to en whatever, but you gotta keep him happy. When ee says jump, you jump, mind.' I was moved that he'd thought to do this; it was like being given a map of buried treasure. P, when I made contact, had been primed and was expecting me.

He was a tough nut, undisputed leader of a large tribe; he had cold, unsmiling eyes and there was something chilling about him. For years he'd fished a spot where the canal spilled over into the Parrett, luring the elvers to the sweet, fresh water. He caught consistently, and his fish were very good, well caught and unstressed. It was a little gold mine and no-one ever tried to dislodge P and his family, once ensconced for the season. In fact, he was organised and reliable, straight in his dealings. With P, you never haggled: he just told you his price — top whack - and that was it. At the end of every night, on our way home, I'd call by to collect from him, waiting in a wreckers yard, a graveyard of cars, cliffs of crushed and busted vehicles and twisted metal on all sides. It was a soulless, god-forsaken place. If anyone had wanted to do a spot of mugging, this would have been the place. Usually he sent his son to weigh in. In complete darkness, I'd sit in silence until the tap on the side of the van and the door would slide open. Terry had been right: his catch was invaluable, helping me to secure at least some share of what came off the river. Through all the turbulent times, I managed to hang on to him almost to the end.

P was our back marker; when he packed in, it was time to head home. I used to love the drive back, up the riverbank road this time, quickly into country, shedding the ugliness of town. I drove very slowly, bone weary, looking forward to bed. Almost on auto, the van knew its own way, along willowy lanes, their boughs pollarded like old knuckles. Often the headlights picked out a pair of barn owls in a tree at the entrance to a farm, beautiful creatures, blinking in the lights. Back home, stealing in as quietly as I could without turning on lights, I would be greeted by a heavy pat on the head from a sizeable paw. This was Ginge, our large, striped ginger tom who slept by the back door in a basket full of gloves and hats fixed high on the wall. He'd purr in welcome, short bursts like a machine gun, land another affectionate thud on my head, and resume his slumbers.

★★★★★

In the early summer of '92, we held a pond fish sale. And it was to set off a train of events that were to transform the business.

221

For some years each spring and summer I'd been selling ornamental fish, golden orfe, rudd, koi, and tench to the garden centres: not the most profitable enterprise by the time the herons had taken their toll, but at least it was another iron in the fire and helped cover our overheads. The fish were held in earth ponds at a site near home where a local farmer had created a coarse fishery with good access and car park. It was one of our students from Sparsholt, busy putting up a heron-proof cage, who came up with the idea of setting up our tanks in the car park and selling direct to the public. Rather hesitantly, with the farmer's approval, we decided to give it a go. To our astonishment, the public arrived by the carload. We sold more fish than I'd ever thought possible and at the end of the day counted a bundle of cash - duly gobbled by the overdraft but nonetheless encouraging. Suddenly it made us think: if the fish sale worked, then perhaps it could be applied to the smoker. We could open it up, perhaps, show people round, offer them samples of what we produced and they could buy from us directly.

We planned a set of three Open Days, enclosing the invitation in the seasonal newsletter. I feared that as our customers bought from us by mail order, they wouldn't be interested. But it was a revelation. They came in their droves. They were curious. Many had been using us for years; they wanted to see what the smokery was all about, where it happened, how it was done, to taste some of the other things we did. They came from all over the south of England, from London and Oxford and south Wales. For all of us helping, it was not only exciting but intriguing also to meet people whom we had known until then only by letter or phone. As soon as they arrived they were given a glass of wine and made their way round the plates of samples laid out on tables. Emily was old enough to help and with skills honed from selling apples and plums from the gate at home, was a natural sales person; the eel pate she'd tell people was her favourite. On her recommendation we sold it by the bucketful. She was, I noted, very steady under pressure, good too with the mental arithmetic and change; far swifter than Utta or I. Meanwhile, I did tours of the smokers, showing so many people round, I was hoarse at the end of each day. And they spent. They bought in multiples, by the bagful. I gutted and smoked eels in the evenings to keep up with the demand. Open Days, we decided were definitely a good thing and were to become a feature for years to come.

But something else had happened. An advert in the local press had attracted many more visitors from the surrounding area. 'This is marvellous,' they said, 'We didn't know you were here, but where can we buy your stuff? Do you have a shop?' To have to reply, as was then the case, 'No, we only do mail order,' seemed such a blatant missed opportunity. But just through the wall, and tacked on to the side of the barn, was Ernie's old tractor shed. With a bit of work, and some knocking through, it would make a perfect shop. It would be the next project. For the time being however, it would have to wait till the funds were available. Funds in fact were very short: between '87 and '92 interest rates never fell below 10%, even peaked at fifteen, and ours were pegged by the bank at four above the going rate. Things were very tight, especially as we had just had an official visit from Environmental Health and were, as a result, required to carry out necessary, but very substantial, improvements to the smokery in compliance with new legislation.

That visit would be remembered for a long time. Checked regularly each year by our nice lady EHO, the smokery, though very basic and simple in its health and hygiene practices, had passed without incident. But in 1990 a major piece of legislation, the Food Safety Act, had appeared, affecting the whole of the food industry throughout the EC. I was given notice of a major inspection, a whole day booked for a major audit. A senior EHO, a quietly-spoken man in white coat and hat, spent hours poring over each area of the barn, making detailed plans, asking Viv and Sally, working there that day, about the processes involved so that he could understand the flow of production. The longer he stayed, the more anxious I became; I wasn't sure quite what this was all leading up to. From his silent working, the sheets of notes, the plans, whatever it was, seemed pretty major. Then, I suppose it was inevitable since we'd plied him with coffee and tea, he asked,

'May I use your toilet, please?'

My heart sank.

'Er, yes of course, er, it's this way, follow me.' And I took him round the corner to the shed I'd built against the wall of the barn outside. There was very limited drainage in the barn. Actually none at all. Only the gutting room had a sink and waste. So the shed housed a chemical loo, set up on blocks. Years before, Ernie's boys had used it for rifle practice, fortunately not while anyone was in it, and it was peppered with small holes through which one could enjoy limited views of the orchard and fields beyond. I found it a peaceful, contemplative place as evidently did the spiders and other flora and fauna that had taken up residence there.

'I have a horrible feeling,' I said to them as I returned to the barn, 'That this is it. We're going to be shut down. He's in there. He'll have a fit.'

We waited. He didn't appear; he was taking a very long time. Maybe he had fallen in.

At last he returned. I waited for an outburst but he didn't say a word, just washed his hands, looking rather thoughtful and continued with his survey. At length, he announced, 'Well, I think that's it. I'm going to go away and send you a list of measures, works you must carry out in order to comply with the new regulations, which will have to be completed within a fixed time-frame. In the meantime you will be able to apply for derogation so that you can continue production in the present state. But,' and he smiled, looking me straight in the eye, 'the first thing you're going to have to install is a proper toilet.'

The Open Days had given us a taste for selling to the public. Now, as time allowed, armed with a fridge, a table and a large wicker basket to display our wares, I began to do small local shows, the odd market, plant sale, charity event or tastings like the annual one at Avery's, wine merchants in Bristol, held in their vaulted brick cellars. The takings were pretty modest, but I loved the selling, sampling, meeting people, telling them about the mail order or the next open days. It was all part of laying the groundwork, building the customer-base, spreading the word.

In the autumn the Christmas food fairs and charity shows began; it was only possible to do a few and they had to earn their keep for they required a huge amount of preparation just at the busiest time of year in the smokery. Quite apart from packing the range of goods to sell at the show, there was all the other display kit to remember -we always managed to forget something and became past masters at improvisation - and the staffing of them to consider.

There were times when I'd wonder why the hell I was doing them: held up by traffic, or road closure, or flood, or all three, I'd arrive late to find our pitch in some inaccessible spot in some school or hall, lugging fridges, tables, and boxes from miles away in pouring rain. But I always relented for in those days, before farmers' markets, they were well attended, the cost of a stall still reasonable and they generated vital revenue, desperately needed to reduce the overdraft - fat and well-fed at this time of year - and to fund the buying of eels. They were vital too for the growth of the mail order; those who bought from us could well become mail order customers for years to come. From dealing direct with the general public we learned, too, that you could never judge by appearances or make assumptions. An expensively-dressed lady might appear on the stand, closely perusing our various packs and then, just as we were sure she was about to buy, murmur, 'All lovely stuff, thank you,' and drift away to the next stall. As she left, there'd be another figure, hardly noticed, an elderly man in a shabby coat who'd have been quietly browsing and who'd start, 'I'd like three of these, please,' picking the packs of eel fillet, 'and two of the duck breast, and oh yes, three of these...'

The Christmas shows were a world of their own. Over the years, we got to know stallholders, many small businesses like ourselves, some of them husband and wife teams, retired with careers behind them, or casualties of some financial misfortune, who sold exclusively through shows, leading exhausting nomadic lives as they did the season, moving from one event to another, like circus travellers, setting up and taking down. I couldn't have imagined anything more ghastly, yet they worked incredibly hard, deserved every penny they earned. Like all of us, in a way, they were hooked on hitting the jackpot, finding the perfect show - like the elver fishermen finding the right spot. We'd swap news on the current form; there'd be much talk of the latest find, a new show, the flavour of the season, where they'd managed to get a pitch, very excited; apparently it was a goldmine. When I met them at a later date, it would turn out that it hadn't been that special, no, but there was talk of another that you just had to go to; people spending like no tomorrow. It was like chasing rainbows; always the next one.

Though we took our whole range of products, it was the smoked eel that attracted most interest. And there were two standard responses: they were those that knew it and were hooked on it, and there were those who had never tried it before, and never wanted to, associating it with jellied eel, with all things slithery. Getting them to try it, making a sale, was wonderfully satisfying, like casting the fly and landing the fish.

'Just try some. Go on.' And when they did, in a surprised tone, 'Oh, that's not bad, rather good in fact. Hmm. Might try another piece.' Then turning to their husband, 'Perhaps we should take some home for supper, darling.'

People's likes and dislikes when it came to food were so much to do with their own preconceptions: it was all in the mind. I once attended a small charity event where the lady of the house in which it was held discovered my plate of eel samples, returning again and again to graze on them. She apologised but couldn't stop herself; 'Oh, so more-ish,' she'd say, popping in another piece, so much so that I was having to fillet eels just to keep up with her. It was like feeding a gannet. In the end she found her husband and dragged him over to introduce him to the new found delicacy.

'Darling,' she said, 'You must try the smoked trout.'

'But that's not smoked trout,' darling replied, 'that's smoked eel.' At which her ladyship, who up to that point had probably consumed about a pound's weight of smoked eel samples, gasped, 'Oh my God,' and, as if she'd just swallowed arsenic, spat out the offending morsel she'd just put in her mouth like a regurgitating sea bird.

Looking back, we were lucky with our timing. There was an excitement, a buzz in the world of food; things were changing fast. Consumers were becoming more daring, more discerning, eager to try new things, to find the richness and variety of food they found on their travels on the continent that had character and individuality. Small specialist producers were experimenting, digging up old recipes, making food in small batches, doing it with love and care, proud of what they produced. It bore their stamp, their own identity. One of the champions of these changes was the food presenter, Derek Cooper, with his weekly Food Programme on Radio Four on Sunday mornings. I liked his rich voice, his unpretentious style and integrity, his willingness to take on officialdom, and his enjoyment of good things to eat. It was just the sort of programme we'd have loved to feature the smoked eel.

By then, national advertising, even in the classified sections, I'd discovered, was a total waste of our meagre resources; much more effective was to send a Press Release, for the cost of a stamp, to the food editors of newspapers and magazines - and always to the *Food Programme* on BBC Radio 4. The eel was so much part of the Somerset Levels, I could tell them about the eel fishery at the nearby abbey of Muchelney mentioned in the Domesday Book, about hot smoking learned on the continent, and collecting the chalk stream eels. It was a colourful story and it seemed to appeal to journalists – especially when backed up by the offer of a sample.

Over time we received generous coverage from food writers like Philippa Davenport, who wrote for both the *FT* and *Country Living*, from Sue Lawrence of *The Times*, from Hattie Ellis, freelance, and later, from Tamsin Day-Lewis of the *Weekend Telegraph*. They were all hugely supportive and took us to a far wider audience and market than we could have ever reached on our own. Sometimes we had no idea the press release had even been received and a piece would appear unannounced, galvanising the mail order, sending it into overdrive, especially at Christmas. Others would phone up wanting more detail, or visit us at the smokery. To be picked up by someone knowledgeable about food gave such encouragement. It was the same with the enthusiasm of chefs like Joyce Molyneux who found us through the mail order and who'd order for her restaurant The Carved Angel in Dartmouth, or nearer to home, Phil Vickery from the Castle Hotel in Taunton, and later some of the top London chefs. Their endorsement gave us much-needed confidence that what we were producing was good and made us want to get better still.

Yet I was never as excited as when I was contacted by the BBC to arrange an interview at the smokery with Sheila Dillon from the *Food Programme*. I was gutting eels when she arrived, accompanied by her colleague, Henrietta Green, whom I'd also heard on the programme. They watched the eels being smoked, then tasted them after, devouring them while they were still hot. All this they described in the programme when it went out. Not much came of it in the form of direct sales: there was of course no phone number or address given, and I learned that the shelf life of a programme, radio or TV, is ephemeral. And yet indirectly, a great deal came out of it. People remembered it and would say, at a show, or on the phone, 'Oh yes, the smokery was on that programme ....' It reaffirmed their confidence in us. But it had another consequence, much more lasting. I didn't know it at the time but Henrietta Green was compiling a guide of interesting food producers and food shops in the country. Published in '93, we found we had been included, one of over 600 entries. Well-written and researched, *The Food Lover's Guide* heralded the emergence of small food producers, and it became the bible of any buyer looking for new and interesting suppliers.

Not long after its publication, I began to be contacted by restaurants, distributors, and other smokehouses. In particular, we were visited by the buyer from Fortnum and Mason. He liked the eel and later phoned to place a sizeable, regular order. Alone in the barn, I danced for joy. All these new markets helped consolidate the wholesale side of the business, which though small, added another flow of income in addition to the existing mail order and the shows. We knew how vulnerable we'd been relying solely on the elvers for our living; it was reassuring gradually to see the growing strength of the smokery with its various strands of income.

The Guide brought other visitors too. I was quietly gutting eels – I always seemed to be gutting eels in those days – when the owner of a northern smokehouse, John Ward, appeared at the door of the barn. Continuing the family business of bacon curing and smoking, a craft that his grandfather, an orphan, had learned in Canada, he'd established a smokehouse, just outside Wilmslow, south of Manchester, with a population of four million on the doorstep. Up to then he'd been supplying the trade, hotels and restaurants, but with his son, he was about to open a small speciality food shop on-site, for which he wanted to buy our smoked eel. A lot older than us, John used to say he ought really to be retiring not opening shops. I liked his openness and curiosity, his sense of humour. It was the start of a long friendship, and a rare and valuable thing for a small business: someone to turn to for all sorts of advice and practical help.

In the first place the encounter helped us to enlarge our product range; everything they produced seemed delicious. We bought their air-dried ham, every bit as good as Parma ham, also their Kasseler, smoked loin of pork, and their dry-cured bacon and added them to our mailing list; we also bought their smoked duck breast, whole, and sliced it ourselves. It was immediately popular. Brined in a rich marinade, then hot smoked, it was wonderfully succulent. After a while, we started smoking it ourselves and John gave us advice on the method and the recipe for the brine, which needed the addition of saltpetre, potassium nitrate, to penetrate the denser flesh. This was remarkably generous: technical know-how special to a small business, is hard-won, gained from years of trial and error, kept secret not to be shared.

The duck, and soon after, the chicken breast that we added to our list, would emerge from the hot smoker, roasted a golden brown, the ends crispy and bubbling hot. The eels too, hanging to cool, were irresistible;

the skin peeled back easily and the flesh so succulent and creamy was addictive, especially around lunch time. I was always saying to Utta, 'if only our customers could try it like this.' And we'd joke that we ought to open a restaurant, before being seized by common sense, rolling our eyes in mock horror, 'Not bloody likely.' But the smoker's perk, sampling what came out of the smoker actually had a more serious purpose, an essential part of quality control. You could pick up a problem before it became a real problem. Our production wasn't automated; it used a live fire and every smoke was different. As with cooking, you had to put love into the smoking. The challenge was to get as close as possible to perfection and to help, each step of the smoke was logged, the time and temperature recorded. The tasting made it possible to react immediately, to cook or smoke for longer, or alter slightly the brine or marinade.

I loved the physical business of smoking, splitting logs, getting the fire going, monitoring the eel or duck as they cooked; the pleasure of watching thick smoke from the heap of apple twigs coiling up through the eel. Whatever the pressures of the moment, it was absorbing, thera- peutic; things untangled in the mind. In the early days, I did as much as I could on my own but as the smokery grew, I had to find help especially in the build-up to Christmas. For several years in the early1990s, a bright young man, Jonathan Starling, son of an old friend from Devon days, would come in his holidays, each year becoming more and more useful as he learned the ropes, until he could gut and smoke the eels perfectly. Energetic and good natured, as well as his smoking duties, he looked after us all, brought us teas and coffees and ran errands in answer to our shouts, 'Jonathan, can you get me....,' In the end he was with us for some five years through school and university until the real world claimed him. He was greatly missed by all, especially the woman folk. And there was no-one left to call for, or to fetch and carry.

★★★★★

By now we had a computer, an Amstrad, into which I laboriously entered the two and a half thousand names and addresses of the mail order customers we had gathered since we began and which, up to then, had been stored on index cards in shoe boxes. It was a momentous moment. At the press of a button we were now going to be able to print them all off onto labels; a job that would have taken us days, hand-writing the envelopes round the kitchen table with Biddy, Sally, Pat and Vivienne. But it never quite worked like that. It had a temperamental, stubborn streak. All would go well for a while as page upon page of labels piled up neatly on the floor below the printer, then – and I'm sure it could see me - as soon as I turned my back, it would jam, printing three hundred names onto two labels. What made it worse was that I could never get it to print from where it had faulted, so it would go right back to the beginning and start all over again. I ran through millions of labels. Frequently I'd phone Bernard, in Langport, from whom I'd bought it, a real wizard on computers; remarkably long-suffering. He'd come out at all hours and muttering to it, coax it back to life.

This was as nothing, however, compared to what happened a few years later in the autumn of '94. We had by then been adding names, updating addresses directly onto the computer and the shoe boxes had long since gone. But I hadn't backed up. When I pressed the button to print our Christmas mailing, it froze, had a nervous breakdown, perhaps it couldn't face Christmas; whatever, nothing would rouse it. It was dead with our whole mail order business firmly locked inside. Bernard, normally, so positive, looked worried. 'I'll have to take it away,' he said, 'I'll see what I can do.' He didn't sound very confident. Again, as in times of crises, the phone would ring, family and friends, 'Any news?' Like waiting for someone in a coma to come round. Filled with dread, wondering how to rebuild the list, we waited for days. Then Bernard phoned late one evening, 'I've got them back, it's working.' I learned a bitter lesson about backing up, but it also reinforced my dislike of a machine capable of causing so much grief, and on which we were increasingly so dependent. I was a pen and ink man and felt comfortable that way; all of us did then at the smokery. For a long time, whilst the computer printed the labels for each mailing, when Pat or Biddy took orders over the phone, everything was handwritten, paper-based. It might have been slower but at least we had the hard copy that couldn't vanish into the ether.

★★★★★

For several years, in addition to Utta's nursing, we had made our living from four activities – elvers, ornamentals, crayfish and smokery - but central to our thinking and focus of our attention was the smokery. Between '87 and '94 its turnover had more than doubled. But not its profit: it seemed to eat money, and like a drunk against a lamppost it needed constant propping up by the other activities and the nursing. Yet I was beginning to be increasingly aware that juggling them all was fast becoming counterproductive. I was forever rushing from one to another, delivering ornamentals, setting crayfish traps, doing a smoke, packing orders, collecting elvers from the river. It was time to make radical choices: financially I couldn't yet leave the elvering, but I could at least drop the other activities and concentrate on the smokery. I remember feeling distinctly nervous about removing the props, letting go parts of the business that had helped keep us afloat. Yet the effect was immediate. Given proper time and attention, the smokery responded like a plant under sunlight. Turnover bounced, activity grew; there was a renewed vigour, new markets. And a new shop.

Ernie's old tractor shed had long been earmarked. Henry and Richard, who had now taken over the farm from Anthony, were fully in approval and as my new landlords, they carried out the building works. Ernie would have been intrigued to see what had become of his old shed: the stone walls whitewashed, natural light streaming in through windows at one end, our goods displayed in chill display cabinets down either side. Other works took place as well. Upstairs, the storage loft, where we had once slept on elver duty, was now our new office. Reached by an ingenious single flight of short stairs, designed to save space, you had to start with the correct foot. Hapless visitors, clutching briefcases, would arrive at the top breathless and confused with legs in a corkscrew. With the office transferred from home to smokery, everything was now together and more coherent. Instead of phoning an order from home through to the packing team at Bowdens, Pat could now take it downstairs. But Pat, very fit, never walked when she could run and a sure sign of busy times was the rap of her shoes as she scampered up and down those stairs like a mouse on a tread wheel. Office intercom was yet to come.

The shop bought a new regime of set opening hours and a sign at the bottom of the drive. And it put us on the map. 'So this is where you are!' people would exclaim as they entered to the tinkle of a bell we'd found for the door. Some came just to buy, some would ask to look round. A new leaflet sent to all the tourist information centres invited visitors to the 'Smokery you can Visit' where they could sample, buy smoked food and see how the smoking was done. If I was on my own, I'd have to stop what I was doing, and wind up the energy to show them round. But once started, enthusiasm would catch and fire up. Most had never been into a smokehouse before, were genuinely fascinated, awed when they saw the smoker full of eels. Frequently visitors had their own eel stories, like the fisheries officer from New Zealand researching into the age of fish populations who'd come across an eel, 'as thick as a man's thigh,' that was 120 years old; or the person walking on a river bank when an eel landed on his head – presumably dropped by a startled heron. And always, if they'd been shown round, they went on to buy in the shop, and took away the mail order details. I was glad, though, when Oliver was old enough to help in his holidays, sharing the tours when he wasn't gutting eels. He was a natural performer with a seamless patter and if he didn't know it, he just made it up.

By the end of '95, the shop, providing a new flow of income, had helped increase turnover significantly, once again we got within a whisker of going into the black. Not for long, but it gave us hope. Yet growth meant gearing up, the need for more space for a cold room, and a new smoking area. In this we were lucky, for the original barn had already been extended, long ago, with a series of smaller, separate sheds built on to it for cattle and sheep. By knocking through, laying new floors, these could be incorporated without difficulty into the body of the main building. The problem was finding someone to help full time with the smoking as well as someone who could build our next generation of smokers. Just by chance, through the elvering, I was to meet a man who could do both.

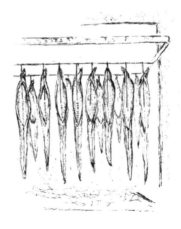

Chapter Twelve

I met Keith during the elver season of '93 when he was fishing for elvers and weighing in to us. With his dark looks, wicked smile and swagger, there was something of the pirate about him, a larger-than-life character. For his age - he was only in his late twenties - he'd managed to fit in an awful lot of living and though he had no qualifications, he could turn his hand to anything: welder, metalworker, carpenter, antique restorer, leatherworker, a good cook. He was also very successful with women. He loved their company and he'd often start the story of a different part of his tangled life with, 'Well I'd met this woman, see...' followed by a long and complicated tale of romance and moving on.

Keen to find more permanent work, he'd heard about the smokery and asked if there was anything going. It was agreed that he would join us for a trial period. Quick to learn, he was soon able to gut eels and prepare trout and salmon as if he'd done it all his life. Furthermore, he had a real affinity for making and working a fire. Having lived for spells of his life out of caravans, cooked and kept warm on fires, he quickly saw that when hot smoking, especially the eel, you needed a big mature fire, one that was kept throttled back but could be quickly encouraged if the need arose to give more heat. In fact once he'd got the hang of hot smoking the eels, it was I who learned from him.

Keith joined us just as we were expanding and making alterations to the other parts of the barn to give us more space for chillers, storage and a new hot smoker. I had already seen the type of kiln I wanted. Earlier that year, I had flown with Peter Wood to see Rosengarten in Hamburg to discuss his elver requirements for restocking for the coming season. At my request, Rosengarten had taken us to see one of the biggest, traditional eel smokehouses in the Hamburg area. The basement of the building, like a medieval dungeon, contained ten brick kilns, side by side, each one capable of smoking hundreds of kilos of eel at a time. In just one day at peak production, they could produce more than our entire annual output. They were just the design that would suit us well.

On return I showed the photos I'd taken of the Hamburg smokery to Keith who was confident he could replicate one with a few modifications. Most of the materials were to hand. The body of the smoker he built from the bricks that had formed the dividing walls of the old cow stalls; they had beautiful rounded ends that he was able to use on the corners. Built against the solid wall of the stable, it only needed three sides. For the front, he found several thick steel plates that he'd hoarded in his garden, too precious to throw away, and which he fashioned into two doors on massive hinges, with a smaller set of doors below for feeding the fire.

Having made and sold wood burners at some stage in his life, he created a much-improved draught mechanism to control the fire and a loading frame that slid out like the drawer of a filing cabinet so that you could hang the eels without being overcome by smoke and flame – always a hazard before. The final touch was the little inspection door to check the cooking of the eel. When it was finished, it looked as if it had been there forever and it worked perfectly, holding the heat far more efficiently than my previous two models and with a far bigger capacity, capable of a good 50 kilo-load of eel, a huge boost to production. Not counting his time, it came to about a hundred pounds. By contrast, a computer-controlled smoker from Germany would have cost roughly the same as a small house. And I had no doubt which would do the better job.

Meanwhile, our cold smoker, the wooden cupboard, was now beginning to look very old and forlorn. Certainly, given the popularity of the cold smoked trout and the use it was getting, it too needed replacing. This time I turned to Pete, a local builder, to install a new one. He had already carried out most of the improvements stipulated by the new health regulations - including the new loo; his charges were very reasonable, he came out-of-hours, and was quite undeterred by little things like floors that weren't level, or roofs that weren't supported by very much. He'd pause and consider the problem, 'Tidn quite the same height-th' he'd say, 'But don't worry, we'll just have to tiddle it.' And tiddle it he did, his renovations successfully getting us past all EHO inspections.

With our first cold smoker, the smoke entered indirectly through a pipe from the old wood burner placed alongside. Now, though, there was no room for such an arrangement. Instead I got Pete to build what was essentially a large brick chamber about a metre and a half across, with a wooden door - not dissimilar to an outside shed - where the smoke rose directly from the sawdust smouldering on the floor beneath the hanging sides of salmon, or racks of cheese or garlic. It was a simple method of smoking based on the London Brick Kilns, introduced in the early 1900's by Jewish refugees from the pogroms in Russia. Settling in London's East End, they brought with them their culinary traditions and love of things smoked, especially their taste for smoked salmon.

From the outset, the new cold smoker worked well and soon the walls and door were covered with the patina of shiny black tar. I loved the sight of the smoke drifting up through sides of salmon or trout that hung like great pink leaves against the tar-black surround. It made me feel I had reached some sort of professionalism. In fact the tar was one of the things that always intrigued visitors when we showed them round: I remember an American visitor, perhaps eager to use it on his apartment, once asking, 'Gee, where d'ya get your paint from?'

Only in the summer did this new smoker give us problems. The ideal temperature for cold smoking, particularly salmon, is 20–25°C; above that it starts to cook, the flesh turns flaccid and becomes difficult to carve cleanly. As it warmed up, the humidity increased and when that happened, the sides could tear from their hooks and drop to the floor or the cheese turn to fondu. It was around this time that we were beginning to smoke fish that customers had caught themselves, useful additional business while we were still growing: there was no purchase cost involved, just our time, it made good use of the smoker and often led to customers buying other things from us. But it did demand a certain diplomacy. Every fisherman's catch was special, an object of pride, and often came with a story that had to be listened to: which fly they'd used, how hard the fight. They would appear at the smokery carrying their fish like babes in arms, swaddled in paper or foil or tailor-made bags. The catch came in all shapes and sizes: tired old salmon, lean and spent; fishing lake trout, fat as pigs, full of pellets, and now and then, superb, wild salmon like bars of silver.

One day an elderly colonel turned up bearing just such a fish, a beautiful spring-run salmon of about 12lbs, which he'd caught on the Tweed. 'Bloody expensive fish,' he grumbled, 'Only one I caught all bloody week and the rod costs me six thousand a year.' In those terms, I hardly needed a calculator to work out its value. Mindful of the enormous responsibility and with the utmost care we gutted and brined it and hung it to smoke. The weather was very warm and as a precaution I laid less sawdust in an attempt to reduce the temperature. Even so I was a little apprehensive as I opened the door to the smoker in the morning. But I couldn't believe what I saw. There on the floor, both sides were lying face down in the sawdust. Not only were they caked in sawdust, they were also badly mangled by the fall. Totally irretrievable. The thought of imparting this information to the colonel was not terribly appealing. I rang Coln Valley who now supplied us with our smoked salmon. Michael Henriquez was very understanding. Two large whole sides were on their way forthwith. The colonel collected 'his salmon' and went away rejoicing. A week later he phoned to congratulate us on the quality of the smoke. It is, as they say, all in the mind. Yet from this unfortunate episode I learned one vital lesson: that in warm conditions, it was far safer to lay the fish flat on racks, skin down, flesh uppermost. That way they could not fall and they seemed to smoke just as well as if they'd been hung. I learned too over time that salmon smokes best when not hurried; there is an old saying that three days – a day to dry after curing, a day to smoke, and a day to rest after smoking – give the best result.

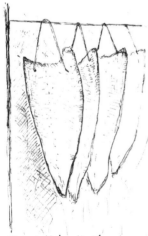

Trout sides in the new cold smoker

Keith was to work with us on and off for nearly four years to '98. Beside his natural talent as a smoker, he was a huge help in this time of expansion, helping to build much-needed storage rooms and shelving, fitting out the new shop. Furthermore, employed by Peter and UK Glass Eel in Gloucester, he helped me each season with the elvers. These were frantic years, with intense competition amongst all the buyers in the UK, France and Spain to supply the Chinese eel farms. To enable them to meet demand, UK Glass Eel were now importing elvers from the continent before their own season started – latterly in their own aeroplane – resting them in quarantine in Gloucester before air freighting them to the Far East or to eel farms in Europe. The seasons in Somerset were starting earlier and earlier, the fishermen, lured by ever higher prices, starting to catch in January and carrying on till well into May, and wherever possible fishing both the night and the morning tides. It was relentless work and I couldn't have done it on my own. Keith and I did alternate nights through the season and when there was enough on board, he would run them up to Gloucester. We were a good team: on busy nights we worked together on the van, one of us weighing, one of us paying. Having been an elver fishermen himself, he was privy to a lot of inside information, ground talk, some of it of a more personal nature. 'See this bloke coming now Mike,' I looked where his gaze was directed to an innocent figure carrying his catch to the van, 'Well they say,' his voice dropped to a whisper, 'they say 'is todger is so big, it's like a bloody donkey, and it'd well weigh over a kilo if you put it on them there scales.' How anyone should know the weight of another's willie was beyond me. 'Be worth a lot more than his elvers,' he murmured as we paid the man for his meagre catch.

But there were times, too, when I was very glad of his company, like the night we were told by Gloucester to drop the price – the Chinese had suddenly stopped buying. There was a near riot; tempers flared, the fuck rate went off the Richter scale and this time it was directed at us. Fists clenched. The van began to rock. Keith was a strong man, with biceps like Popeye. I took shelter behind him, minding the cash box while he faced the throng at the door of the van until the moment passed.

With Keith, conversation was always enlivened by his encyclopaedic knowledge of women generally, and tales of his various romantic entanglements in particular. In fact he relieved me of the task of delivering to Oliver the parental homily about the birds and the bees, what my father's generation had called 'having a chat'. Working alongside him, gutting eels in his holidays, Oliver received the complete theory part of his sexual education. I'd walk in on them, interrupting particularly graphic details and then, intrigued by astonishing things I'd never dreamed of, try nonchalantly to hang about in earshot, ears flapping, hoping to pick up useful tips.

Yet for all his qualities, it was not always an easy working relationship. The first two years were the best. He was happy at the smokery as part of a team that valued him, and surrounded by lovely ladies he must have thought he'd landed in heaven. It was the elvering that changed him, just as I'd seen it do to others in the past. It was always the money that got in the way. What was difficult for him was paying out to the fishermen more in a night than he might earn in a month or two of hard slog. It soured him; it was like grit in his shoe, a nagging discontent. Nor did it help that he was not good with his own money, he'd often spent his wages in advance of receiving them. Sometimes when things were not going well in his domestic life, his temper flared, his work at the smokery became erratic and unreliable. It was time, we both felt, that he moved on to pastures new. We parted on good terms; he'd seen us through a critical stage of the smokery's expansion, built us a magnificent new smoker and raised our skills at smoking to a new level. Happily he has done well since.

★★★★★

In the old days the busiest time of the year had always been the elver season in the spring; it was what we planned for and worked around. It had dominated our lives. There was still an elver season and it was now nearly five months of long hard slog but it wasn't quite the same for it wasn't my own business. The balance of the year had shifted. What had now become the focus of all our energy and emotion was the build up to Christmas at the smokery with the shop, the shows, the wholesale and above all the mail order, all going full bore. It was a time of intensity, often chaotic, of living on the edge, all leave cancelled, the adrenalin flowing. So much depended on it: the three months leading up to Christmas accounted for 50% of our annual turnover, 25% in December alone.

The preparation began as early as July and August, the opening moves the same each year: putting together a packing team for the mail order, deciding the content of the of the Christmas list, composing the customer letter then the licking sticking and stuffing – no longer handled by Emily and Laura White – but by the more composed group of Pat, Sally and Biddy. From the dispatch of the mailing – nearly a thousand pounds of postage – the response was immediate, a first wave of orders, providing vital cash to fund the outgoings, especially the buying of the eels. As Christmas approached, there were always seasonal worries that kept me awake me at night: the post office threatening to strike or one of those long dry spells when not an eel was caught and our stocks shrank to danger levels; or simply the fact that we were teetering on the brink of the overdraft limit.

In the final weeks, it reminded me of the old style elver seasons: the avalanche of incoming orders like the elvers arriving, eliciting just the same mix of excitement and dread: wonderful to have, yet how the hell were we going to deal with them all? Yet there was one big difference. The Christmas deadline. Everything had to be out by the last posting date. Each time I went upstairs to the office the number of boxes in which the orders were filed seemed to grow and grow. In my dreams at night they filled the room and overflowed down the stairs.

With one week to go there seemed to be an absolute mountain of orders to pack. Would we ever get through them? It was a race against time. The packers would be flying. In all parts of the barn, every surface, nook and cranny was used, all the packing tables, cubby holes in store rooms, the tops of freezers, for the weighing, labelling, wrapping, boxing, sticking, ticking, all the while trying to remember to enclose the tag or card or special message. Upstairs in the office, Pat and Biddy were never off the phone as the orders kept coming; the knack, that I never really mastered, was knowing when to stop taking them; it was like raising and lowering a hatch to control the river; if you left it open too long, you could drown. The mail order frenzy had a way, too, of sucking people into the maelstrom: visitors, friends, would innocently call by to see how things were going and be grabbed, press ganged into washing hooks and racks, or running vital errands, emerging days later, dishevelled and blinking, as from a strange dream.

Of the packers, Sally was the fastest, working with a kind of silent intensity, fuelled by black coffee, Holly the neatest, Laura Burne scattering jokes and keeping us sane. Usually it was freezing, the barn unheated, and we worked muffled and wrapped like polar explorers. At full bore it was a cacophony of sound, the squeak of sellotape dispensers, muttered oaths at the weighing machine, rip of packaging tape, the clack and thump of lids going on, like the whirr and clatter of some old-fashioned industrial machinery. Through all this, Vivienne in the processing area kept cool as a cucumber, filleting mountains of eel or trout, trying to keep everyone supplied and happy. Inevitably, we were always running out of things; they were waiting to be smoked, or still in the smoker, or too hot to fillet and send out. Each day the pace quickened as the afternoon deadline of postal collection approached. In the early days I used to load the van with parcels and race them into the Taunton depot to catch the nightly post but as our volume grew, the RML lorry came to us, and then it was a case of delaying the driver with tea and biscuits while the last parcels were feverishly packed.

A major handicap – like driving with the brake on - was the time wasted each day getting hold of our eel and salmon stocks: with limited freezer capacity on site, I'd transfer all our raw material about a month before Christmas off-site to a huge cold store on the other side of Taunton, at least an hour's round trip through heavy traffic with the obligatory wait while they located what we needed for the day. When finally I was able to buy our own blast freezer in '98, it was a huge relief, a giant step forward. What I also overlooked in the early days of its existence was the volume of business that was generated by the new shop right up to Christmas Eve – the first year I was totally thrown and found myself gutting and smoking right to the wire to keep it stocked.

At last, a week before Christmas, the orders would slow, then stop and the queries begin: Who was it from? Had it been sent? How do I eat it? How long does it keep? And just as thoughts turned to Christmas and family and what to put in Mrs Brown's stocking, the phone would go and it'd be a fisherman: he was catching elvers and were we interested? Too early, I'd say, see you later, but it was a grim reminder that the elver season was there, just waiting round the corner.

★★★★★

By now we were very much on the radar as producers of smoked eel – the best – and looking to buy in five to six tonnes a year, tiny when compared to the big Dutch and German smokehouses who could get through that in a week, but significant nonetheless. Then something happened that was to put us in a much stronger position. Fred Cook, who for years had taken all the eels from the big racks on the Test, retired. For a year or so the river keepers dealt with a Dutchman but that hadn't gone too smoothly and to cap it all the poor man had been robbed, done over, as he came off the ferry in Ireland, his money stolen, some of which was owed to the keepers. They'd been paid in the end but they'd decided to try someone else. I was approached.

It couldn't have come at a more appropriate time. There were three racks centred around Stockbridge: the Leckford estate (owned by John Lewis), the Houghton Club and the Fairey estate. Together they produced a steady three tonnes a year. I loved the Test - it was a beautiful river, I almost felt it a privilege to go there. Not that I always had the time to collect the eels; in my place I'd often send, while on their various student vacations, Emily or Laura Burne or Charlie, Biddy's daughter, all lovely ambassadors for the business. For the river keepers, their appearance was undoubtedly the best bit about dealing with Brown and Forrest :much preferred to a visit by the boring old boss himself. When I did go, I could see their faces fall, sense the disappointment in the slightly wistful greeting, 'Oh, it's you today is it; we were hoping, er, thinking, it might have been one of the girls.'

Many of the keepers were born to the life, brought up on the river, some third, even fourth generation, following in the family footsteps, men like Mick Lunn: though long retired and well into his eighties by the time I met him, his grandfather and father had both been head keepers of the Houghton Club on the Test before him. 'It was a wonderful life for a young lad, right on the river, ' he recalled. He could remember seeing elvers as a boy, as late as July, going up the side of the weir on the moss. Later, as head keeper, the eels they caught were sent up to Billingsgate by train in wooden boxes but they were always being told the quality wasn't very good or that some had died. In the end Mick had decided to go up and see for himself what was going on. It was there that he'd met Fred Cook and it'd been agreed that Fred would collect off the Test, in

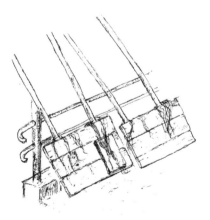

return for all the eel off the river. When it came to catching, 'You always knew when the eels were going to run, you got a sort of feeling, knew they'd be there.' Their biggest single night was one November during the dark, back in the 1980s. There'd been a lot of rain, the river had lifted, there'd been a few the night before but this time they were early, barely time to prepare the rack before they came and kept on coming, a huge run, over two thousand eels, well over a tonne in a single night.

Wooden hatchboards after the run

By coincidence, or perhaps through proximity to Portsmouth and Southampton, the river seemed to have strong connections with the early aircraft industry. The Fairey estate that supplied us belonged to the engineering family famous for the biplane torpedo bombers that crippled the Bismark in 1941 and their stretch of the river bordered that of the Sopwiths, of Sopwith Camel fame. But the estate with the longest history was the Houghton Club. Formed in 1822, based in Stockbridge, it was probably one of the most exclusive in the country; non-profit-making, with just 26 members, it owned a priceless twelve miles (24 bank miles) of the Test along with some 600 acres of adjoining land. Ray Harris, the current head keeper explained to me that in the old days they used to fish everything, trout, grayling, salmon, pike. Salmon were vermin and used to be knocked on the head; they weren't wanted as they were trying to build up a trout fishery. It was mostly dry fly but nymph fishing was allowed too. The club's logbooks record every fish ever caught on this stretch of the river since the club began. The original Commonplace Book is, as Ray described it, a fascinating and extraordinary historical document, sprinkled with brief references by members to some of the great events of the day in which they were often directly or indirectly involved: battles, disasters, changes of government, Jutland, the sinking of the Titanic, all earn brief mention followed by fulsome commentary on the fishing of the day. The visitors are equally interesting: the landscape painters Edwin Landseer and J.M.Turner appear as guests, so too the scientist Sir Humphrey Davey. Their priceless sketches and drawings feature in the early pages, while a brief entry also records in June 1944 that around the time of D-Day, General Eisenhower fished the river as a guest. In a way, the records are a testament to the peace and recuperative power of fishing.

★★★★★

Over the years, our corner of Somerset reflected rural changes taking place in the 1990s up and down the country: on the way to the smokery there had been seven dairy farms in the 1980s, now there was just one; many orchards had vanished, grubbed up, and there was only one remaining withy bed on the moor; the village shops where our children had bought their sweets had long since gone, so too the village post offices.

Yet for all that, there were things that didn't change. The longer we lived at Willow Cottage, the more we loved the place, the friends and community around us, and the moor that lay across the road, its wilderness of meadow, sedge and water under wide open skies. We never tired of walking there, and there was always something: the chit-chit calls of the secretive warblers; the creaking wings of the swans in flight, a skylark singing or the flash of the kingfisher on the river. Most evenings I'd run with Lilly, our lurcher, padding along the river bank or on the grassy droves. When it was hectic at the smokery or during the elver seasons, I found problems and worries dissolved in the rhythm of running. We loved too the seasons and their changes: the gathering of elderflower, blackberries, or driftwood after the floods. And then there were mushrooms, furtively picked, the best spots kept secret, surreptitiously checked after rain in case they might have suddenly appeared. Most exciting of all was the occasional encounter with an otter. It could happen at any time. The first sign was the disturbance in the river, a bow wave like a boat, then a stream of bubbles before a head appeared. They were big, the males over a metre long. If it was dark, all you'd hear was their splashing as they worked the river, the sound of their breathing, heavy and nasal. In the sensuous roll of the body and tail as they dived, they reminded us of the very food they hunted – the eel; but they also fished the big fresh water mussels, leaving the empty shells, big as ash trays, strewn along the banks.

Each May we were still making the journey to the Laxford in Sutherland. But by the mid 1990s it was for a holiday, not to fish the elvers. They still came, but the migration was a whisper of the past, a fraction of the quantities that we had first known in '75. It was incredible to think that in just a quarter of a century a migration that had taken place, undisturbed, unbroken for thousands of years, had almost dried up, and, while this was part of the overall decline in stock, the fact that we were probably the only people who'd ever fished elvers on the Laxford made us in some way feel directly responsible for their demise. It was sobering and it made us acutely aware of this living world's vulnerability to the things we do to it, take from it. As a consequence, we started from this time on, in a very small, unofficial way, to restock the moors and rivers, to put something back.

In nearby Kinlochbervie too there were signs that stocks of fish were down; it was a duplicate picture of the elver situation: the same increased catch effort, that same sense of scraping the barrel for higher prices but leaner catches. It was quieter than we'd ever seen it, fewer boats and the great auction shed echoingly empty save for a few boxes landed. The local trawler Loch Inchard was still there tucked against the quay like a moorhen to the bank, but the other boats were far larger now, built to stay out at sea for long stretches at a time with bigger gear and blast freeze facilities so they could fish far out into the north and west, saving time and fuel by not having to run for home to unload. Things were tougher, you could sense it in the faces; boom time was over. But managed properly, given time to rest, the fish stocks could still return. In one of the shops there was a postcard, a reminder of another boom a century before: an old photo taken around the 1890's of the fishing port of Wick along the coast where the herring fleet gathered; so many boats, it was said, to fish those massive shoals, you could walk from one side of the harbour to the other over their decks without getting your feet wet.

★★★★★

It was around this time that I received a fascinating phone call. A voice from the past. It was late one summer's afternoon at the smokery, all the team had gone home and I was up in the office finishing some work. The voice on the phone was that of an elderly man, a lovely soft Highland accent, and it belonged to Gilbert Skinner, a retired fish merchant from Inverness-shire. He'd read an article about our eel smokery and eels generally, and the possibility that the Loch Ness monster might have been an eel. It was a piece of family history that my grandfather, an Inspector of Lifeboats for Scotland in the 1930s, and a reliable witness, had seen a strange shape on the Loch and had always held that there was definitely something there. This had really interested Mr Skinner and having just read the piece, he was phoning to tell me his own story.

His grandfather had been part of the west coast herring fleet before the First World War. Once, on their way back from the Outer Isles through the Caledonian canal, the fleet had been becalmed on Loch Ness. Each boat carried, in addition to the herring fishing gear, two baskets of baited hooks, great lines with 3–4,000 hooks for white fish. Two of the boats in the fleet decided that since they were becalmed, they might as well set the lines which they baited with mussel and crab and which they paid out nearly to the bottom of the loch. What they caught was to remain indelibly printed on their memories.

'Not just eels, but huge eels, as long as the boat', so long in fact that they had to cut the lines for fear of being swamped.

Years later when the first sightings on the loch were made in the early 1930s, grandfather Skinner always insisted that this monster they were all talking about was nothing more than one of those great eels. His story is backed up in other ways too. Divers in the loch have on occasion seem massive eels lying deep down on the rock shelves of the loch side. And at the hydro-electric station at the outlet of the loch, sections of eel sometimes appear, chopped up by the turbine blades, sections that would equally come from creatures of enormous size and several metres long. One theory is that the great depth and cold in the loch deaden the migratory instincts of the eel which then gradually grows to reach this legendary size.

★★★★★

For many years the Christmas shows provided vital and timely seasonal income for the business. Then Henrietta Green, following the success of her Food Guide, launched a series of shows held throughout the year under her Food Lovers brand. Unlike the Christmas shows, these were devoted entirely to food and small producers. They had something of the circus about them: a colourful corral of tents and marquees in the grounds of some big house on the edge of town in the southern counties. Well organised, usually held over three days, they were well-attended and in their early years before they had their imitators, very worthwhile not only for the amount we sold but for the number of new mail order customers we gathered from them.

Best of all, however, were the ones in London, like the Food Lovers Fair in Covent Garden, always held over the first weekend in November, hugely successful in its early years. It had a wonderful atmosphere, the perfect setting; it was free to the punters and it stayed open till late; crowds poured into the square, many of them passing by on their way to and from work, pausing to browse for their evening meal. Set up all round the colonnades of the central buildings, the stalls were canopied over but open on all sides to the autumnal weather. Muffled against the cold, selling hard, you never cared, with customers standing deep, lining up waiting to buy. At times like those, it was as if there was magic in the air, you felt on a high, as if you could sell anything.

It wasn't always so. Once, when Biddy and Vivienne were running the stall, there was a royal visit by Prince Charles. We had been primed and sworn to secrecy but it was still very exciting and a great honour. He took time to talk to each one of a number of stalls, of which we were one. However, rare occasions can come with a price: the security arrangements were so tight, we were fenced off and no customers were able to reach us for several hours before or after his appearance with the result that we lost half a day's trading. But then, you don't get to meet Himself just any day of the week.

And then there was one show memorable above all the others and that was the Borough Market. It was an inspired choice for a Food Lovers Fair. A market has existed on or near the site for over a thousand years and Southwark, on the river by London Bridge, has always been associated with food, often known as London's larder. Shabby and rundown, full of atmosphere, the Borough was still active overnight as a wholesale fruit and vegetable market but quiet by day. We Food Lover stallholders packed inside in rows like medieval streets. Henrietta must have done her publicity well for from the City, over London Bridge, came a grey suited army from banks and businesses across the river. Stopping only at the cash machines en route to pick up crisp new notes, they spent as we'd never seen before. On this occasion Utta was manning the stand with my cousin Rupert while I was back in Somerset standing by ready to smoke more if it was needed. Rupert rang during the first afternoon to report breathlessly, 'Michael, we're running out of everything, including change; I've never seen anything like it, they don't even ask the price, they just buy. When do you think you can you get here?' Ready for this possibility, we smoked and filleted a whole new batch of stock which I drove up overnight. It was unforgettable, it was the big one; we never ever did so well at any show. Nor did any of the other stallholders. It was the success of that show, Henrietta's inspiration, that led to the Trustees of the Borough setting up their own regular monthly market for small producers. At the outset it was held on just one Saturday in every month.

Regular attendance at the Borough was the beginning of a new era for us, an extraordinary opportunity to get right into the heart of London to sell and showcase our goods. Once a month all through the year was a big commitment but just manageable in the context of the smokery workload, helped by the fact the stallholder's fee was then very reasonable, much less than other shows we attended. It made for a long but satisfying day. Having loaded the van the night before, Utta and I would leave at around four on the Saturday morning. It was like the old days, delivering the elvers to the airport, driving through the dark, seeing the dawn coming up over the Wiltshire downs.

We'd get to Southwark just after seven. Other stallholders would be arriving, some having driven all night, from way up north. A lot of stretching and yawning; we'd find our pitch and start setting up; not much chat in the cool, grey light; delicious smells of coffee, bread still warm from ovens. The regulars came early, knew just what they wanted. 'This is such good stuff, all delicious, I can really recommend it,' they'd say, turning to on-lookers. You wanted to hug them for it, this personal endorsement. Late morning was the busiest, people were hungry and bought more freely. I loved the buzz, the noise, meeting people, above all the selling, especially when Emily or Oliver were with us too, it was very special working together. Every now and then, wafts of song, snatches of aria, would rise from one of the veggie stalls nearby that employed opera students. On the way home, like Scrooge, I'd count the takings in the wooden cashbox and fish out the wads of notes hidden in numerous pockets. In those early years the Borough was a little goldmine. Gradually though, as the market grew, upping its pace from once a month to once a week, with more and more stallholders, our takings dropped; it was as if the customers' spend was spread ever more thinly over the goods available. As long, however, as we more than covered our costs, there were other benefits, for besides picking up hundreds of new customers to add to the mail order, it was here too that chefs would browse on the lookout for new products and there were restaurants we would supply for years to come as a result of the Borough. We loved it also for the chance meetings with friends and family who'd suddenly appear out of the blue in front of the stall, and sometimes, after a good day, we'd celebrate with them in the restaurant on site before returning home to Somerset. It was called eating the profit.

It was all a far cry from the first pond fish sale.

By now the smokery was growing so rapidly that I took the decision to give up the elvering; after 25 years, it was time to leave. Having been propped up for so long, the smokery had at last come of age and could stand on its own. I owed a huge amount to the elvering, it had supported our lives, given us our daily bread, but I had few regrets leaving, for it had changed so much since I first arrived in Somerset. Then, it had still been deeply rooted in country life and rural tradition, now it was something that took place downriver, kidnapped by the town of Bridgwater, an urban affair. Most worrying was the decline not in adult eel, which still seemed unaffected, but in elver stocks. There were many possible causes: habitat loss, obstruction of migration by barriers on rivers, insufficient restocking and conservation work, shift of the Gulf Stream, and above all, over-fishing of the species as a whole. When I first came to Somerset in '73, we weighed to the nearest kilo; now we weighed to the nearest gram. In the old days the price to the fishermen for elvers was fifty pence a kilo; in my last year, in '98, it rose for a brief spell to a staggering £285 per kilo, a sure measure of a dwindling and increasingly scarce resource. Yet nothing was ever done about it; in the eyes of the authorities at the time, there wasn't a problem, the elvers still seemed plentiful. They were too busy doing other things. To give them their due, much of their energy was given to controlling the use of illegal nets, the flow nets, used to catch elvers, but the big picture – the over-fishing, the need to preserve European stocks of elver and eel - was neglected. Looking back I wished I'd been more farsighted, persistent, especially in the 1980s, in trying to set such measures in motion. But like the authorities, I was too busy with other things.

There was another good reason for giving up the elvering. A combination of circumstances had lead to a significant development in the life of the smokery. For some time now when visitors came to the shop they'd look at the smoked food displayed in the chill cabinets and say, 'Oh, my goodness, seeing all this lovely food is making us hungry, where can we eat round here?' And we'd point them off in the direction of various pubs. It began to happen so often and with such regularity that we began to be aware that we really were missing an opportunity. I had always said to Utta that there was nothing quite like the duck, the eel or the chicken when they emerged from the smoker, the flesh still hot, the skin crispy, and had often joked that we should open a restaurant so that people could try it. In fact there was proof positive that it would work: the restaurant that John and Darren Ward at Cheshire Smokehouse had added on to their shop had turned out to be a great success.

It was just as we began to consider the idea seriously, turning it over in conversation at home with the family around the kitchen table, when Richard and Henry Lang approached us with the news that the old granary adjoining our part of the barn complex us was shortly to become vacant. Would we be interested in using it? It had indeed been a granary when I first came to Somerset, but part of it had been turned into a milking parlour and for many years leased to a hardworking young dairy farmer who had now found his own farm and would be leaving within six months. Without much hesitation we accepted the Lang's offer: we would take it on. The existing business, we felt confident, was strong enough to survive even if the new project turned out to be a failure. Much more to the point, we thought, where else might we find such a perfect location for a restaurant? We wouldn't have to move, it was right next-door and could be easily incorporated into the smokery; it had acres of parking and one of the best views in Somerset.

For all that, we had done no proper research. I was just wondering how I was going to present the idea to the Bank without factual support when the phone rang and a young man, Peter Mullineux, in the midst of his Business Studies A level year, asked if he could do his project on some aspect of our smokery. For a moment, I groaned inwardly; there were frequent such requests and whilst I was keen to help young people, it could also be very time-consuming. And then I had a thought: rather than creating some hypothetical task, why not get him to do something really useful, a feasibility study into starting up a restaurant. And that is precisely what he did. In fact he did it very well, designing an excellent questionnaire, which we asked customers to fill in when they came to the shop, something they did with a surprising degree of thought and imagination. The response was overwhelmingly positive. In their view a restaurant serving smoked food straight out of the smokers was a wonderful idea, and yes, they would come and eat there and if they did, they would like it to be relaxed and informal, not just a restaurant serving food but somewhere they could have a coffee with the papers, with a sofa, child friendly, but no piped music. And definitely no smoking.

When we spoke to our own customers about the restaurant project there were several who'd lived in Germany and had first-hand experience of smokehouses where you could eat on site. One delightful ex-serviceman strongly recommended that we visited a place in Germany called Stein-hudermeer, west of Hanover, where he'd been stationed after the war. The following year, in May '99, Utta and I went to see for ourselves.

We stayed in a small guesthouse on the edge of Steinhudermeer's circular lake, several miles round but shallow as a saucer, the water not much deeper than a man standing so that it warmed to a rich soup of nutrients. Fish thrived in it and it was full of eels with special wooden boats used to set the fyke nets that caught them. All round were villages and smokehouses producing all sorts of smoked fish, but specialising in smoked eel sold whole like baguettes, slipped into long clear bags. It was a beautiful day, the sun sparkled on the lake as we cycled round. Each smokehouse had a restaurant or kiosk, serving what they produced fresh from the kiln; for lunch, we stopped at one, knocked on a window and were handed an Aalbrötchen, eel in a bun, which we ate on a bench by the water. The bread was freshly-made, the eel hot out of the smoker. Washed down with a glass of beer, it was one of those memorable meals. The simplicity, freshness, the immediacy of it all, this was exactly what we wanted to recreate. We felt that we were on the right track.

Utta had already handed in her notice at work. We weren't going to need a chef in our new restaurant, because much of it came ready to eat straight from the smokers, but we did need a team to put it together, to make the soups, the salads and the desserts we aimed to serve as well. And we needed someone to manage it. Earlier, in the New Year, I'd asked her, 'So who's going to run this restaurant?' and she'd replied, 'I will, I'm fed up with psych. nursing; I've had enough.'

We were complete beginners; we had an idea, a vision but that was about all. Looking at the suppliers' catalogues, it was immediately evident that you could spend a small fortune setting up a restaurant with seating for around fifty; in no time at all, you could clock up forty thousand on seating, tables, cutlery and crockery and you hadn't even got to the kitchen. None of what we saw we liked anyway, it was all too stiff and formal; we wanted something very simple and in-keeping with the building where work had already begun. The milking parlour and the old granary had been stripped away revealing a large L-shaped space enclosed by walls of stone and brick under fine old wooden beams - still marked for assembly by the chisel of some long ago carpenter. A new stone flag floor was laid and the plaster chipped off the walls to show the old brick beneath. It had a simple feel, warm and friendly.

All through the summer of '99, Utta scoured the charity shops and markets for tables and chairs, just a few pounds each, sanding them down, re-seating the chairs, making acres of tablecloths from pink and white gingham. She was also planning and sourcing the kitchen, putting together menus and a team to work with her, and acquiring her wine licence. One of our customers, Peter Dixon, a retired Royal Marine from our old village of Drayton, built us a long serving counter, beautifully made. A small grant from some obscure EC funding helped us to buy the coffee machine and fit out the kitchen. Significantly, we moved the shop from Ernie's old tractor shed and repositioned it, chill cabinets and shelves, to one end of the L-shape by the counter and till. The positioning was important: Cheshire Smokehouse advised us that shop and restaurant worked off each other: people came to eat then shopped to buy what they'd enjoyed; while visitors coming to shop, saw the restaurant and wanted to eat.

We might not have needed a chef for our restaurant but we did need a full time smoker. Since Keith's departure I was back to gutting and smoking with various help from casual labour, and from Oliver, saving up for travels between school and university. Working with him, needing to rely on him was good bonding time; he learned to smoke well and was a tower of strength to have around. Helping us part time was William White, whose sisters had been part of the mail order assembly gang, and whom we had known since Drayton days when his family lived opposite us. When his other commitments came to an end, he asked if he might work for us permanently. It was perfect timing; he was just the man, in fact almost family, we'd known him so long. Will was practical, interested in food and a keen cook, a natural with fires and the smoking and soon he was fully in charge of production. With his quiet charm and easy manner, he was very popular with other members of the team and the ladies loved him. It was something of a family affair for his mother, Ingrid, was helping Utta in the kitchen whilst his sister, Laura, the only person we knew with any waitressing experience, gave us a hand, in a break from her medical studies, to set up a simple system for serving customers and recording what they had ordered.

It was one thing to plan and set up the restaurant; it was quite another to open the doors and go live. It reminded us of one of the stories we used to read the children, 'Mrs Wobble the Waitress' where the family open a tea shop in their house to the refrain, 'Today's the Big Day, Ma.' It was indeed. And we were terrified.

We opened in November '99. To warm up gently, the first week was a kind of dress rehearsal for which we didn't charge, when friends and acquaintances - many of whom thought privately we were quite bonkers and making a big mistake - came to eat and gave us feedback, while Utta and her team got used to the new kitchen, resolved inevitable teething troubles, sorted suppliers.

Apart from the smoked food, her team made wonderful soups and puddings, including a golden syrup bread and butter pudding that was never to come off the menu. The salad served with the main course was an instant success, carefully made from different leaves to give flavour, texture and colour, and dressed with a delicious vinaigrette, the recipe for which had been given to us, fittingly, by the young French couple who'd helped us fish for elvers in the pouring rain way back in '75. To accompany the smoked eel, Utta painstakingly made her own horseradish, digging the plant that grew on our riverbank, cleaning and preparing it, eyes streaming from the fumes, before mixing it with a little plain yoghurt, which helped it to keep. It was served with the eel on rye bread, locally made, with a tiny swirl of beetroot and onion. It looked and tasted fantastic.

The first few weeks were slow: ten lunches a day was the norm, then it crept up to fifteen. Recorded in our daily sales log as B.O.S. – Bums on Seats - the absolute record for that time was 24 and we were very proud of it; it was the one to beat. Still very green and learning all the time, we felt we were doing something right because so many people would say as they settled up, 'That was really the best meal I've had in a long time.' Steadily word got around and numbers grew. Just as Cheshire Smokehouse had predicted, the sales in the shop increased in tandem. Then came the first of the Open Days since the restaurant had opened. Our mail order customers, loyal as ever, curious to try it out, came in their droves from all parts of the land. They jammed the car park. We must have done over 80 lunches both days, at least we thought we did, it may have been a lot more for we lost count in the confusion and scrum, the till jammed, the till roll ran out, the coffee machine nearly blew up but the food kept coming. The team were exhausted but the takings were an absolute record. The experience stretched us, highlighted the weak points, took us to new levels, above all showed us we could do the numbers. And survive.

For Utta and I, involved in the different parts of the smokery, it felt almost surreal; this new creature, the restaurant, Utta's creation, had sprung to life and now devoured our lives. Yet it was a time of intense excitement; and working together as we'd done in the early days when we had first flown the elvers to Rosengarten reminded us that in a way the restaurant was a direct descendant of those early beginnings.

★★★★★

It was a year or so later; there had been a full page write-up in the restaurant review of the *Weekend Telegraph*, a glowing piece by Alice Thomson; it had had people queuing for a table. The number of bums on seats had lifted to a new level. I stood at the counter listening to the hum of voices like contented bees in a hive, and thought to myself, 'I think we're getting there.' Not quite over the line, a lot yet to do, but the overdraft was in remission, for the first time in our lives we were paying ourselves a salary. It had been a long journey from the first elvers, to the smokery, and now to the restaurant, and a memorable one and it could never have happened without Utta, who had been with me every step of the way.

There was, however, just one sadness: that my parents who had supported us in spirit all along had not lived to see the restaurant nor had the chance to enjoy its welcome, eat its food; it would have made them very happy. And Ernie would have loved it too - dropping by for frequent chats and cuppas, maybe even to try 'another bit of that there eel.'

Postscript

And after years of decline, how fares old eel now? Well, perhaps not in the best of shape but at last receiving attention.

Since 2000, there had been a growing awareness that all was not well, much debate and plans deferred, but little action. Not helped by the pull of vested interests – the conflicting elver and adult eel lobbies – each blaming the other for the situation. Then, in 2007, the industry received a mighty wake-up call when the European eel, *Anguilla anguilla*, was placed on the endangered list by several international wildlife bodies.

About the same time, the European Commission issued a Regulation requiring all member states to produce Eel Recovery Plans. Varying in degree, some tougher than others, these represented for the first time a concerted effort to address the survival of the species by reducing commercial fisheries, actively restocking with glass eels, improving habitat and migratory pathways, and allowing a 40% escapement of adult silver eel.

Implementing such measures hasn't always been easy. Of the plans that came into force in 2010, by far the most significant was a total ban on the sale of European glass eels to China and the Far East, a massive and lucrative trade. The doors on illegal sales are closing. Without the Chinese market, elver prices became more stable and the elvers that would have vanished overseas have now gone for restocking and for eel farming within Europe. France meanwhile has been compensating fishermen to take boats out of production to reduce the national catch. Ireland has stopped all commercial exploitation of eel to concentrate on restocking (though catches were reportedly healthier than ever up to the imposition of the ban). In the UK, research through tagging has yielded new insights into the behaviour of the eel that will help shape its recovery.

Much needs still to be done especially on improving habitat and migratory pathways, but at last things are happening. Given its longevity, full recovery will take time – years. A total ban on fishing may yet be necessary but the best way forward is surely a well-managed, sustainable European eel fishery: a healthy species needs a healthy industry. Aside from some unforeseen threat to its existence, I believe this wondrous creature, one of the great survivors, will recover.

Also published by Merlin Unwin Books
Further details – www.merlinunwin.co.uk

Over the Farmer's Gate
Roger Evans £12

Fishing with Harry
A Tale of Piscatorial Mayhem
Tony Baws £15.99

A Countryman's Creel
Conor Farrington £14.99

The Countryman's Bedside Book
BB £18.95

The Naturalist's Bedside Book
BB £17.99

The Best of BB
An anthology
Denys Watkins Pitchford £18.95

That Strange Alchemy
Pheasants, Trout and a Middle-aged Man
Laurence Catlow £17.99

Advice from a Gamekeeper
John Cowan £20

The Brewer's Tale
Frank Priestley £10

The Otter
James Willliams £20

The Hare
Jill Mason £20

The Private Life of Adders
Rodger McPhail £14.99